THE INTROVERTED LAWYER

A Seven-Step Journey Toward Authentically Empowered Advocacy

HEIDI K. BROWN

Cover design by Elmarie Jara/ABA Design

The materials contained herein represent the opinions of the authors and/or the editors, and should not be construed to be the views or opinions of the law firms or companies with whom such persons are in partnership with, associated with, or employed by, nor of the American Bar Association unless adopted pursuant to the bylaws of the Association.

Nothing contained in this book is to be considered as the rendering of legal advice for specific cases, or psychological advice, and readers are responsible for obtaining such advice from their own legal counsel, medical professionals, or psychological counselors. This book is intended for educational and informational purposes only.

To protect the privacy of some of the individuals referenced in this book, the author has altered certain identifiable characteristics.

Printed in the United States of America.

25 24   10 9

ISBN: 978-1-63425-772-5

e-ISBN: 978-1-63425–773-2

Discounts are available for books ordered in bulk. Special consideration is given to state bars, CLE programs, and other bar-related organizations. Inquire at Book Publishing, ABA Publishing, American Bar Association, 321 N. Clark Street, Chicago, Illinois 60654-7598.

www.shopABA.org

Contents

Preface

The introverted lawyer: an oxymoron? The American typecast of the effective lawyer conjures images of an extroverted, confident, prolix, podium-pounding orator. Hollywood stars like Ryan Gosling, Matthew McConaughey, Reese Witherspoon, and George Clooney portray gregarious exemplars of the profession on the big screen. Art reflects life. A stereotype bias in law school and legal practice favors the talkative extrovert. While naturally loquacious professors, students, lawyers, and judges thrive in a world dominated by the Socratic question-and-answer method and rapid-fire oral discourse, quiet thinkers and writers can be sidelined. Introverts are "frequently overlooked and underestimated by organizations and colleagues who buy into the idea that talking reigns supreme."[1] Introverted or otherwise interpersonally reserved (perhaps shy or socially anxious) law students and lawyers often struggle to find their place in the legal arena. Research indicates, however, that they bring impactful gifts to the profession, such as active listening, empathy, deliberate thinking, and insightful writing. As legal education and law practice adjust to changing law school enrollment trends, and as academic institutions and law firms reevaluate business models, the legal community is primed to make room for subtler voices.

The impetus for this book is both personal and professional. I was an introverted law student, and I remain an introverted lawyer and law professor today. I feared the Socratic Method in law school, fumbled my 1L (first-year) oral argument, dreaded most deposition and court appearances in the first 15 years of my litigation career, fretted about commanding a classroom in my first year of teaching law, and rarely spoke in contentious faculty meetings. Much of the time, I felt like a fraud, faking extroversion to strive and achieve. Yet, from the beginning of my legal career, my brain happily buzzed with complex legal issues, theories, and strategies. When I sat down to write lengthy briefs as a junior associate at the law firm, my thoughts flowed and I communicated legal concepts in a persuasive manner to advocate passionately for my clients. I read, listened, contemplated, analyzed, and wrote. Over the past two decades, I have composed reams of briefs, and penned law review articles and books to help novice lawyers litigate. However, in frequent flashes of self-doubt, I continued to worry: was there no true place for me in the law because

I flinched in the throes of a Socratic grilling by a professor, colleague, opposing counsel, or judge?

Well-meaning, extroverted mentors throughout my legal career have urged: "Just speak up!" "Get your nose out of that book and spout an opinion!" "Grow a thicker skin!" "Just do it!" . . . As if I could just tie on a pair of Nikes and bungee-jump my way into the Socratic bonanza with zest. I thought there was something wrong with me. There wasn't. I am an introverted lawyer and law professor, and I am good at my job. I just do it quietly. And deeply.

In many law school and law office communities, students and lawyers who are introverted, shy, or socially anxious—three distinct categories, with important differences explored in Chapter 1—experience high levels of stress. Many of these individuals worry that they are not cut out for the practice of law. Some extroverted professors and lawyers unconsciously or unwittingly reinforce this message in classrooms, law offices, and courtrooms every day, not yet understanding the valuable assets that quiet individuals bring to our profession. In faculty meetings and academic conferences, some extroverted law professor colleagues have questioned why some students never volunteer in class. "If these students don't want to speak or participate," these confident academics query, "why choose law school?" Some professors cold-call students in class, schedule in-class oral argument assignments without realizing that students first need more context and training, and seem surprised if a student does not readily share a gusto for oral advocacy. Their argument in support of that pedagogical approach is that law school trains students to "think like lawyers," and thus, the classroom should mirror the "rigor" of the courtroom or boardroom.[2] Some professors argue that cold-calling—and the attendant heightened level of anxiety—is the best way to ensure students are prepared for class. Meanwhile, ever since I outed myself in the legal academy as an introverted and formerly shy lawyer who overcame an extreme case of public speaking anxiety, smart but reticent students email me, confiding internal conflict; they are petrified about oral argument assignments and cold-calling in Socratic Method–run classes, yet they yearn to share their budding ideas about the law. To not miss out on the bounty of these thinkers, we need to bridge this divide and help introverted, shy, and socially anxious law students and lawyers find their authentic lawyer voices.

As a card-carrying introvert and someone who struggled with severe anxiety toward public speaking for too many years in the legal context—where extemporaneous discourse is lauded—I fell victim to the pressure to be something I was not. "Fake it till you make it!" many extroverted coworkers, friends, and acquaintances exclaim, clinking glasses and high-fiving. That approach does not work for introverts, and it is not a realistic long-term solution for those who suffer from anxiety toward interpersonal interaction in the legal arena.

Susan Cain, renowned author on introversion, validates that "the bias against quiet can cause deep psychic pain."[3] By pushing introverted law students and lawyers to feign extroversion, we do many intelligent and hard-working individuals—and the legal profession—a serious disservice.

Through extensive psychology-based research and self-study, digging into my personal history to understand the roots of my preference for quiet and my instinctive resistance toward instantaneous legal discourse before my thoughts are fully shaped, I now embrace introversion as an asset in teaching and litigating. Do I often still blush and break out in blotchy hives when I voice legal opinions and teach law? Yes, routinely. But I convey my passion for and commitment to the might of the legal profession by finally being genuine: analyzing legal concepts quietly, appropriating the time I need to reflect before speaking, and communicating when ready, using the power of the written word to amplify my voice. A voice does not need to boom to have an impact. Nor do the words or delivery need to be perfect. As activist Maggie Kuhn once said, "Speak your mind—even if your voice shakes."

This book champions the power of introversion within the legal profession, urging the legal academy and law practice to make room for the quiet thinkers and writers. Through this book, I endeavor to instigate my fellow introverts to *seize* your quiet space. This manifesto is for the many law students and new lawyers who experience overwhelming anxiety in a Socratic dialogue, who feel they have to force an extrovert persona, and who ride tsunamis of self-doubt over their chosen profession. Introversion in the law profession is a gift.

The journey of this book has two parts. The first half: (1) explains the differences among introversion, shyness, and social anxiety and how each can manifest in the legal context, (2) explores the impact on quiet individuals of the push toward extroversion in law school and law practice, and (3) highlights greatly valued proficiencies (i.e., active listening, deep thinking, sensitivity, empathy, thoughtful writing, etc.) that introverts (and shy or socially anxious individuals) can offer to the legal profession, by nurturing instead of repressing innate strengths. As Voltaire said in *Candide*, "Il faut cultiver notre jardin": "We must cultivate our garden," or "We need to work our fields."[4] While literati interpret this line multiple ways (some of which imply self-absorption to the exclusion of others—which is not my aspiration or exhortation), I instead translate it as a message of emancipation. No longer bound by the expectation to don a fake extrovert mantle, and instead free to incubate germinating ideas about the law and nourish alternative problem-solving techniques, introverts can transform our profession.

Of course, in numerous circumstances, lawyers must be equipped to interact interpersonally with confidence and vigor. Thus, to help quiet law students and lawyers become authentically powerful advocates in both deed *and word*, the second half of this book outlines a practical seven-step process to help introverted, shy, and socially anxious individuals amplify their voices without compromising or suppressing their quiet strengths—repackaging their perceived challenges into valuable lawyering competencies.

Stress is already a hallmark of legal education and practice. According to the Dave Nee Foundation, studies show that: (1) matriculating law students exhibit a collective psychological profile reflective of that of the general population, yet, after graduation, 20 to 40 percent of graduates indicate a psychological dysfunction, (2) 26 percent of attorneys who pursue counseling reference anxiety and depression, (3) 19 percent of lawyers struggle with "statistically significant" heightened depression levels, and (4) "[l]awyers are 3.6 times more likely to suffer from depression than non-lawyers."[5] According to the website LawyersWithDepression.com, an estimated 30,000 to 60,000 American law students battle depression during their law school tenure.[6] Numerous surveys reveal "high levels of unhappiness, stress, and depression among lawyers and law students."[7] Studies show that "[a]ttorney distress is an empirically documented phenomenon. Depression and alcoholism, for example, appear to occur among attorneys at about twice the rate found in the general population."[8] Statistics confirm that divorce rates of attorneys exceed those of the general population and other professionals.[9] Professor Larry Krieger of Florida State University College of Law, who studies the mental health of law students and lawyers, "reported that between 20 and 40 percent of law students suffer from clinical depression by the time they graduate; that the incidence of clinically elevated anxiety, hostility, and depression among students is eight to 15 times that of the general population; and that, out of 104 occupational groups, lawyers rank the highest in depression and fifth in incidence of suicide."[10] Sadly, research indicates that "[l]awyers, as a group, are twice as likely to commit suicide as the general public."[11] With these statistics as a backdrop, the legal community owes our newest and next generations of lawyers our most profound commitment to seeking ways to reduce unnecessary stress. Introverted, shy, and socially anxious law students and lawyers, whom we goad into forced extroversion—without honoring differences in the ways humans learn, process, and debate complex analytical concepts—are at risk of needless anxiety and depression.

This book aims to empower educators to adjust the way we teach law: rather than expecting all new students to leap immediately at the opportunity for a Socratic drilling starting on the first day of law school, we first should overtly teach the *purpose*—and transparently model the Q and A *pattern*—of this type of legal query. By expressly explaining *why* and *how* we use this teaching technique, and arming students with sufficient knowledge of how best to prepare for class (and handle situations in which they might not know how to answer a professor's question), we can peel away at least one layer of the anxiety associated with learning an unfamiliar legal language and mode of communication. Without sacrificing any rigor of the law school experience, we also can afford naturally quiet but thoughtful individuals time and space to contemplate thorny legal concepts, and then experiment with communicating legal theories in their own authentic voices. This book also aspires to spark a refreshed perspective in law firm managers about junior associates who prefer to squirrel away in the library, or behind a closed office door. These quiet thinkers just might generate a brief or a solution to a legal problem that will stun the world. Appendices A and B provide key takeaways and practical suggestions for educators and practice mentors who hope to effectively tap into these quiet voices in a healthy and productive manner. Most importantly, this book rallies quiet law students and lawyers to embrace their potent traits and use them to recalibrate the profession—through thoughtful pondering of tough legal principles, active listening to clients, empathy, "sensitivity to nuance,"[12] instrumental legal writing, collaborative resolution of disputes, and artful persuasion.

Marti Olsen Laney, Psy.D., author of *The Introvert Advantage: How to Thrive in an Extrovert World*, quotes Michael Pollan's *The Botany of Desire*, in stating, "The tulip is an introvert among flowers."[13] Noting how tulips hibernate all winter before blooming in colorful flourish every spring, Dr. Laney observes, "Given the right conditions, tulips are hardy and bloom longer than many other flowers. But they won't bloom at all if conditions are inhospitable. Introverts are like that, too."[14] By shaping a conducive intellectual and interpersonal climate where introverts can thrive, they will revolutionize the legal profession. Let the quiet upspring begin.

Acknowledgments

This book has been a labor of love for nine years, sprouting from that impossibly hot California day in August 2008 when I stepped into my first classroom as a law professor—blushing, sweating, and rattling with nerves, once again chiding myself, "Why can't I *just do it* like everyone else?" Over that year, I witnessed many strong legal writing students battling public speaking anxiety in the face of the Socratic Method and oral arguments. Those students, and many more quiet impassioned ones since then, empowered me to study the phenomena of introversion, shyness, and social anxiety in the legal arena, leading me to finally understand that quietude does not equal weakness, but in fact can represent remarkable power, strength, and impact. Thank you to all my students at Chapman University School of Law, New York Law School, and Brooklyn Law School; without you, this book remains a mere thought. You made me a better teacher, lawyer, writer, and human. Thank you to the New York State Bar Association for supporting our Overcoming Public Speaking Anxiety (OPSA) workshops at New York Law School, and to all my student participants for bravely sharing your stories.

Thank you to all the authors listed in the bibliography, especially Susan Cain, Steve Flowers, Erika Hilliard, and Ivy Naistadt; your work switched on the light bulb over my head, illuminating important truths.

On the writing front, I am thankful for my first legal writing teacher, Professor Jan Levine, who ignited the initial spark of my love for legal writing (and writing in general) at The University of Virginia School of Law, giving me a vehicle to experiment with my lawyer voice. I appreciate the *Journal of the Legal Writing Institute* for publishing my first article on the topic of the silent law student, and the *Duquesne Law Review* for publishing a follow-up article on empowering law students to overcome extreme public speaking anxiety. These two pieces shaped the early bases of my research, and many concepts explored in the two articles evolve further in this book. I greatly cherish my legal writing colleagues nationally and internationally who provide unparalleled collaborative support for the variety of individual scholarly interests blossoming and flourishing within our academy. I am grateful for the important venues—such as the Global Legal Skills Conference—provided by the legal writing community where we can share our research, written work, and voices.

I extend particular thanks to Professor Richard K. Neumann, Jr. of the Maurice A. Deane School of Law at Hofstra University and Professor Robin Wellford Slocum of Chapman University School of Law for providing invaluable feedback on early versions of the book manuscript.

I also appreciate my fellow members of the Board of the Association of American Law Schools' Section on Balance in Legal Education, whose commitment to the well-being of our nation's law students and new lawyers kept me plugging ahead on this project.

Thank you to my research assistant, Jessica Laredo, of Brooklyn Law School, for her attention to detail in checking my citations, and to Loreen Peritz, Brooklyn Law School librarian and research professor, for locating numerous elusive research sources.

I treasure my Brooklyn Law School colleagues (notably, Professor Jodi Balsam, Professor Maryellen Fullerton, Professor Heidi Gilchrist, Professor Linda Feldman, Dean Nick Allard and his wife Marla Allard, Professor Dana Brakman-Reiser, Professor Jayne Ressler, Professor Gregg Macey, Professor Ted Janger, Professor Maria Termini, Professor Carrie Teitcher, Linda Harvey, Joanne Tapia, and all my legal writing colleagues), my former New York Law School colleagues (notably, Professor Kim Hawkins, Professor Anne Goldstein, Professor Erika Wood, Professor Doni Gewirtzman, Professor Lynn Su, Professor David Epstein, Professor Lynnise Pantin, and Dean Vicki Eastus), and my former Chapman University School of Law colleagues (Professor Carolyn Larmore and Professor Rita Barnett-Rose) for their support and encouragement of my writing and teaching projects.

Thank you to my agent, Jessica Faust of BookEnds Literary Agency, for seeing value in this project and for pushing me to make tough edits to the book proposal. Thank you to my wonderful publisher, Jon Malysiak at Ankerwycke Books, for believing in the message of this book from the beginning, and for reading early manuscript drafts so carefully. Thank you to Kristine Toliver for improving the manuscript through the copyediting process.

Thank you to my creative, brilliant, hilarious, and unconditionally supportive friends who constantly check in on me and make sure I am still breathing every time I go off-grid and retreat into my introvert/writer cave, especially Clay Edmonds (introvert extraordinaire), Melissa Jangl, Lauren Brownstein, Susan Silver, Kelly Woods, Anna Miller, Todd Flournoy, Lucinda Heidsieck Bhavsar, Tim Erblich, Jess Rothschild (my website designer), and Krista Bonura (my headshot/bio photographer). Your check-ins motivated me to get up each day, shove that stubborn pen onto that resistant paper, and eventually dig into the draft reviews and copyedits when I was scared to look. To my family, *omnia vincit amor. Vi ringrazio molto.*

To all the quiet law students and lawyers out there—when you're ready, shine that bright, oh so bright, light.

I Walked the Quiet Walk

If you are an introverted, shy, or socially anxious individual considering or wading through law school or law practice, and wondering whether this career path is truly for you, I understand. You *are* on the right journey. I was you. Please allow me to share my serpentine story.

For nearly two decades, I believed my introversion and social anxiety were flaws. I worried that colleagues would determine I was not cut out for practicing or teaching law and eject me from the profession. I kept "just doing it" as the rousing Nike brand inspires us, and "just failing." When forced to feign extroversion to fit the lawyer stereotype, my nerves frayed and the palpable desire to work alone persisted. Eventually, after studying the science of introversion and the origins of my deep-seated fear of judgment that fueled my social anxiety, I finally understood that I could be my most effective self—as a client advocate and an educator—by being authentic. I stopped trying to fake extroversion, mined my personal history for the origins of my interpersonal anxiety, and quietly reinvented myself.

Entering law school at 21, I let the Socratic Method bully me. I never grasped that it had a discernable pattern; I operated in a fugue state and regarded my law professors at The University of Virginia School of Law as enigmatic gurus dangling nuggets of knowledge beyond my reach. In class, my body rattled like a turbulent airplane. My Civil Procedure professor cold-called me to explain the concept of federal diversity jurisdiction to my 65 peers. Although I understood this rule completely, having bullet-pointed, flow-charted, and practically story-boarded the assigned reading, I delivered a barely audible response based entirely on the faulty geographical premise that Seattle and Portland occupied the same state. Red stress blotches speckled my neck and cheeks daily. In my first-year oral argument, I developed a nervous tic of yanking on my hair. Even though I had over-prepared and brandished impeccable outlines, I could not access the names of cases or respond coherently to layup questions. My 1L year was a nine-month migraine.

I landed a summer associate position with a Washington, DC–area law firm, a fraternity of aggressive, confident, ambitious, "work hard/play hard" partners and associates practicing construction contract litigation. Our softball jerseys taunted, "Losing is not an option." The firm represented developers, owners, builders, architects, and engineers in transactional contract-drafting and multimillion-dollar lawsuits involving complex breach of contract issues related to power plant, hospital, assisted-living facility, and sports stadium projects. We resolved conflicts over late payments, completion delays, faulty designs, weather events, unanticipated underground obstructions, and other disruptions.

The partners and senior associates dispensed difficult legal research assignments to the summer associates, requiring us to delve into the nuances of multifaceted construction and government contracts disputes. With each research and writing project, I raced to the law library—in my cornflower-blue mini-suits, channeling actor Calista Flockhart's character on the 1990s TV show *Ally McBeal*—nestling into the quiet stacks to find the answers. I loved poring through the burgundy casebooks and online judicial opinions, ascertaining the big picture of the client's circumstances, and brainstorming possible solutions to the legal dilemmas facing the client at each incremental stage of the case. I was happy writing, and circumvented most command speaking performances that first summer, letting my memoranda and briefs do the talking.

After an additional summer at the firm that culminated in a full-time job offer that I hungrily accepted (student loans looming), law school graduation, and a successful bar exam, my supervising attorneys and mentors chucked off my training wheels and heaved me into a hefty lineup of depositions, client meetings, and court appearances. I developed an elegant pre-game ritual of throwing up. Although I loved the substance of my work and the research and writing process, the often stubborn and combative construction industry was a tough junket for an introverted young female associate. I wanted to write, but needed to fight. I believed I had to fake an extrovert persona in every interaction with a construction client or opposing counsel. It was inauthentic, draining, and ineffective. Although I adored and respected my fellow junior associates, I sought solitude in my workspace, preferring to hole up in the library or my office and research and write alone.

The construction clients were smart and tough, and generally had strong personalities, as did the lawyers and project representatives on opposing sides of every case; the cast was predominantly alpha-male across the board (with the exception of a few vivacious, whip-smart, and assertive female partners and senior associates at our firm). Contract negotiations for new construction projects and contentious lawsuits over troubled jobsites typically involved armies of extroverts, and they tended not to be happy-go-lucky folk. When too many dominant characters were involved, negotiation and litigation positions quickly cemented on all sides, forestalling progress or reasonable compromise and costing the parties and players additional money and stress.

For six years, I felt happy and calm researching and writing client opinion letters, memoranda, and briefs, yet sick and stressed arguing, negotiating, and performing (and, like other associates, absorbing verbal blows from a particularly volatile partner). My personal relationships suffered greatly. During my life's most traumatic breakup of a 12-year relationship—which still feels like I hacked off a limb with a rough saw—I left everything and moved to New York. I accepted a new job in a law firm on a mid-level floor of Tower Two of the World Trade Center. My office abutted a senior partner's office, and unfortunately he was another unpredictable and often explosive character. Each day, while I grieved my relationship and former life, I stared out the waffle windows at sailboats circling the Statue of Liberty and wished I could trade places with the boatmen. For nearly a year, I flinched every time the senior partner erupted at associates and staff over mishaps as minor as misaligned staples. Each night, I escaped by placing my handbag in a Redweld folder and marching with purpose toward the back staircase. In late summer 2001, I decided I needed time off to regroup. I booked a spontaneous trip to Greece and was flying back home on a Lufthansa plane, after connecting through Frankfurt, Germany, when the towers fell. My pilot diverted the plane to Gander, Newfoundland, joining 38 flights and 6,000 grounded passengers and crew. The Canadians fed, clothed, and boarded us at schools and churches. Eventually, five days later, I returned to New York, after first having to fly back to Frankfurt due to border closures and then hopping on the next flight home. 9/11 smacked me out of my self-absorbed grief; I no longer had any excuse to feel sorry for myself. My sadness, anxiety, and depression had saved me from being in my tower office that day, and I happened to be on the right plane, not the wrong one. It was time to get on with it, and to be grateful for my life. I quit the law firm (which had relocated to midtown after we thankfully and miraculously lost no employees), took time off to write my first litigation book and feel mentally strong again, and thereafter joined a small firm as a brief writer.

Fourteen years into my litigation career (still battling anxiety during performance-oriented events), I was living out West working on a California-based lawsuit for the law firm, and a West Coast law school hired me to teach legal writing. Armed with three-ring binders of lecture outlines in large typeface and color-coded highlighting, I stepped into my first classroom as a teacher rather than a student. Staring from the podium at what I worried were a sea of skeptical 1Ls, hives crept around my neck. My face sizzled. I gulped and started speaking. I explained who I was, where I came from, that this was my first day of teaching, that I loved legal writing, and that I wanted to help them love it too. My academic career launched.

Although I often reveled in the classroom environment, especially those light-bulb moments when students grasped a legal rule framework or crafted a creative public policy argument, the nerves lingered. I overprepared and believed every class needed to be perfect or the students would deem me a fraud. In my mind, no amount of pre-planning could avert an "epic classroom fail" if students simply were overstressed that day, or I flubbed an answer, or an interactive experiment flopped. In the early semesters, I turned scarlet in those instances, every time, and worried my students perceived me a charlatan. They didn't. After a semester or two, when an awkward moment arose in the classroom—a student posed a question I hadn't thought of, classmates battled a little too heatedly over a controversial topic, or I misplaced my next page of teaching notes—I began sharing my internal dialogue instead of faking through it. I would say, "OK, I'm turning red right now, and there's nothing I can do about it, so I'm going to keep on going." Students laughed. We exhaled, bonded, and opened up a communication flow, committing to making our classroom a place where everyone could be themselves. We worked hard to understand the law and how to talk and write about it, and tried to eliminate intimidation or a tenor of judgment that could lead to self-censorship.

Ultimately, my *students* instigated my own introvert revolution and reinvention journey. Observing many of my quiet students—who were often my strongest writers—stress about class participation and oral arguments, I finally snapped into action and began studying introversion, shyness, and social anxiety. Thanks to myriad helpful psychology resources, it finally made sense why authenticity and vulnerability felt good and bonded me to my students, but faking it in the law classroom, office, courtroom, and faculty meetings felt bad. I began to strive to be myself in every legal encounter, even if I blushed or took a while to formulate a coherent thought. Meanwhile, at the suggestions of the many authors whose books on social psychology, shyness, and anxiety I devoured, I undertook the not-so-pleasant task of quarrying my personal history. I reflected back and identified antiquated toxic messages that derailed my present-day confidence: sarcastic comments by middle school teachers, disapproval from well-meaning formative influencers, and judgment from high school "cool kids" and "friends" whose stinging words chopped the legs out from under my blossoming ideas and individual opinions. I eventually realized that their obsolete words about my quiet inquisitive nature and nascent independent thoughts no longer had any relevance in my life in the law. It was time to delete and overwrite. I also began to notice that some of the loudest lawyers I had encountered over many years were not necessarily the smartest—about life or the law. I had been confusing brawn and belligerence with brains.

While my introversion research gained traction, I continued to practice and teach law simultaneously, which provided real-life opportunities to test new mental and physical strategies for optimizing assets and managing anxiety as a naturally quiet advocate. Through trial-and-error and continuous personal reframing, I adjusted my approach to the substantive legal work, flexing instead of suppressing my introvert strengths. My law firm's practice, although litigation-heavy, entailed a significant amount of transactional work: negotiating high-level, multimillion-dollar (sometimes even billion-dollar), construction-related contracts among various players. Having litigated disputes involving these types of agreements for years, I had learned the many ins and outs of what made a strong contract, or one that best protected the interests of my client, which-ever side of the transaction he or she (usually he) represented. Instead of engaging in my well-practiced stress-out meltdown routine in anticipation of a fight with opposing counsel over language and content, I started tapping into my quiet power, focusing on the intellectual enjoyment of scrutinizing every word of these sometimes 80-page agreements and carefully crafting proposed changes.

While previously I believed (based on my litigation training at three dif-ferent firms) that I had to adopt the most aggressive, client-favorable stance and dig in my heels to battle for every word (which went completely against my nature), my drafting and negotiation strategy shifted. Instead, I com-menced each contract negotiation by letting my writing do the talking; I took the lead on drafting reasonable but firm client-favorable language and circu-lating a redlined version—electronically—to the opposing party for review. Dueling redlines can easily devolve into an all-out brawl if opposing lawyers will not budge from their perceived client-biased positions. I used to think I had to meet an opposing counsel's tone with a similarly resistant attitude. But instead, when a party's lawyer proposed alternative language, I took the time to consider each word or sentence. If I agreed that the new phrasing added clarity and did not detrimentally affect my client's contractual rights or negotiating stance, I accepted the change. If I disagreed with the revision being pushed by opposing counsel, instead of faking outrage and stoking temper flare-ups in others (techniques I had observed in mentors at all three firms and believed (correctly or incorrectly) that I was expected to mirror), I calmly explained as transparently as possible why the new language did not work for my client, or offered an example of how such language had fomented unnecessary litigation in the past. Instead of digging in like many of my counterparts across the negotiating table, I communicated reasons for my position, and invited opposing counsel to do the same: "Hmm, can you send me the statutory language you are relying upon? I'd love to take a look. Do you have a sample of an alternate contractual provision that has worked better in the past?" By not just asserting "no," and instead saying, "well, I acknowledge what you are saying, yet the reasons why I have an issue with this language are (a) . . . (b) . . . and (c)," dialogue usually continued instead of ending in a stalemate.

Of course, some clients wanted a hard-hitting negotiation, no matter what—on the phone, or in person. Welcome to the introvert's nightmare: the dreaded multiparty conference call, where loud voices often browbeat like bullies on a playground, and introverts who cannot stand interrupting people could flail. Jumping into the mayhem to interject a thought among clashing dominant voices is, in the words of one of my favorite law students, "so not my jam." Even worse, when I negotiate face-to-face, each time I try to fake a rigid immovable negotiating position, I blush—a lovely biological lie detector. While I worked on understanding my natural habits and traits and cultivating my introvert fortitude, my strategy for telephonic and in-person contract negotiation also transformed. I realized that speaking in a calm friendly voice—if on a conference call, while physically *standing up* in the privacy of my home or office to garner a boost of energy—lent authentic power to my ideas. In preparation, I wrote out the reasons underlying my proposed contractual language; I never demanded a term simply to win (that will never be my style) but rather, I always had a justification for why the provision was fair. I stated my position steadily and clearly, and I did not demand acceptance on the spot. If someone interrupted me, and someone always did, I continued talking in my composed and slightly amplified voice and did not stop. Once I stated my piece, I gave the other side time to mull my ideas over, even if it meant scheduling a follow-up exchange of emails or another conference call. This strategy puzzled some participants; they were not always sure how to handle the soft-spoken female on the line or the serial blusher in the room. At first, many pushed back, stamping their feet and repeating their positions. If that happened, instead of letting rigid or increasingly antagonistic stances begin to unravel me, I ignited newly adopted mental and physical strategies (explained in the seven-step process in the second half of this book) to manage my instinctive anxiety responses. I restated my position, and explained that yes, I *heard* their contention, and already accounted for that in either my language or my thought process.

With repeated practice, although it wasn't always smooth, this method began to work for me. I experienced much greater success using my authentic voice than I ever did trying to act like an argumentative jerk. My contracts eventually got signed, and I unexpectedly had opposing counsel and project representatives send me "thank-you" emails, commenting on how refreshing it was to engage in productive and reasonable negotiations in our often-bellicose industry. An executive vice president of one of my construction clients once wrote, "You have a talent that not many have to understand and respond to a client's needs."

Likewise, in my litigation role, instead of immediately adopting a combative "attack dog" persona when ghostwriting letters for clients to their counterparts in a construction dispute, or when crafting my own emails to opposing counsel to resolve discovery disagreements, I tried to diffuse personality conflicts caused by too many raucous voices talking over one another. Instead, I attempted to suss out the real root of the clash. I engaged the introverted preference for internal methodical thinking *before* speaking (a tendency described in Chapter 1). I carefully processed the applicable facts and law. I tried to employ empathy (another trait of many introverts and individuals who struggle with anxiety, as explored in Chapter 3) to consider what aspects of human nature were holding the key players back from resolving the conflict. I then used my all-time favorite skill of artful legal writing as a tool to try to move the case forward instead of just churning the status quo with unhelpful rhetoric. Of course, this aspiration does not always work; some clients (and bosses and co-workers) were accustomed to the fight, and—100 percent of the time—resisted the kinder, gentler approach, demanding a tougher tone. But often, my letters and briefs laid stepping stones of progress toward a successful resolution.

Now that I have I transitioned out of law practice entirely to focus on full-time law teaching and writing, I continue to hone my introvert strengths so that I can be my most impactful self when interacting with students and faculty colleagues. Still prone to anxiety, I work out every day, continuously learning how to channel physical strength to power my authentic voice (techniques discussed in Chapter 8), calm my constantly racing mind, and corral my nerves. I try to model vulnerability and honesty in my interactions with students, so they know that their worries about law school in no way make them unfit to be transformational lawyers. Continuously making peace with my past, I aspire to be present in my interactions with others, exhibit empathy and a collaborative inclusive mindset, and look *forward* to great things instead of backwards. Yes, there are hiccups and bumps in the road, but (to paraphrase my favorite role model, Bono of the Irish rock band U2 as he regards "friends and enemies") "all of them useful."

My evolution was not an overnight metamorphosis. So far, this has been a nine-year journey of self-discovery—using the seven-part transformative process described in the second half of this book—and continues to be a work-in-progress. Every week, I encounter a new introverted challenge in the legal world. But I am much happier, calmer, healthier, and successful being my authentically quiet lawyer self than I ever was trying to "just do it" and "fake it till I made it."

If you are a fellow quiet soul, come join me on this voyage.

PART I

QUIET LAW STUDENTS AND LAWYERS: CHANGE AGENTS FOR THE PROFESSION

CHAPTER 1

Shades of Quiet: Distinctions Among Introversion, Shyness, and Social Anxiety

Society tends to clump together the classifications of introversion, shyness, and social anxiety when labeling quiet individuals.[15] Quiet folks frequently are branded as introverted, shy, distant, standoffish, unapproachable, antisocial, or aloof, or they are tagged as wallflowers, loners, recluses, or outsiders. These hasty characterizations often are technically inaccurate, and they jumble distinct psychological classifications and personality traits. Each categorization invokes discrete manifestations, implications, strengths, and challenges for law students and lawyers. An individual might fall into just one, or more than one, category. For instance, many introverted law students and lawyers are not shy or socially anxious at all; they are confident speakers when they are ready to communicate. By nature, they simply prefer thinking and writing over talking. They are *internally* methodical and, therefore, they might appear to take longer than some extroverts in processing complex legal analyses (extroverts tend to think aloud). Further, introverts renew their energy through solitude instead of social engagement. In contrast, other introverted law students and lawyers suffer a substantial amount of stress when pressured into mimicking an extroverted lawyer role or persona; fear of judgment sparks shyness or a more extreme state known as social anxiety. This chapter explains the science behind all three categories. For quiet law students and lawyers who seek to better understand the impactful roles they can play in the legal profession, an important first step is enhanced self-awareness to determine which of these categories resonate.

As a law professor over the past nine years at three schools in New York and California (and as a visiting professor at a law school in Italy), I can confirm that introverted, shy, and socially anxious students occupy our law school classrooms. Many such students tarry outside my faculty office doorway, awaiting a lull in writing conferences. They flock to public speaking anxiety workshops.

Some struggle in oral arguments, despite excellent brief writing and valiant and dogged preparation. They dispatch countless emails, confiding that they need help but do not know where to turn. Further validating my conviction about the prevalence of these students in the law school environment, befuddled yet determined legal writing professors often gather around the podium after presentations on this topic at legal conferences around the country. They aspire to know how they might better help their anxious students cope with the Socratic Method and oral advocacy assignments.

In a research survey I conducted in 2010 and 2011, when I began to study introversion in the law context, I queried deans of students and directors of academic support at the nation's top 100 law schools. I asked them whether their students seek assistance with public speaking anxiety, and if their schools offer any formal program, workshop, or course to focus on this issue. Forty-two of the schools responded: The majority of respondents acknowledged that yes, a number of students seek guidance for this concern every year; and no, unfortunately, their schools do not provide formal programs to address anxiety toward interpersonal interaction in the legal context. Most law schools furnish academic support programs in which trained advisors mentor students in test taking, outlining, fundamental writing skills, and bar exam strategy. Further, most law schools provide substantive, procedural, and stylistic instruction in the 1L year on how to deliver an oral argument. However, my survey indicated that at that time, very few law schools tackled the public speaking anxiety component from an underlying psychological standpoint. Only two schools confirmed that they offered mentoring and one-on-one workshops, to give students a forum for practicing oral arguments with the specific aim of reducing anxiety toward the assignment. Although law school academic support programs and mental health support groups within bar associations aspire to reduce students' and lawyers' anxiety, a specific focus on introversion, shyness, and social anxiety is relatively new to the profession. Lately, the legal community has begun to take notice. In February 2016, the American Bar Association (ABA) Young Lawyers Division and the *ABA Journal* teamed up to offer a webinar that addressed the impactful role that introversion and introverts can and should play in the legal profession.

Part of the problem historically has been that not everyone understands the important distinctions among extroversion, introversion, shyness, and social anxiety. This is especially true in the legal context, in which quietude and self-reflection traditionally have not been emphasized. Further, the common misbelief is that everyone can push through interpersonal reticence with enough moxie, preparation, or rehearsal. This "just do it" approach—without self-awareness and strategic planning to address and manage the roots of an individual's instinctive resistance toward social interaction—can heighten instead of mitigate anxiety.

Instead, quiet law students and lawyers who yearn to tap into their formidable lawyer voices *first* must learn the differentiations among extroversion, introversion, shyness, and social anxiety—to self-assess. *Then*, they can embark on a personally tailored path to capitalize effectively on innate strengths and reduce anxiety toward interactive legal discourse. Understanding the scientific difference between introversion and extroversion can be transformative in a quiet lawyer's professional development. It can illuminate the internal conflict that naturally flares when an individual attempts to force extroversion instead of realizing, appreciating, and cultivating one's effectiveness as an introverted advocate. After recognizing this friction—perhaps for the first time—and subsequently reevaluating the role of quiet strength in the legal arena, introverts can make subtle adjustments in attitude, mental and physical approaches, and communication techniques to showcase a more naturally powerful persona, which inevitably reduces stress. The second half of this book describes a seven-step process for achieving this goal.

In contrast to introverts, shy and socially anxious individuals manifest a more deeply rooted fear of judgment and criticism that fosters self-censorship and restraint in interpersonal interaction. With similar self-study (through the seven steps) and increased conscious attention, individuals who experience a more intense version of stress in law-related performance events can work on identifying the historical roots of their apprehension, and then make potent changes to mental and physical approaches to interpersonal exchanges in the legal arena. For now, let's start by differentiating introversion, shyness, and social anxiety.

INTROVERSION

So, what precisely is an introvert, and who are the introverted law students and lawyers? In everyday parlance, we stereotype extroverts as gregarious and outgoing, and introverts as reserved and possibly even socially detached. These definitions are not accurate or complete. According to the Myers & Briggs Foundation,[16] Swiss psychiatrist Carl Jung originally "used the words to describe the preferred focus of one's energy on either the outer or the inner world. Extraverts[17] [sic] orient their energy to the outer world, while [i]ntroverts orient their energy to the inner world."[18] Extroverts ramp up and maintain energy by infiltrating and soaking up their surroundings, intermingling with people, engaging, talking, and interacting—through coffee dates, parties, group exercise classes, teamwork, FaceTime, or Skype telephone chats.

An extrovert is more likely than an introvert to perk up at the idea of scheduling a first date, attending a party where many guests are strangers, chatting with a fellow passenger on an airplane, cheering in a spinning class, talking to newcomers at the dog park, shaking hands with or hugging a neighbor at church during introductions, working in pairs or on teams in an interactive classroom exercise, or tossing around ideas in an office brainstorming session.

Introverts certainly are capable of exerting energy in public, and they can be quite adept in the art of social engagement when they want or need to be. However, eventually, a long span of human interface saps an introvert's energy, like air escaping from a punctured inflatable raft. Introverts' social engagements typically have a shorter shelf life than their extroverted counterparts. An expiration alarm eventually sounds in the introvert's mind, signaling the time to retreat to a quiet haven for reenergization.[19] Because introverts' energy drains more swiftly than extroverts',[20] at some point, they slam into a wall of social exhaustion and must retreat or their temperaments can shift rapidly. Sophia Dembling, author on introversion, sums it up perfectly: "We're fine, we're fine, we're fine, we're okay, we're kind of okay, we're getting tired, we're getting really tired, *boom*, we're bitchy."[21]

In the recovery stage, introverts stockpile renewed verve through solitude, quiet, and internal sanctuary. After a social or professional foray, an introvert might hibernate at home, take a walk alone, spend time with a pet (who might stare reverently but won't expect energetic conversation), listen to music, paint, strum a guitar, exercise, read, write, binge-watch a favorite television show, or simply rest. An introvert might turn off or avoid the phone, or communicate solely through text messaging or email, rather than live or by speaking on the phone, to the chagrin of extroverted friends and family who "just want to hear your voice."

On a day-to-day basis, an introvert might be perfectly happy and anxiety-free researching and writing, texting and emailing, sitting quietly in a meeting while pondering ideas and taking notes, engaging with a close friend or colleague one-on-one in attentive exchange, sampling hors-d'oeuvres at a cocktail party without feeling compelled to chat with anyone yet, and working independently. This behavior does not make the introvert antisocial or misanthropic. Dr. Laney vividly notes that introverts "are not scaredy cats, shrinking violets, or self-absorbed loners."[22] Yet, force an introvert into a lengthy multi-party conference call, group work, sharing ideas before she is ready, party games, ice-breakers, or role play? Internal cringe for many of us. Pressuring an introvert to play a trust game too soon with a co-worker or high-five a sweaty stranger in a spinning class can launch a prickly case of hives.[23]

The divergence in the way introverts and extroverts produce, derive, and sustain energy has very tangible manifestations in how these two categories of people navigate life, process complex information, communicate thoughts and opinions, make decisions, and interact with other humans. These are highly relevant considerations when analyzing the differences in how introverts and extroverts approach—and will thrive best in—law school and law practice. Generally, according to Cain, introverts "listen more than they talk, think before they speak, and often feel as if they express themselves better in writing than in conversation."[24] As we explore in Chapter 3, these traits are well-suited for the legal profession. Yet, law school and law practice tend to push the extrovert exemplar. Many introverted law students and lawyers are patient listeners, deep thinkers, methodical processors of information, careful decision-makers, and thoughtful speakers—when they are ready to share. To accomplish these tasks, these individuals crave quiet, they limit overstimulation, they minimize interruptions (to self and to others), and they work in solitude. They treasure authenticity (and therefore experience internal conflict at advice like "fake it till you make it"), and they resist pressure to be something they are not. The next few sections of this chapter place each of these introvert traits and tendencies within the current context of legal education and practice. Chapter 2 then analyzes the effects of traditional legal education models and law practice on the stress and anxiety levels of quiet individuals. Chapter 3 rouses introverted, shy, and socially anxious law students and lawyers to serve as change agents—fostering greater empathy, intellectual humility, and inclusion within our profession—leading into the seven-step process in the second half of the book. Finally, Appendices A and B offer suggestions for legal educators and law practice mentors to champion impactful, quiet advocates.

INTROVERTS PREFER LISTENING TO TALKING, AND PROCESS INFORMATION INTERNALLY, METHODICALLY, AND DEEPLY

Introverts are good listeners[25] and deep thinkers.[26] Although being a rapt listener is an asset as a lawyer, the act of listening also can be energy-depleting for introverts because "we pay attention."[27] We process significant amounts of data before we speak. In dialogue, many introverts naturally listen, pause, think, anticipate, reflect, sometimes reconsider, and possibly even mentally rehearse phrasing and language choices before reacting to a question or statement.[28] Some extroverts might perceive this sequence as socially sluggish or uncommunicative. However, Dr. Laurie Helgoe notes that "[i]ntroverts think before speaking, and need time *within* conversations to develop their ideas and responses";[29] they are not avoiding communication but rather internally gearing up in an effort to do it well. Dr. Jennifer Kahnweiler agrees: "Even in casual conversations, they consider others' comments carefully and stop and reflect before responding. They know how to use the power of the pause."[30] The character John Cage on the popular 1990s television legal drama *Ally McBeal* was a quirky introverted trial lawyer known for announcing in open court, "I'm going to take a moment," or "I need to take a moment," while pondering his next riposte. The pause gave his brain the power surge to craft an ensuing legal zinger.

Because introverts habitually seize mental lulls to reflect,[31] their thinking process can appear slower than extroverts', who often muse aloud, firing off thoughts and ideas more rapidly. As Dembling points out, "Introverts are kinda slowpokey in our thinking. Gears in our heads seem to turn long and ponderously before cranking out an idea. When we're concentrating, we can't easily switch attention from that task to another."[32] Introverts deliberate before reacting to a thought;[33] they mull "things around to examine every angle first."[34] Some introverts rework and vet thoughts in their heads so extensively that they "edit [themselves] into silence."[35]

Science explains the introvert's assiduous thinking process. Researchers indicate that introverts have more blood coursing to their brains[36] than extroverts, which links to intensified stimulation and sensitivity. Further (and fascinatingly!), introverts' and extroverts' blood apparently journeys along diverse brain highways.[37] Dr. Laney describes an experiment by Dr. Debra Johnson that contrasts introverts' and extroverts' blood movement:[38]

> *The introverts' blood flowed to the parts of the brain involved with internal experiences like remembering, solving problems, and planning. This pathway is long and complex . . . The extroverts' blood flowed to the areas of the brain where visual, auditory, touch, and taste (excluding smell) sensory processing occurs. Their main pathway is short and less complicated.*[39]

Scientists also note that introverts' and extroverts' "dominant" brain passageways employ different neurotransmitters:[40] acetylcholine for introverts, which influences the ability to access long-term memory;[41] and dopamine for extroverts,[42] which fuels "energy, excitement about new ideas, and motivation."[43]

Against this backdrop of introverts' natural tendencies to listen and contemplate before communicating, many law professors, supervising attorneys, and judges expect law students and lawyers to engage in and excel at spontaneous discourse. In the law classroom, law office (often governed by the billable hour), and courtroom, slow thinking is not typically encouraged or understood. Quicker thinkers erroneously might leap to the conclusion that a cautious-thinking law student or lawyer is not that smart. This book aims to upturn that misperception *while at the same time* empowering quiet advocates to more effectively (and authentically) demonstrate the depth of their thinking.

INTROVERTS ARE GRADUAL DECISION-MAKERS

Although introverts do not need to hem and haw for weeks or months to make a decision, instantaneous decisiveness can be inharmonious with an introvert's nature. Dr. Laney emphasizes that "introverts require time to form and articulate opinions."[44] Because of their need "to let information percolate,"[45] introverts do not delight in immediate decision-making[46] or in thinking "on their feet." Coercing an introvert to make a knee-jerk assessment or a spontaneous choice might yield a completely different result than if the introvert's normal marinating process ran its course. Thus, the pressure to draw immediate legal conclusions in the law classroom, or to make on-the-spot tactical choices in a negotiation or courtroom, can run contrary to an introvert's natural preference for measured decision-making. However, with enhanced awareness of this conflict, plus forethought and strategic planning, introverts can be sound legal decision-makers, even in scenarios where spontaneous decisiveness is warranted or expected.

INTROVERTS ARE SELECTIVE WITH WORDS

Introverts are choosy about their outlay of words; they "don't talk for talk's sake."[47] Introverts value words expended, and therefore, they reserve speech for ideas that will add to a dialogue meaningfully and that exhibit merit. Cain describes one introvert she encountered as "prefer[ring] to contribute only when he believes he has something insightful to add, or honest-to-God disagrees with someone."[48] Likewise, Mark Tanner, author of a book on introversion in the church, notes that introverts proceed guardedly, and resist sharing thoughts, ideas, and solutions to problems "until [such concepts] are robust enough to stand up to public scrutiny."[49]

Because of introverts' "constant distilling process"[50]—instinctively cataloguing, sorting, and sifting internally—Cain acknowledges that introverts might not thrive in "speaking extemporaneously."[51] Because introverts think deeply and "value meaning, they want to be precise and select just the right words to express [thoughts and ideas]."[52] The Edge, guitarist of U2, reinforces this notion of stewardship of words, or in his case, musical notes:

Notes actually do mean something. They have power. I think of notes as being expensive. You don't just throw them around. I find the ones that do the best job and that's what I use. I suppose I'm a minimalist instinctively. I don't like to be inefficient if I can get away with it . . . I'm a musician. I'm not a gunslinger. That's the difference between what I do and what a lot of guitar heroes do.[53]

The Edge's respect for the worth of each musical note parallels introverts' judiciousness with words. Nonetheless, this language economy and conservationism can prompt some extroverts—especially in the legal arena—to incorrectly regard introverts as "hesitant and uncertain of their opinion[s]."[54] With enhanced awareness and recognition of the purpose (and benefits) of introverted advocates' selectiveness in word choice and timing of expression, we can change this potential misperception.

INTROVERTS ARE NATURALLY CAUTIOUS IN GROUP MEETINGS AND BRAINSTORMING SESSIONS

The innate need for unpressured reflective time and a reliance on long-term memory[55] can menace introverts in group meetings where spontaneous banter often is expected within the "cut and thrust of debate."[56] The pressure to be "on" in a meeting resembling a verbal volleyball match can be rattling, not to mention antithetical to introverts' deep thinking and internal decision-making. In group discussions, introverts "usually find it hard to both absorb all the new information *and* formulate an opinion about it."[57] They might be keen listeners and prolific note-takers, but require a post-meeting contemplative period to assimilate the information gathered, synthesize new concepts with past experiences, develop stand-alone opinions, strategize about appropriate follow-up action, and then craft the best way to phrase a responsive idea to others so that it will be correctly received and implemented.[58]

The same principle applies to the (dreaded) collective brainstorming session. Dembling affirms that "there's not an introvert alive who can think clearly in free-for-all brainstorming sessions."[59] Dr. Kahnweiler concurs: "For introverts, this team-heavy approach presents a problem. Not only does being intertwined with others deplete their reserves of people energy, it also takes them away from the physical and intellectual space, where they do their best thinking."[60]

Although the power of the billable hour discourages many lawyers from overscheduling meetings, trial and transactional deal teams inevitably must convene for group strategy sessions. Similarly, law students often must work in teams and groups. In such dynamics, the talents of the quiet thinkers are not always optimized. Again, however, with increased awareness of the assets introverts bring to teams and groups throughout law school and practice, and strategic planning by introverts to carve out impactful roles in these sometimes challenging settings, output and effectiveness can be enhanced for all participants.

INTROVERTS CRAVE REDUCED STIMULATION AND QUIET

Cain defines stimulation[61] as "the amount of input we have coming in from the outside world."[62] Introverts "can be easily overstimulated by the external world, experiencing the uncomfortable feeling of 'too much'"[63]—like nap-inducing bloat after a holiday meal. As Dr. Laney notes, when enough is enough, "the introvert's mind can shut down, saying, No more input, please. It goes dark."[64] Under these circumstances, an introvert's productivity can suffer.

When some extrovert friends hear that in the later years of my litigation career I worked remotely from New York City for a Washington, DC-area law firm, researching, writing, and editing briefs 8–10 hours a day in the solitude of my Manhattan apartment, they remark, "How isolating! Why didn't you go to Starbucks and work?" If I trotted off to Starbucks to draft a motion for summary judgment, my brain would not be able to process legal rules, case law, or persuasive arguments. Instead, the jazz music lilting from the speakers, baristas crooning "half-caf soy latte," playwrights clacking on their laptops, and rowdy toddlers playing bumper cars with strollers would consume me like a tornado. Dembling shares this sentiment: "I can't write with music playing. Actually, I can't write with anything going on around me."[65]

Introverts thrive in a quiet, reflective, private workspace, and function well operating solo.[66] The quiet "provides energy, increases self-awareness, and spurs creativity."[67] Unless introverts can minimize external stimuli, "their inner thoughts, feelings, and impressions will never bubble up to the surface."[68] With excess environmental distraction, introverts' ideas can fumble around blindly, with no clear path outward. Of course, after several hours working in isolation, the introvert likely will seek out human contact, but to get the real work done, she disappears back into her office cave. Luckily for introverts, most law firms have rejected the open cubicle/bullpen workspace concept that marketing agencies and other creative companies have embraced, ostensibly to enhance communication and idea sharing. However, introverted lawyers still must battle against the perception of being antisocial or "not a team player" when working quietly behind a closed door or in a remote library carrel to tune out the world and concentrate.

INTROVERTS RESIST INTERRUPTION TO OTHERS AND THEMSELVES

With a proclivity for deep thinking, methodical internal processing, and minimizing distraction, introverts bristle at interruption,[69] to others and themselves. In meetings, an introvert might wait for a turn to speak, or until a lull—which might never come. He might try to interject softly (and be overshadowed or glossed over by the more dominant voices),[70] or take advantage of a momentary pause to speak about an earlier topic, when the group has long since moved *en masse* onto another matter.[71] Interrupting a loquacious extrovert or a clamorous group demands a bundle of energy, which introverts are loath to expend haphazardly.

Likewise, interrupting introverts "causes them to lose their place, and they have to exert extra energy and concentration to retrieve their thoughts."[72] The intrusion "is like a blanket that silences his or her voice."[73] After an interruption, introverts must ramp up energy to reboot the conversation[74] and, thus, such interference with thought flow can be "a big drain on productivity."[75]

Consider the telephone. An extrovert might welcome a midday surprise FaceTime chat. To an introvert immersed in a research or writing project, the buzzing of a cellphone is an immediate arrest of concentration and depletion of energy.[76] The phone call becomes a command performance, "requiring expending energy for 'on-the-feet thinking.'"[77] To muster the momentum or vigor for a phone call, some introverts feel compelled to stand up and move around during the conversation, to make their voices heard. Introverts are known for screening calls, letting voicemail messages accumulate, and then scheduling time to return a series of phone calls one after the other, curtailing intermittent interruption and energy deficit.

Unfortunately, interruption abounds in legal education and practice. Some exuberant advocates have trouble waiting patiently for an introverted conversation partner to complete a thought before interjecting a point or counterpoint. Many lawyers pepper depositions and trials with objections, strategically disrupting opposing counsel's flow. Likewise, oral arguments are interspersed with interludes of judges' questions, which can pose a challenge for intro-verted advocates. Introverts can engage in strategic planning to minimize, and also manage, interruptions in the law context.

INTROVERTS CHERISH AUTHENTICITY

When introverts confide apprehension toward taxing group dynamics or daunting public speaking scenarios, some (well-meaning) advisors coach: "Fake it till you make it!" "Act *as if*!" "Pretend you are a Hollywood actor playing a role!" Yet, because introverts revere genuineness,[78] they resist these prompts. Cain acknowledges that introverts "have trouble projecting artificial enthusiasm."[79]

I always knew I was averse to the "just fake it" approach, but I wasn't sure why. My resistance resurfaces each time I need to facilitate classroom simula-tions to model lawyering techniques. Many faculty colleagues share vignettes of classroom success teaching class "in role" as a supervising attorney. Even though I was a supervising attorney in real life for years, I routinely shy away from play-acting the part in the law school classroom; I teach legal writing in the role of a professor, not as a hypothetical law firm partner. I craft assignment instructions as if they were written by real lawyers doling out work to junior associates, but when exploring foundational writing tasks with students, my delivery comes from "Professor Brown," not from "Attorney Brown." A quiet law student shed light on, and validated, my internal opposition to teaching "in role." This student excelled and thrived in all her legal writing projects but dreaded an upcoming simulated (and graded) client interview and a final oral argument assignment—the capstone to our 1L legal writing course. She confided, "I just hate the fakeness of both scenarios. It ruins the experience knowing that the client is just an actor being paid to challenge me. In the argument, it just feels so phony to stand up there in a suit I borrowed from my mom, and say the words 'May it please the court' to my Property professor wearing a judge's robe."

I never had analyzed the roots of my aversion toward teaching "in role" until this introverted student propounded the perfect summary. She said, "Playing a role in this context just feels inauthentic. It feels bad—physically and mentally." She wanted to be herself. She cared about the substance of the assignment and toiled to get her message right, but she wanted to convey it only in her own persona and voice. While of course, authenticity and genu-ineness are not exclusive to introverted individuals, it is helpful for introverts to note, acknowledge, and understand feelings of internal resistance toward playing a "role" or a "character" in the legal arena.

THE DANGER OF SOCIETY'S OBSESSION WITH CONVERSION OF INTROVERTS

Some people erroneously perceive introverts "as shy, anxious misanthropes instead of competent, thoughtful individuals."[80] They assume introverts need to be fixed. Well-intentioned but misguided mentors prod introverts: "Smile!" "Cheer up!" "Speak up!" "Chime in!" "Get involved!" "Have an opinion!" "Be assertive!" "Participate!" "Get out there!" "Be social!" "Be approachable!" "Just do it!" Unfortunately, as Dembling affirms, "Many introverts have internalized society's message that their way of being is wrong and that extroversion is bet-ter."[81] They are pushed to change who they fundamentally are.[82] Dr. Kahnweiler reiterates, "[I]ntroverts are indeed continually asked to adapt to an extrovert-centric workplace that rewards being out there and on stage."[83] Many introverts try for years (myself, for nearly two decades) to adopt extrovert standards[84] of socializing, working, and striving for success. They wonder why they are exhausted, frustrated, stressed, anxious, or depressed.

Shame is a dangerous by-product of the push toward introversion conver-sion. As children, many introverts are made to feel ashamed for simply being their quiet selves in our loud American culture,[85] "receiving the message overtly and covertly that something is wrong with them."[86] Notably, Carl Jung warned of the harm in "push[ing] a child outside of the natural range of his or her temperament."[87]

Speaking from personal experience, plus observation of and open con-versations with my law students, children disparaged by authority figures for exhibiting introvert traits and habits "can become shy, inhibited, or afraid."[88] Some quiet law students with a crushing fear of public speaking have verified this causal connection after mining their childhood experiences and recall-ing specific instances of self-silencing after repeated interactions with criti-cal authority figures such as coaches, teachers, or dominant family members. Reaching back to my own educational journey as an introverted child (as part of my self-evaluation along the seven-step journey toward finding my authentic lawyer voice), I vividly remembered a popular middle-school teacher publicly mocking me twice: after I mustered the courage to verbalize outward excite-ment over the results of a science experiment, and upon the joyous discovery that the largest Secret Santa gift under the classroom tree miraculously was for me. Later, in high school and college, when influential, formative figures admonished and withdrew from me when I marshaled the nerve to express blossoming political thoughts about election candidates and public policy issues that differed from their beliefs, such as the death penalty or abortion, I burned with shame, and lost the nascent trust germinating in my young voice.

When I got to law school, the shame entrenched. Overwhelmed by a cacophony of classmates bandying about constitutional levels of scrutiny, I retreated off-grid into my textbooks. When cold-called in class, I flash-blushed, and hives curled my neck like vines. Researching, writing, and quietly thinking about the law offered solace.

Shame is a particularly important emotion for determined introverts to note and process because it "is related to *being*. We feel shame when we think we are unworthy or innately flawed."[89] Rather than a fleeting sensation of temporary embarrassment because a person cannot *do* something correctly or has committed an erroneous *act* (an external representation), shame derives from a belief of *being* an inherently defective person (an internal entrenchment). Using a religious theme, it is the contrast between committing a sin versus being a punishable sinner. Or, committing a crime versus being a criminal.

Imbedded childhood shame can rear its monstrous head many years later in adult social and professional circumstances, holding us back from asserting ourselves, taking a stand, expressing an opinion, or making a decision. One outstanding yet nervous law student shared his utter confusion at a newly triggered extraordinary fear of public speaking in the law classroom. He marveled at how he had navigated college with no anxiety or performance issues whatsoever. Through surveying his personal history, he realized that the tenor of judgment and competition in the law classroom had reignited childhood shame linked to harsh criticism by coaches he worked with as an accomplished child athlete.

Dr. Peter Breggin, who writes about the "legacy emotions" of guilt, shame, and anxiety, explains that some individuals "learned in childhood to feel shameful at the very thought of standing up to authority."[90] Perhaps parents, teachers, coaches, religious advisors, babysitters, or other authority figures rebuked an introverted child for stating an opinion that differed from theirs, after the child carefully and methodically molded that belief and rallied the energy and courage to express it. After repeated similar censorship experiences, the introverted child began to doubt his viewpoints and decision-making ability. Naturally, developing a personal perspective or making an individualized choice became scary, associated with a risk of withdrawal of love or approval. Logically, to sidestep shame, adults with such history might unconsciously resist sharing thoughts and observations with others,[91] especially in the legal arena, where thought-sharing quickly can transform into heated debate and (perceived) judgment.

Emotions like shame and anxiety pose barriers to "adult self-assertiveness even when it is rational, ethical, or needed for self-defense and the promotion of our higher ideals."[92] In the legal context, law students and lawyers are expected to assert strong opinions about societal issues. To do so comfortably and genuinely, introverted advocates first might need to peel back a layer of shame or anxiety painted by a lifetime of being told to change. The great news is: childhood messages that underscore the notion that introverts need to be fixed or should harbor shame for being themselves can be overwritten. The second half of this book offers one tangible plan for quiet law students and attorneys to embrace their authentic personas and unveil their mighty lawyer voices.

SHYNESS

Introversion, which epitomizes the way many of us expend and rekindle energy, and how we process and share ideas, is different from shyness, defined as "an extreme self-consciousness when one is around people."[93] Shyness stems from a dread of "rejection, ridicule, or embarrassment"[94]—a fear of judgment.[95] Of course, judgment permeates the legal world: through competition for law school grades, law review and moot court accolades, job placement, bonuses in law practice, partnership decisions, etc. We even refer to a case outcome as a *judgment* in one litigant's favor. Although some people mistakenly interchange the terminology of introversion and shyness, some individuals might be both introverted *and* shy, but not all introverts are shy. Non-shy introverts socially engage, and many can do so masterfully, investing in each interpersonal interaction with a "pace of high social energy."[96] Eventually, they simply need solitude to decompress. As marriage and family therapist Steve Flowers, author of a transformative book, *The Mindful Path Through Shyness*, explains, "Introverts prefer solitary rather than social activities because that's satisfying for them; people who feel shy, on the other hand, choose solitary activities out of fear or anxiety."[97]

When we think of shy children, we envision cautious tots clinging to their parents' legs. When children don't respond readily to adult questions, parents step in and quip, "Oh, she's just shy." When we use the verb "shy," as in "to shy away from," we imply avoidance, evasion, circumvention. In some cultures, shyness connotes positive characteristics, such as modesty, respect for others, and humility. In American society, shyness is undesirable, especially when linked to perceived unsociable behavior or to a more intense fear of social interaction.

Distinct from introversion, some individuals dodge social interaction not because they have reached their mixing-and-mingling limit and crave a battery recharge, but because they dread sensing initial or lingering judgment, feeling lesser than the other person, or being perceived as weak, perhaps nerdy, unintelligent, unattractive, awkward, weird, or unlikeable. Flowers explains that some people experience "problematic shyness," marked by "feelings of being unsafe in interpersonal relationships."[98] Flowers, Dr. Barbara G. Markway, and Dr. Gregory P. Markway use the term "painfully shy."[99] Flowers reiterates, "It's painful to feel anxious and unsafe in the world, and to think there's something wrong with you."[100]

Painfully shy individuals grapple with feeling evaluated, judged, critiqued, shamed, and rejected in their everyday interfaces with other human beings— some on a merely unpleasant level and others on a potentially debilitating level.[101] This adult pattern can originate in childhood through messages conveyed by parents, caretakers, teachers, coaches, siblings, or other influential figures. Many individuals "learn to be shy because of criticism, shaming, and rejection."[102] These messages are reinforced both externally and internally, and become ingrained in the way shy individuals interact with others. Shy folks hear a forceful and prolific internal critical voice that constantly castigates them for everyday actions, speech, and behavior.[103] Not only is the shy person's mental script harsh, but shyness can spark unpleasant *physical* responses like a rapid heartbeat, shortness of breath, facial redness, perspiration, and trembling.[104]

Like the root of some introverts' self-censorship, shyness stems from feelings of shame,[105] invoked by historical criticism or rebuke from others. Shame makes an individual feel unworthy,[106] and "powerless or insignificant."[107] Because shame obviously does not feel good, the more we felt shame as children, the harder we strive as adults to avoid any form of that emotion. Consciously or subconsciously, we flee situations that potentially might trigger shameful feelings, such as social interaction or public speaking scenarios that inevitably invite judgment. Shy persons "are afraid of the consequences of being more open, forthright, or assertive."[108] To protect oneself from circumstances that summon knee-jerk habits of "self-blaming and self-shaming," these individuals isolate, relentlessly "building the walls of the prison that is shyness."[109]

The distinction between introversion and shyness is important for quiet law students and lawyers to know. The non-shy introvert's developmental arc toward increasing impact as an advocate will involve: (1) realizing the pivotal role that introverts can and should play in the legal profession (described further in Chapter 3); (2) increasing awareness of and honing natural proficiencies like active listening, deep analysis, thoughtful writing, etc.; and (3) making conscious mental and physical adjustments (described in the second half of this book) when anticipating and participating in interpersonal exchanges, to amplify one's authentic voice. However, shy and socially anxious law students and lawyers likely *first* will need to go *deeper*, to unearth root causes of fear of judgment, clear out the mental detritus from the past that is no longer relevant in our law-related lives, and *then* jump into the foregoing steps.

SOCIAL ANXIETY DISORDER AND SOCIAL PHOBIA

Anxiety is ubiquitous in American society, which is no shock considering our daily news injection of global and domestic conflict, plus the rollercoaster of personal pressures and responsibilities we all ride daily. The competitive legal world is no stranger to anxiety (or depression). As noted in this book's introduction, studies show that matriculating law students exhibit a psychological profile reflective of the general population.[110] Yet, after graduation, 20 to 40 percent indicate "a psychological dysfunction."[111] Research further reveals that 26 percent of lawyers who pursue counseling reference anxiety and depression, and 19 percent of lawyers struggle with "statistically significant elevated levels of depression."[112] Remarkably, experts indicate that "anxiety is the most common emotional problem in our society, if not the entire world. Yet, only twenty-five percent of people with anxiety seek professional guidance, and only a fraction [of these] receive effective help."[113]

Social anxiety disorder is a variation of shyness, in clinical form.[114] Shyness and social anxiety "are among the most debilitating forms of anxiety."[115] Flowers provides the American Psychiatric Association's definition of social anxiety disorder:

> *Social anxiety disorder, also called social phobia, is an intense fear or even terror of humiliation or embarrassment in relation to groups of people. It's very difficult to overcome and can be very disabling. For this reason, social phobia is substantially different from shyness and is classified as a mental health disorder in the* Diagnostic and Statistical Manual of Mental Disorders.[116]

Like shyness (and the roots of self-censorship by introverts), social anxiety propagates from negative, self-critical, and self-shaming words, phrases, and messages that individuals accepted as truths earlier in life, and which they replay over and over in their minds throughout adulthood.[117] Socially anxious individuals fear "being negatively judged by others and humiliated. They may have panic attacks or severe anxiety when they are in or anticipate being in social situations."[118] Social anxiety that rises to the level of detrimentally affecting an individual's personal and professional engagements qualifies as social phobia or social anxiety disorder.[119]

Experts estimate that social phobia affects up to 13 percent of the American population,[120] which means there is a strong likelihood that socially phobic individuals sit in every law school classroom and law office. However, this condition is rarely if ever discussed in the law context, in which immediate interpersonal interaction in the classroom, courtroom, or conference room is expected. Happily, social anxiety disorder is treatable,[121] through reframing mental and physical habits and behaviors. Social anxiety is "not a fixed state. *It is fluid.* [An individual] can change its shape and its quantity."[122]

HOW INTROVERSION, SHYNESS, AND SOCIAL ANXIETY CAN MANIFEST INTO PUBLIC SPEAKING ANXIETY IN THE LEGAL CONTEXT

In American legal education, public speaking is mandatory in the Socratic classroom and in oral argument assignments. In law practice, litigators engage in public debate through depositions, courtroom arguments, trials, and settlement negotiations. Transactional attorneys deliver client presentations and negotiate orally. Some introverted, shy, and socially anxious individuals struggle in the legal public speaking arena, no matter how large or how small the audience, and no matter how high-stakes or how low-stakes the engagement. Even in one-on-one encounters or in small-group settings around a conference table, introverts can experience anxiety toward public speaking because of their tendency toward methodical *internal* thinking, their habit of pausing and reflecting, the time they need to process information before responding, and a reluctance to speak prior to vetting ideas. In larger settings, such as in an auditorium or courtroom, introverts can become overstimulated by crowd noise, bright lights, technology overload, and commotion. Likewise, for shy and socially anxious law students and lawyers, fear of judgment and criticism invoked by a one-on-one encounter or a small or large group audience can trigger past shame feelings that are capable of derailing even the most prepared speaker. The good news is, after we understand the triggers of public speaking anxiety, we can adopt mental and physical strategies to optimize our quiet strengths and become truly impactful orators.

CULTURAL INTROVERSION

The phenomenon of "cultural introversion" can occur in English as a Second Language (ESL) students studying law in the United States or non-native-English-speakers pursuing law courses taught in English in non-U.S. law schools. Students who are confident, talkative extroverts in their native environments and languages can self-censor into quietude, embarrassed by, or worse, ashamed of accents or a shaky command of English. These students fear being perceived by professors and classmates as less intelligent than their peers. A different form of cultural introversion can occur in international students studying in American law classrooms who hail from countries in which disagreeing with or engaging in debate with a professor is considered rude or disrespectful. Unless teachers provide adequate context for, and model, the Socratic dialogue *first*, the expectation to speak extemporaneously in the American classroom, and to challenge statements made by professors and classmates, can trigger stress and anxiety in some of these students.

Participants in my public speaking anxiety workshops have offered examples of cultural introversion. For three consecutive years, 2012–2014, in anticipation of the spring oral argument competition at New York Law School, where I taught legal writing, I conducted a five-part Overcoming Public Speaking Anxiety (OPSA) workshop series, with funding from the New York State Bar Association (in the latter two years). The workshop participants included mostly women, many minorities, and several students with upbringings—either cultural or religious—that reinforced quiet personas. One participant shared her version of cultural introversion. She moved to the United States from Germany when she was in junior high school; learning English, she spoke with a heavy accent. Her classmates teased her to the point that she self-censored. Even though her adult voice evinced not a trace of an accent, her cultural introversion lingered in the law school classroom, triggering fear toward the Socratic Method and the 1L oral argument assignment.

More recently, I taught a workshop on English legal writing to law students in southern Italy. My own stereotype of and enamoredness with the boisterous Italian persona intact, I did not anticipate encountering introversion in this particular classroom. For the final assignment in our curriculum on persuasion, I asked my students to prepare and perform a five-minute oral argument on a topic of their choice. Given my personal history and research focus on introversion and interpersonal anxiety, and because the course was fast-tracked into a short, four-week schedule with limited time for real, oral advocacy training, I also offered an alternative: students could participate in a small-group workshop on public speaking anxiety in the legal arena if the oral argument assignment presented personal challenges. Four students confided that they felt substantial apprehension toward the oral argument assignment. One of the four (a male student) opted not to participate in the workshop and performed the oral argument anyway. Three female students participated in the workshop (one of whom additionally performed the oral argument). Two of the female students shared that their anxiety toward public speaking stemmed from fear of judgment by their classmates about their substantive command of legal topics. The third female student—one of the top writers in the class—disclosed that her fear sprang not from anticipated public perception of her substantive knowledge, but from embarrassment about her Italian accent and stilted grammar when she spoke English. Interestingly, several students I met during my teaching in Italy confided that they experienced marked anxiety toward the Italian model of *oral* exams required in the majority of their classes, but reported that—to their knowledge—no programs yet existed to address the psychological aspect of this type of student stress.

Building on the foregoing foundation of the distinctions among introverted, shy, and socially anxious individuals, let's now look at the challenges facing these law students and lawyers in the legal context. Then we'll examine how quiet individuals—with increased self-awareness and a holistic approach, and buoyed by compassionate and motivating professors and law office mentors—can transform the legal profession.

CHAPTER 2

Challenges Quiet Law Students and Lawyers Face

I owe Socrates an apology. For two decades, I was mad at him for inventing the Socratic Method—his intellectual dialogue technique adopted by law professors and judges for use in the classroom and courtroom. As an introverted law student and attorney, I viewed the Socratic Method as a weapon of mass destruction. But then I read *Socrates Café* by Christopher Phillips[123] and discovered my gaffe. Socrates' original method is quite compatible with the quiet, thinking lawyer's approach to the law, a reassuring notion for introverted law students and attorneys. By modeling Socrates' intellectual humility (a trait defined by former justice of the Supreme Court of Wisconsin, William A. Bablitch, as "an awareness of what we do not know, and an awareness that what we think we know might well be incorrect"[124]) and a mutually respectful approach to engaging with others in the law, introverts can pack a big punch.

Socrates (c. 469–399 BC), a founder of Western philosophy, hailed from Athens. No Clooney of his time, the public often mocked him—in plays and social gatherings—for being unsightly according the aesthetic standards of fifth-century, BC, Greece.[125] He didn't care much about creature comforts,[126] but garnered personal fulfilment from interacting with a motley assortment of people. Socratic scholar, Paul Johnson, describes Socrates as "a sensible, practical, down-to-earth man, interested in usefulness, not perfection, and inclined to make allowances for the infinite variety of human nature."[127] Notably, Socrates did not consider himself brilliant; in fact, he "didn't think he knew the answers, or that knowledge was the rarified domain of so-called intellectuals."[128]

As the story goes, there were Seven Sages, wise men of ancient Greece—philosophers, politicians, and legislators—who assembled periodically in the southern city of Delphi to share practical wisdom with the masses. One or more of the sages (possibly Solon of Athens and/or Thales of Miletus) espoused a motto: "Know thyself." The sages inscribed this adage on the entrance of the

Temple of Apollo in Delphi, an imposing edifice poised on a summit over-looking the Mediterranean Sea.[129] Socrates was a humble, middle-class guy,[130] and once noted, "I am not yet able, as the Delphic inscription has it, to know myself."[131] Aspiring to expand the boundaries of his intellect, however, he emphasized the importance of seeking to learn what he didn't know. In his quest to know himself, Socrates realized he had an instinct for questioning himself and others; "the investigation of the internal world of man was some-thing he could do and wanted to do."[132] Thus sparked his Socratic Method of Q&A. Ever modest, he "did not contend that following him was 'the way'—just *a* way to find *your* way."[133]

Daily, Socrates roamed Athens asking questions of people in all walks of life, not just elite illuminati but street vendors, friends, and playwrights. Why? According to Phillips, "Socrates didn't just question for the sake of question-ing. He questioned out of conviction. He questioned in order to become the best human being possible."[134] He used his queries "to help people gain a better understanding of themselves and their nature and their potential for excellence."[135] As Phillips eloquently describes: "The Socratic Method is a way to seek truths by your own lights."[136]

For introverted lawyers who are naturally resistant to the law school version of the Socratic Method, which requires participants to engage in *instantaneous* public discourse about complex legal topics without much time to think and process, studying exactly how Socrates' *original* method worked can help alter our perspective and better prepare us to handle questions. Although the Soc-ratic Method in the law classroom or courtroom can be intimidating for the questionee, Socrates reportedly was kind in his inquisitions, even as he gently exposed flawed assumptions and intellectual contradictions. Scholars refer to the technical logistics of the method as *elenchus*, "Hellenistic Greek for *inquiry* or *cross-examination*."[137] Again, while modern courtroom or deposition cross-examination can at times be grueling or embarrassing for the witness, Socrates was a benevolent inquisitor. Ronald Gross, author of *Socrates' Way*, summarizes the method in the following chronological steps:

- State a declaration that seems obvious and infallible.
- Next, regard the declaration as if it were untrue, i.e., brainstorm scenar-ios in which the statement would not hold up.
- Notice how the counter-examples show that defined terms within the original declaration might be insufficient, too broad, or vague.
- Revise the original declaration.
- Push further to identify a variety of alternate circumstances that help fine-tune the original notion.[138]

Phillips outlines Socrates' method similarly:

- Commence by posing a question on any topic.
- Then, scrutinize the question for:
  - Embedded terms that should be defined more specifically
  - Shades and nuances that should be fleshed out
  - Logic flaws, paradoxes, and contradictions
  - Implanted (false) assumptions
- Define terms in the question by "separating out the concepts and exploring them individually."[139]
- Continue testing "alternate viewpoints"[140] to better define the original question.

Here is an example of a Socratic inquiry, exposing assumptions, embedded concepts, overbroad generalizations, exceptions, contradictions, and flawed logic:

Q: Can a naturally **quiet** person be a **great** lawyer?

A: That seems contradictory. Lawyers are outwardly **intelligent**, **confident**, like to **debate**, and have a lot to **say**.

Q: If someone is **quiet**, does that mean she is not **intelligent**?

A: No, but lawyers need to **talk** to do their jobs.

Q: Are there any parts of a lawyer's **job** that do not require talking?

A: Yes. **Reading**. **Listening** to a client's story. **Researching**. **Writing a contract or a brief**. **Outlining** an argument.

Q: Are these **quiet** tasks important to lawyering?

A: Yes.

Q: What does it mean to be a **great** lawyer?

A: **Winning** cases.

Q: Are there any circumstances in which a lawyer that wins cases is not great?

A: I guess if he is **unethical** in how he won the case.

Q: Any other circumstances?

A: If he didn't **listen** to the client's wishes, or treated his team poorly.

Q: Are there any circumstances in which a lawyer can be **great** without winning cases?

A: Well first, there are a lot of transactional lawyers who don't do trials that are **great** lawyers.

Q: And why are they **great**?

A: They **listen** to their clients, obtain **agreements** with other parties, and **write** good contracts.

Q: Can a lawyer who loses a case be **great**?

A: I suppose.

Q: How?

A: If she did the best **job** possible with difficult facts or law, **worked** hard, and brainstormed **creative** solutions. Even if the solutions didn't work in the end, I suppose the lawyer still did a **great** job for the client. And maybe paved the way for a future change in the law.

Q: If a lawyer is **quiet**, does that always mean he doesn't have a lot to **say**?

A: Not necessarily. I guess it could mean he is **thinking**.

Q: Do **great** lawyers **think**?

A: Of course, yes.

Q: If a person is **quiet**, does that always mean she is not **confident**?

A: Not necessarily. It could mean she is **thinking** about how to respond powerfully to an argument.

Q: Have you ever had a **debate** with a **quiet** person?

A: Actually, yes. It was with a close friend I have known forever.

Q: Was the **debate** superficial or deep?

A: Pretty deep. My friend doesn't say a lot when he's in large groups, but when it's just the two of us, our conversations can get pretty heavy.

Q: Are there occasions in which lawyers interact one-on-one or in small groups rather than large groups?

A: Yes, in client interviews, depositions, negotiations, some oral arguments . . .

Importantly, even while revealing "discrepancies, contradictions, and consequences"[141] in a dialogue, which possibly could trigger embarrassment, shame, or defensive pride causing a communicator to shut down, Socrates "made the people he questioned, and cross-questioned, feel important, and he seemed to find their answers valuable."[142] When he interacted with others, he showed "courtesy, patience, sensitivity, and calmness."[143] He "rarely if ever snapped" in a conversation.[144] Phillips describes the original Socratic dynamic as:

> *a paradigm of communication that calls on all participants in a dialogue to participate fully, and in an egalitarian way. And it requires that participants* help one another *articulate and then examine their perspectives, as well as the implications for society of these perspectives, and the assumptions within these perspectives.*[145]

This type of thought exchange sounds lovely, inviting, and collaborative, and different in tone from the Socratic Method I feared in law school and still observe in some classrooms, conference rooms, and courtrooms. Socrates aspired to be an excellent human being. To him, excellence meant "striv[ing] to acquire certain virtues, such as temperance, courage, and wisdom. Why? Because the acquisition of such virtues creates a different kind of wealth—a wealth of empathy, of imaginative vision, of self-discovery."[146] So how did we evolve from Socrates' aspirational methodology to the way a Socratic interaction often transpires in the legal world now?

QUIET LAW STUDENTS AND THE MODERN SOCRATIC METHOD

Of course there are exceptions—every law professor has a personal style, and many are nurturing and encouraging to *all* students—but the traditional law school method of classroom interaction, governed by the Socratic Method, pressures students to act like extroverts. Numerous law school lecture courses are managed by an intense Q&A in which professors—often intimidating because of academic pedigree, tenured status, intellect, or tone—choose a student either through an alphabetical process, a seating chart, or at random ("cold-calling"), and then question the student about a precedential case, a legal rule, or a public policy concept from that day's assigned reading. The inquiry might focus on a jurisprudential theory, elements or factors of a governing rule, a court's decision, the bases for such decision, and how that result might change in various hypothetical scenarios. Students have little time to think. Professors expect immediate responses based on the assumption that the student on-call has completed the assigned reading and prepared adequately for class. Notwithstanding even the best efforts of a caring professor who is attuned to internal and external influences that can affect classroom temperament, the overall tenor can be competitive and judgmental, especially in the 1L year, when students feel pressure to jockey for grades, class ranking, interviews, summer jobs, and promotion to law review and moot court teams, but are not yet sure where they fit. For a new 1L law student struggling to find her lawyer voice, some law classrooms do not readily offer a collaborative dynamic of "participants help[ing] one another articulate and then examine their perspectives,"[147] as Socrates designed.

Further, unfortunately, not all law professors embrace Socrates' humble acknowledgment of not knowing themselves, and instead seem, in the students' eyes, to know *everything*, at least about Contracts, Torts, Property, Civil Procedure, Criminal Law, or Constitutional Law. As Phillips describes: "While today's academic elite ballyhoo their 'Socratic heritage' at every opportunity [Canadian novelist and essayist John Ralston Saul] holds that 'the way they teach' is the antithesis of the Socratic way. 'In the Athenian's case every answer raised a question. With the contemporary elites, every question produces an answer.'"[148] Gross also acknowledges that "in the wrong hands, the Socratic Method can be abused."[149]

Some law professors regard the Socratic classroom technique as a rite of passage every student must endure, without sufficient and transparent accounting for differences in individual students' abilities to process challenging legal concepts extemporaneously, speak spontaneously in a new legal language before a large number of peers, or stay cool under pressure when stumped. At some point during a Socratic query, despite dogged preparation, a student might not know the answer to the professor's question, or stay calm enough to articulate an answer that is still gaining traction in his mind. But instead of fostering an environment in which we overtly acknowledge that we all have limits to our knowledge—as Socrates did—law school classrooms often unwittingly can create a dynamic of shaming a faltering student. Professors feel pressure to cover the scheduled amount of material during each class period and can become frustrated with hesitant responders, sometimes jumping to the mistaken conclusion that the reticent are unprepared, less capable, or just not ultimately tough enough to withstand legal debate. Introverted, shy, or socially anxious students who stumble during a Socratic Q&A worry they are perceived as less intelligent than their peers. Quiet or hesitant law students can be misjudged by professors and contemporaries (or even themselves) as ill-equipped for the practice of law—a serious misperception.

In law school, the professor standing at the podium logically expects an answer within seconds, or at least a minute or two, to keep the class session moving forward. While extroverts comfortably shape budding answers by speaking aloud, our traditional American style of legal instruction does not allow room for the typical introvert's most effective mode of learning or analytical processing: deep internal thinking rather than spontaneous volley. While the law school version of the Socratic Method inhibits and discourages contemplative pauses, Socrates himself was "a slow, careful thinker."[150] He took time to ponder, and considered himself a cogitator.[151] In fact, his "insistence on clarity frequently revealed that the people with the instant answers hadn't really thought things through."[152] Introversion author Tanner reverberates this theme: "Words do not have to be spontaneous to be heartfelt and real."[153]

Experts confirm that introverted students use different processes than extroverts for learning[154] and digesting complex information. Cain emphasizes that "[i]ntroverts need different kinds of instruction from extroverts."[155] She quotes education scholars Jill Burruss and Lisa Kaenzig as saying, "[V]ery little is made available to that learner except constant advice on becoming more social and gregarious."[156] Like other forms of American education, the law school instructional model mandates class participation in a manner that runs contrary to the introvert's nature. As Dr. Kozak points out: "The value of participation is so deeply woven into the fabric of academic life that it goes unnoticed, and introverts become the collateral damage."[157] Professor Katherine Schultz, in her *Washington Post* article, "Why Introverts Shouldn't Be Forced to Talk in Class," writes: "There are potentially grave consequences for students when teachers do not understand their silence as a form of participation . . . [S]tudents who are silent might receive low grades for classroom participation, when in fact they are actively engaged in learning."[158]

Consider this example of a quiet law student: She spends most evenings burrowed in a library carrel with a highlighter and a casebook (or four). She underlines rules, outlines rule components on notecards, and contemplates their underlying structure and interplay with public policy. She identifies the key legal issues addressed in each judicial opinion, extracts the elements of the governing rule, discerns how the court applied the rule to the particular case facts, and ascertains the court's reasoning behind its ultimate decision. Having sat through weeks of class already, she has monitored and detected a pattern in her professors' lines of questioning, and invests time anticipating the flow of queries that might befall her if she is cold-called in class. She brainstorms possible hypothetical adjustments to each precedent case's facts so she can flexibly maneuver in a dialogue.

Armed with bullet-point outlines, today this student walks into the classroom, shuts down her cell phone and social media, and slides into her assigned seat, poised to capture another day's worth of notes. As class commences, the professor scans the crowd. He calls her name. Her number is up. The Socratic questioning begins. Her nerve endings sizzle. The answers to the professor's inquiries reside within the scrupulous pages arrayed on the desk in front of her, but her brain stalls. Perspiration trickles. A blush starbursts. Her voice quivers. Row-mates shuffle in their seats. Seconds tick. The professor's next move can have an enormous effect on this student's psyche. This student is über-prepared, but this encounter—if it ends badly—can be detrimental to her learning process and future study habits. Imagine if a momentarily stumped law student could simply say, during a Socratic dialogue, with all eyes on her, "I just need a minute. I'm thinking." But she can't.

Another law school initiation rite is the 1L oral argument. Most three-year American law school programs include a mandatory oral argument at the end of the first year as the final assignment in the legal writing course curriculum. Students write a persuasive legal brief, and then are paired against an opponent to present time-capped oral arguments on opposite sides of the same complex legal issue. A panel of three judges—often professors, law school administrators, members of the school's moot court team, alumni, or other distinguished guests—interrupts the student-advocates and peppers them with questions, to test the strengths and weaknesses of the opposing positions. The oral argument experience is wildly different from delivering a prepared speech. In oral advocacy, the orator might have crafted a riveting roadmap and a cogent argument outline, but the unexpected timing, flow, and subject matter of the judges' questions can derail the speaker's control. For introverted, shy, and socially anxious individuals, this exercise can be torturous. There is no time to think, reflect, or process. During this time-sensitive rite in which a "bailiff" counts down the minutes using a timer, warning flash cards, and a stop sign, judges would stare quizzically if the student at the podium paused for a long moment (in the style of John Cage, from *Ally McBeal*) to craft an eloquent response in his head.

Some professors integrate shorter oral argument assignments into regular class sessions. In creative pedagogy workshops, colleagues enthusiastically have shared that they start off the semester requiring their 1L legal writing students to periodically perform 90-second arguments on topics randomly selected from a hat. I listen to these eager colleagues opine, "It's great! It totally forces the nerves out of their systems," and I wince, knowing that for at least a few students on each classroom roster, this command performance so early in the law school experience—without sufficient training or room to find one's voice first—effects exactly the opposite result. I also have heard legal educators urge nervous students to "just get over yourselves." In turn, I beseech teachers to understand that the "just do it" approach does not, and will not ever, eliminate nerves. Hesitant speakers first need to understand precisely where their reticence toward this type of interpersonal engagement is coming from (possibly, natural introvert resistance to speaking without preparation or in an interruption-based dynamic, or deeper-seated fears of judgment lurking in shy and socially anxious students) before they can make conscious mental and physical adjustments and leap into the fracas with purpose. Not every transformative lawyer is a born talker. Countless attorneys joke about how their families knew from their toddler years that they would enter the legal profession due to their natural affinity for argument and bold assertions. Plentiful powerfully quiet advocates never exhibited those childhood behavior patterns. Many of our pensive students have a lot to say and care deeply about legal issues, but they first require space to let their thoughts about the law incubate until they are ready for prime time. These law students, as Socrates and the Seven Sages counseled, need permission to "know thyself" first while they get to know the law.

Phillips, who convenes Q&A gatherings called Socrates Cafés[159] throughout the world, notes, "I never put anyone on the spot and make them feel like they have to talk. You can participate just by listening. In fact, I find that some of the most active participants at Socrates Café are often those who 'just' listen."[160] In law school, we do not always honor our students who "just" listen, at least not enough. In fact, some law school grading structures directly incentivize class participation and performance-oriented events, favoring extroverts who comfortably engage in class discussions, group work, simulated client scenarios, and mock arguments. Cain confirms this partiality toward talking over listening in other academic arenas: "We perceive talkers as smarter than quiet types—even though grade-point averages and SAT and intelligence test scores reveal this perception to be inaccurate."[161] Cain's research indicates that, "[a]t the university level, introversion predicts academic performance better than cognitive ability"[162]—not necessarily because of a higher intelligence level but rather a greater tendency toward careful thinking and persistence.[163] Law schools track correlations between undergraduate GPAs/LSAT scores and law school performance/bar passage rates; it would be interesting to track connections between results on the Myers-Briggs Type Indicator® (MBTI) personality inventory (which can unveil deep insights into personality preferences including the introversion and extroversion dichotomy)[164] and law school success.

In our law school classrooms sit smart, quiet, serious thinkers who have much to contribute—when they are ready and *after* they have had appropriate guidance in how to communicate in their authentic voices. Forcing introverted law students into extroversion triggers anxiety and promotes further censorship. Such internal conflict can have deep psychological repercussions.

Cain's research reveals that "introverts are significantly more likely than extroverts to fear public speaking."[165]

Some professors might suggest that "if these students don't or won't like oral debate, then maybe they shouldn't be in law school." I could not disagree more. Law school should not be an assembly line of loquacious, verbally slick extroverts. We need to make room for the quiet and empathetic writers and thinkers, and for the internally methodical analytical minds, even if they require additional support and training to learn how to express themselves aloud. For these students, we need to invest time and energy in transparently explaining the context and purpose of the Socratic Method and oral arguments, and model their patterns and rhythms (and examples of normal hurdles, pitfalls, triumphs, and joys), *before* thrusting students into these types of performance-oriented events. Such contextual explanations only require 10 or 15 minutes of class time but can achieve great strides in helping students understand how to (1) best prepare substantively, mentally, and physically, (2) realistically (rather than exaggeratedly) visualize the event, and (3) manage challenges. We must exhibit empathy to students who experience anxiety toward and during these scenarios, and help these individuals navigate these engagements successfully (emphasizing that obstacles and glitches are standard—conversations about the law can and should be messy!) so their ideas about legal concepts can take root and bloom. We also need to make it acceptable to admit vulnerability and fears in an educational setting, so we can transform perceived "weaknesses" into powerful strengths in real law practice.

Overall, when we encounter quiet students, we should consider whether they (1) are introverts who learn, process thoughts, and communicate ideas in a different way; or (2) have experienced certain adverse life experiences— perhaps through historical criticism or judgment from others, or a single traumatic event—that imbedded negative messages about their capabilities, which have become further entrenched by intimidation in the law school environment. Many individuals are trying to learn and eventually practice law while battling personal demons, reinforcing messages of meritlessness and shame. Forcing introverted, shy, or socially anxious students to engage in an aggressive Socratic dialogue, interact with intimidating professors before an audience of ambitious peers, or leap into a confrontational oral argument experience (the "just do it" mentality)—without appropriate context, encouragement, and support—will never enable them to "snap out of it." The situation will worsen. By forcing the quiet students to "fake it till they make it" (or maybe not make it), we ignore their authentic potential and further censor these impactful legal minds.

Cain provides sage advice to educators: "If you're a teacher, enjoy your gregarious and participatory students. But don't forget to cultivate the shy, the gentle, the autonomous, the ones with single-minded enthusiasms for chemistry sets or parrot taxonomy or nineteenth-century art. They are the artists, engineers, and thinkers of tomorrow."[166]

QUIET LAWYERS

Like the law school classroom, in many law office environments, the large personalities can dominate. Rainmakers and glad-handers command a presence, filling space and airtime in meetings, conference calls, negotiations, and depositions. Law practice encourages and promotes the extrovert ideal. In my experience, working for over two decades at three different law firms, the hard-charging and sometimes even rude, obnoxious, disrespectful, and occasionally verbally abusive partners were not reprimanded; they were promoted, compensated, and protected as the "eccentric rainmakers." In the three law firms (medium, large, and small, respectively) in Washington, DC and New York City where I worked, three highly successful male partners hurled office supplies across a conference room, screamed at assistants and paralegals, and ranted at associates if they didn't "have their heads stapled to their desks." No one blinked an eye.

Of course, many law offices offer collaborative working environments conducive to positive personal and professional development. But the reign of extroverted personalities permeates many venues in American legal practice, even in constructive and healthy workspaces. In depositions, the loudest and most incessant objector necessarily commands attention. In mediations, the showman litigators can distract from the crux of the case. In negotiations—either live or in conference calls—the dominant voices can drown out the softer ones. As Socrates scholar Gross points out, the aggressive voices are not necessarily the most grounded in truth, but in the legal context, we often perceive them that way:

> We all have been brought up and educated with the "adversarial" model for resolving disputes. This model, based on our legal system, assumes that the truth will emerge through the most vigorous combat between advocates of opposing positions . . . The adversarial model favors the bigger, stronger, louder champion, regardless of his or her views.[167]

Logically, in law practices governed by the billable hour—for many lawyers, recorded in six-minute increments—meeting leaders might "value instant responses over well-thought-out ones that take a little longer."[168] Driven by ambition to propel a case forward, beating rather than meeting deadlines, and litigating proactively instead of reactively, a lead counsel on a case might misjudge the quiet researcher who will not quit hunting until he finds the one case that changes the whole tenor of a brief. The silent brief-writer who plods through transcripts and precedent to craft an advocacy piece that could hew an advancement in an area of law might sink below the radar at bonus-time. In case strategy meetings, extrovert voices can rule, and the introverted thinkers can fade into wallpaper. Additionally, like in any industry, extroverted lawyers publicly share their triumphs and achievements more than introverts do.

So given this backdrop, how can introverted law students and lawyers best contribute to the legal profession without compromising their health and mental well-being? By embracing the Seven Sages' mantra: "Know thyself." By truly understanding ourselves as quiet students and advocates, the ways that we learn and process information differently from extroverts, and the specifics of circumstances that spark our individual interpersonal anxiety, we can construct strategies to maximize our innate strengths and tackle our vulnerabilities. In tandem, forward-thinking law professors and law office leaders—like great athletic coaches—can foster an inclusive learning and training environment in which both extroverts and introverts can excel. The key to this transformative approach is modeling empathy and intellectual humility.

CHAPTER 3

Change Agents for the Profession

Introverts and otherwise quiet advocates are well poised to play an influential role in the legal profession through active listening, analytical thinking, empathy, impactful legal writing, and creative problem-solving. This chapter links effective lawyering traits with the assets many introverts and other quiet individuals bring to the table.

COUNSELORS-AT-LAW

Lawyers perform multiple intellectual activities and serve varied tactical and substantive roles: issue-identifier, fact-gatherer, researcher, analyst, writer, editor, advisor, strategist, negotiator, and advocate. We call ourselves counselors-at-law. "Approach the bench, counselor," judges direct. To "counsel" means "to provide wisdom and advice regarding the judgment and conduct of another."[169] In the legal context, "to counsel is to apply intelligence, experience and forethought to the client's legal challenges resulting in guidance, opinion, suggestion, creativity, ingenuity and assurance as the client decides how to manage these business matters."[170] Depending on a lawyer's subject matter area of practice, she might counsel owners of a mom-and-pop grocery store resisting a forced property sale, a spouse seeking a divorce from an abusive partner, or a person accused of a crime subject to jail time—all stressful scenarios that, purely based on the human element, might naturally invoke empathy in the lawyer. Or, the attorney might represent a technology corporation on the verge of a lucrative merger, a hospital purchasing land for an expansion project, or (like my law practice) a construction contractor embroiled in a conflict with a project owner over lack of payment—circumstances which, at first glance, seem to focus solely on money rather than emotion. However, across the spectrum of corporate, social justice, public interest, and individual representation, all mindful lawyers *listen* to their clients to identify goals, empathize with individuals to understand fears or concerns about adverse outcomes, and go deeper than the obvious surface legal issues to unearth personality conflicts or emotional triggers posing removable barriers to a successful negotiation or conflict resolution.

Often, law students and lawyers consider the law in terms of absolutes: "black letter law," right or wrong, or clear non-negotiable rules with checklists of elements. Yet every legal matter, whether manifested in a transaction or a dispute, is marked by shades, nuances, and layers. The best lawyers keep open minds and step into these intellectual and emotional shadows to elucidate creative outcomes. Unfortunately, the traditional way we teach and train lawyers can reinforce the notion that law is rational and unemotional; some critics say, "rather than broadening a student's mind and heart, legal training tends to narrow the mind and deaden the emotions."[171] That cause-and-effect is easily reversible, with quiet lawyers leading the charge through empathy, intellectual humility, and an inclusive mindset.

The business cards of some lawyers read "Attorney *and* Counselor-at-Law." Why two labels? Attorney Kevin Houchin explains the difference: "As an attorney I'm in the game calling plays on the field as an agent," but "[a]s a counselor I'm a coach—an expert trusted advisor directing from the sidelines."[172] Houchin suggests that "it's more valuable to be a counselor when doing the work is developmental and something that will help the client grow as a person or a professional."[173] Lawyer Jack W. Burtch, Jr. agrees, sharing how he discovered his counseling role early in his legal career:

> *I was a new lawyer. I wasn't a legal genius, but I had blundered onto the revelation that not every legal problem has a legal solution . . . In order to discern client goals, the lawyer has to somehow get inside the client's head and view the issue through the client's eyes. In modern legal counseling theory, this is known as "client-centered counseling."*[174]

Drawing upon the psychological theory of eminent American psychologist Carl Rogers, Burtch explains that the lawyer-as-counselor's "job is to show empathy, respect, and understanding so clients can make healthy decisions for themselves . . ."[175] The best legal counselors listen, empathize, process information, and problem-solve.[176] Attorney Thomas J. Ryan highlights that "[i]t is this listening, caring, and advising aspect of what we do that sets us apart from other professions."[177] Ryan offers an optimistic view of the lawyer's role as counselor:

> *In my particular practice, I have found that emphasizing my role as counselor builds goodwill, trust, and strong, long-term client relationships. In this very real sense, what is good for those who seek our help, can be good for us and, to be sure,*

for society. As lawyers, we are part of the integral system of dispute resolution that ideally serves to make human relations and commerce orderly and better. When we act as counselors, we are reaching out to make this system work even better.[178]

No matter what type of law we practice—from community public interest to the global corporate stage—effective counselors focus on how the law affects human beings.

My law practice involved construction projects, in which owners and contractors entered into agreements to build power plants, bridges, tunnels, hospitals, assisted-living facilities, sports stadiums, and other large structures. The contractual relationships typically progressed like this: An owner bought a plot of land. Architects and engineers designed the structure to be erected on the property. The owner hired a contractor to build the edifice or facility. The contractor engaged subcontractors, material suppliers, and laborers. The project commenced. When legal conflicts arose on the construction job, it often seemed like the answers should be black-and-white—right there in the blueprints, the drawings, the specifications, the contract, or the project correspondence. But inevitably, it was the human component that underlay each construction dispute: the hard-working individuals physically swinging hammers, maneuvering cranes, moving dirt, pouring concrete, sawing wood, laying bricks, turning screwdrivers, checking schedules, managing delays, writing checks, maintaining budgets, auditing costs, etc. The lawyers could argue all they wanted about contractual language but sometimes, to resolve a dispute, it was more important to understand exactly what was happening on a random Tuesday on the job when rain pelted, the trucks containing materials and supplies arrived late, the design was not working although no one could figure out why, stress levels escalated, project personnel fired off emails they wish they hadn't, and the accusations and finger-pointing began.

For a lawyer whose job requires, first, reading a lengthy, sometimes 80-page construction contract, second, learning the technical steps required to fabricate the complicated structure and, third, figuring out how to explain such contract language and engineering techniques in layperson's terms to a trier-of-fact, the lawyer also must take the time to listen to the people working in the trenches to understand the reality and truth about what is driving the conflict. No matter how corporate or financially driven a case might seem on the surface, or how rough-and-tumble the industry, real listening requires empathy for the human beings involved. Even in a seemingly unemotional negotiation or litigation, consideration of the human elements at play can move the legal matter forward for everyone, through collaborative decision-making and conflict resolution.

University of California, Berkeley professors (now emerita and emeritus) Marjorie Shultz and Sheldon Zedeck conducted an empirical study of lawyers, professors, law students, judges, and clients to derive a list of "lawyering effectiveness factors."[179] A review of the Shultz-Zedeck factors illuminates how introverts and other quiet law students and lawyers offer important assets to the legal community. Shultz and Zedeck's inventory includes, among many others, the following characteristics of an effective lawyer:

- **"Able to see the world through the eyes of others:** Understands positions, views, objectives, and goals of others"
- **"Creativity/innovation:** Thinks 'outside the box,' develops innovative approaches and solutions"
- **"Listening:** Accurately perceives what is being said both directly and subtly"
- **"Self-development:** Attends to and initiates self-development"

As explained further below, research indicates that many introverted, shy, and socially anxious people possess the foregoing highly sought-after gifts of empathy, creativity, listening, and self-discovery. Just as Socrates and the Seven Sages encouraged individuals to "know thyself," many quiet advocates already have the instinct for self-reflection that will serve them well in the role of a counselor for others.

THE ROLE OF EMPATHY IN LEGAL EDUCATION AND PRACTICE

As the tectonic plates of legal education and practice continue to shift, some law professors and practitioners have called for a greater emphasis on empathy in law teaching and training: great news for the quiet advocate. First, it is important to note the difference between sympathy and empathy. Sympathy is "the feeling that you care about and are sorry about someone else's trouble, grief, misfortune."[180] In contrast, empathy is "the action of understanding, being aware of, being sensitive to, and vicariously experiencing the feelings, thoughts, and experience of another."[181] As explained on the website TheMindUnleashed.com, "[s]ympathy is the ability to express 'culturally acceptable' condolences to another[']s plight," while "[e]mpathy is the ability to place yourself in someone else's shoes and understand [and] relate as best as you can to how that person feels in the situation."[182] Empathy goes deeper than sympathy. It might demand more conscious effort, patience, and attention. Empathy can be exercised, in a professional manner, through listening, being open-minded to someone else's life trajectory, considering how a particular circumstance might have affected another person (even if the listener would have reacted differently under similar conditions), and not projecting one's personal biases onto the other individual. Notably, lawyers like Pooja Kothari, Esq., founder of a consulting company called Boundless Awareness,[183] are dedicated to helping lawyers identify implicit biases in interacting with clients, colleagues, and other participants in our justice system. A lawyer can be empathetic without being overly emotional or soft, and in doing so, can gain a deeper understanding of the client's influences, perceptions, experiences, goals, struggles, and concerns.

Various experts provide definitions of empathy that are useful for the legal profession in the contexts of persuasion, influence, compromise, and conflict resolution:

- Introversion author Dr. Kahnweiler defines empathy as "the ability to understand the thoughts, feelings, or emotions of others. When you demonstrate empathy for the people you want to influence, you truly understand them as human beings; their motivations, aspirations, joys, worries, and points of pain. You are also able to understand their points of resistance and why they hold on to the positions they do."[184]

- Professor Joshua D. Rosenberg, Professor of Law at the University of San Francisco School of Law, explains, "Empathy . . . is simply the sense, emotional and cognitive, of knowing what it is like to be the other at a particular point in time."[185]

- Emily J. Gould, Esq., Chair of the Vermont Dispute Resolution section of the Vermont Bar Association, characterizes empathy as "both the emotional and intellectual process in which we become attuned to the emotional resonance of another person, and also see and understand from their perspective."[186]

Traditional legal education has not focused on empathy as a lawyering competency; instead, the core doctrinal curriculum orbits around rules, analysis, and critical thinking. Perhaps teaching doctrine and introducing empathy to aspiring attorneys might have been regarded by some educators as mutually exclusive pedagogical pursuits, or the discussion of empathy deemed too "soft" for the rigors of legal education. Some law professors like Professor Ian Gallacher, of Syracuse University College of Law, say "current legal education practices systematically eliminate empathy from law students . . . [T]his is a mistake that can affect a lawyer's ability to communicate with juries, clients, and the other non-lawyers with whom a lawyer comes into contact."[187] Professor Rosenberg explains that empathy requires a "momentary suspension of most of the key cognitive functions we teach (or at least try to teach) in law school"; to feel empathy, we must relinquish the drive to judge, size-up, critique, assess, and solve.[188]

Professor Gallacher urges that "[e]mpathy—just as much as the knowledge of applicable laws and rules and an ability to synthesize and distinguish precedent—is a core lawyering skill."[189] Professor Rosenberg concurs that teaching law students "how to listen and observe, how to know one's behavior and its effect on others, how to know and modify one's own goals, and how to communicate with others effectively" is useful in "negotiation, mediation, client counseling, dealing with other attorneys in one's own firm, and dealing with opposing counsel."[190] Attorney Gould agrees: "Just as empathy is used in marketing, sales, and product development, it has application not only to the client interview and client development, but also to deposition practice, negotiating with our law partners, settlement discussions, and a host of other processes we engage in as lawyers."[191]

With this foundation, some law professors and members of the bar lobby that "[l]aw schools should reverse course and start emphasizing the value of empathy together with the more traditional logic-based approach to legal analysis."[192] Indeed, Gould indicates that "some predict that empathy is the key ingredient to the future of law practice."[193] I concur: an attorney can be simultaneously thoughtful, transformative, influential, brilliant, strong, *and empathetic.* And quiet lawyers are uniquely poised to achieve just that.

THE ROLE OF INTELLECTUAL HUMILITY IN LEGAL EDUCATION AND PRACTICE

In addition to empathy, an individual's capacity for intellectual humility can make all the difference in teaching, learning, and interacting with others to effect positive personal development, conflict resolution, and societal change. Already inclined toward internal reflection, introverted and other quiet law students and lawyers are ideal agents to expand the role of intellectual humility in improving the legal profession.

In Socrates' view, it is impossible to be intellectual without intellectual humility.[194] Former justice of the Supreme Court of Wisconsin, William A. Bablitch defines intellectual humility as "an awareness of what we do not know, and an awareness that what we think we know might well be incorrect. This is particularly important when it comes to the law. The law has a funny way of jumping up and biting you right where it hurts at the most unexpected times."[195] Legal scholars note that the best judges demonstrate intellectual humility.[196] Supreme Court Justice Felix Frankfurter said, "[t]he indispensable judicial requisite is intellectual humility."[197] Others urge that intellectual humility is a necessary constituent to foster a global legal community[198] as "[t]he essence of humility is treating other things—especially other people—as if they really matter."[199] In legal education and practice, where we value critical thinking, both empathy and intellectual humility are crucial. Attorney Phillip Miller asserts that "[c]ritical thinking without fair-mindedness, humility, or empathy is flawed, and while it may seem brilliant to you or me, it may be no more than intellectual manipulation or trickery to jurors."[200] Unfortunately, our American culture often discourages humility and instead drives ego.[201]

Introverts and other quiet individuals already geared toward constant internal self-evaluation can lead the charge to promote an intellectually humble mindset in the law. Importantly, intellectual humility does not connote weakness, or better said, "[b]eing humble does not mean being a doormat."[202] Instead, humility is a platform of strength upon which we can enhance our profession by listening to and being open to one another's creative ideas about the law.

QUIET LAWYERS AS CHANGE AGENTS

Until I started my personal reinvention as a *proudly* introverted lawyer, I fixated on my perceived weaknesses: extreme blushing whenever I was the focus of attention (and sometimes for no reason at all), shaky voicing of nascent opinions to a group, protracted decision-making, and inability to answer rapid-fire legal questions without reflecting and internally vetting my answers. Only through extensive research did I finally understand that my innate inclination to listen and absorb first (before speaking), experience empathy (not always, but more often than not) for others who foster and exude anxiety (even for some volatile bosses and difficult counsel), focus when researching challenging legal problems, and deep-dive into legal writing projects are my greatest assets. And the other stuff? Well, by working the seven-step process in the second half of this book, I reinvented a stronger, more amplified, and less anxious me.

As Dr. Laney points out, introverts "bring important attributes to the party—the ability to focus deeply, an understanding of how a change will affect everyone involved, the capacity to observe, a propensity for thinking outside the box, the strength to make unpopular decisions, and the potential to slow the world down a notch."[203] Introvert assets include "concentration, loyalty, thoughtfulness, persistence, tough-mindedness, creativity, originality, foresight, and a wide range of knowledge."[204] Further, science links introversion and an empathetic mindset. Dr. Kozak indicates that "[i]ntroverts can be highly sensitive to the needs of others."[205] He explains that "[t]he ability to sit still can nurture compassion and empathy."[206] Notably, "[m]any introverts go into fields where empathy skills are required—like counseling. It's a natural fit."[207]

Experts further confirm that empathy and sensitivity to others are not only introvert traits but also are shared by many shy and socially anxious individuals. M. F. Fensholt, author of *The Francis Effect: The Real Reason You Hate Public Speaking and How to Get Over It*, reports that "[c]reativity and emotional sensitivity are two positive traits often shared by people who experience anxiety."[208] Flowers, author of *The Mindful Path Through Shyness*, notes that shyness is a "source of empathy and compassion."[209] Interestingly, Anna LeMind, staff writer for the website TheMindUnleashed.com, reports:

> [R]esearchers from the University of Haifa's Department of Psychology, Haifa, Israel, studied the empathy tendencies of people with social anxiety and found "elevated mentalizing and empathic abilities." This means that those who suffered from this disorder had higher psycho-social awareness and thus showed "sensitivity and attentiveness to other people's states of mind."[210]

Further, Erika B. Hilliard, MSW, RSW, author of *Living Fully with Shyness and Social Anxiety*, describes sensitivity as "that fabulous quality that often accompanies shyness and social anxiety."[211] She encourages that "[a] lot of good qualities go along with shyness. There is sensitivity to nuances, to subtle differences. There is empathy for others."[212]

An attorney's capacity for empathy and intellectual humility through listening to others can be a transformational tool in conflict resolution, transactional engagement, and persuasive advocacy. Dr. Kahnweiler explains that, "Influence is not about forcing people to come to see things your way but about learning from others and negotiating a shared solution. This approach is well suited to the introvert temperament. It involves patience, planning, and perseverance. If we all think that the only way to get things done is to shout louder and louder and take up more center-stage space, we'll miss the opportunities to listen, learn, and respond thoughtfully."[213] She further emphasizes, "Ironically, a powerful tool for influencing people is silence."[214]

Beyond empathy and intellectual humility, introvert gifts correspond directly to the following day-to-day lawyering tasks: active listening, fact-gathering, researching, analyzing, creative problem-solving, legal writing, persuading, resolving conflicts, and impactfully communicating when ready.

Active Listening

To accurately pinpoint a client's legal issue and appropriately address an opportunity, problem, or conflict, law students and lawyers first must *listen*— either to a professor, a supervisor, a colleague, the client, opposing counsel, a witness, or the judge. Instead of racing to speak, introverts "listen carefully";[215] they "have the gift of attention and when [they] learn to give it, it can be gratefully received in a manner which is extraordinarily transformative."[216] A U2 lyric from the song *Every Breaking Wave* reminds us, "It's hard to listen while you preach."[217] By naturally resisting adding unnecessary static to a dialogue, introverted law students and lawyers can *hear* what other human beings say, one-on-one or in group settings, noting themes and patterns. While others talk—often over one another—"introverts are more likely to listen to and process the ideas of an eager team in a deeply engaged way."[218] Cain explains, "Because of their inclination to listen to others and lack of interest in dominating social situations, introverts are more likely to hear and implement suggestions."[219] A listening lawyer can cut through the clamor of competing voices, hear the underlying messages being conveyed, and synthesize them for use in legal analysis. By listening, a lawyer also establishes trust, helps clients move through fears (even lurking within outwardly confident corporate executives), and facilitates truth-sharing. By striving to understand the relationship, the project, the transaction, or the catastrophic event from the individual's point-of-view, and then the opponent's point-of-view, the listening lawyer might identify a tack, a strategy, or an approach that no one previously had considered.

Fact-Gathering

Lawyers grasp the storyline of a client's legal dilemma by immersing themselves in the client's factual circumstances, interviewing client representatives and witnesses, visiting sites such as accident locations or environmental spills, viewing photographs or videos, and poring over reams of written records. Introverts are good perceivers and fact-gatherers. Dr. Kahnweiler indicates, "Introverts take the time to gather pertinent facts so they can present a very strong case for a new way of thinking or a course of action."[220]

Introverts can be more tuned in than some extroverted counterparts to the visual sights, smells, temperatures, details, tastes, and competing sounds in a fact-gathering environment. On a recent vacation, I meandered with a lively friend through the cobblestones of bustling Rome, a cornucopia of sensory treasures in the blaring August heat. While my extroverted pal chatted, I watched bark floating along the shoreline of the Tiber River, smelled chestnuts roasting on a cast iron sidewalk grill, heard the lilt of street vendors taking espresso orders, salivated at pastel pillows of gelato, and ran my fingers along ancient graffiti carvings etched in stone park benches. When we collapsed into wicker seats at a pizzeria in Trastevere, ordering a steamy hot margarita pizza and an ice-cold Peroni, she admitted she had been so busy regaling me with the time she hiked a mountain in Colorado, she hadn't noticed any of the sensory items I mentioned.

In the legal context, senior attorneys typically dispatch junior associates on investigative trips to gather case facts. As a young attorney, I traveled to a shipyard to photograph a rusted and pitted cruise ship rotor and touch the gravelly substance mistakenly used to clean it. I visited a wastewater treatment plant to review documents (that scent, unforgettable). I spent a sweaty few days in a storage warehouse in San Juan, Puerto Rico, where all the files reeked of cigarette smoke. Those documents, sights, senses, and smells enlivened the client's case. The facts jumped off the pictures and pages, enabling me to write about them with fervor. When I later asked extroverted counterparts to recall document review experiences, they recounted the drudgery of paper cuts and Post-it notes.

In addition to empathy, introverts can use their comfort within silence[221] as an asset in fact-gathering. Extroverts often are not as accustomed to or at ease with silence, and naturally might fill space with words. One of the most effective techniques I adopted as an introverted deposition-taker—a fact-gathering task—was simply to stop talking. I invoked the mantra of my wonderful Washington, DC-based therapist, Barbara Roberts: "Tolerate the discomfort."[222] In a deposition, a lawyer asks a witness—the deponent—questions. Opposing counsel periodically objects to the form of the questions, and the deponent answers the questions, either directly or artfully dodging the probing. In many depositions of strong-willed deponents represented by extroverted counsel, silence triggered my opponents' and counterparts' discomfort, yet soothed mine. Instead of pushing forward into each verbal conflict with an immediate follow-up question, I experimented with sitting quietly, reviewing my carefully typed deposition outline to decide my next avenue of inquiry. Many deponents reacted by filling the verbal void, chatting and chattering about case facts, much to the dismay of their jumpy attorneys. Through silence, I reasserted control of the deposition, gathered robust facts, and obtained more effective answers to use in resolving the case.

Creative Researching

Sometimes legal rules are clear and muster into a neat checklist of required elements, but more often they resemble a murky bog. During the research process, a law firm partner might summon a young associate to his office and instruct, "Find me a case that says X! There has to be one out there." The associate races back to her office, jumps on Westlaw, Lexis, or Bloomberg Law, and scours judicial precedent for that one perfect case. That judicial unicorn might not exist. Good researchers are creative and flexible—happy news for introverted lawyers.

Indeed, "[a]rguments have been made for the superior creativity of introverts."[223] Introverts possess the natural lone wolf working style and internal trial-and-error method of intellectual processing necessary to take a complicated legal research issue, enter the quiet research zone alone, and dig like an archaeologist for a stubborn buried answer. Dr. Laney reiterates that "[i]ntroverted people who balance their energy have perseverance and the ability to think independently, focus deeply, and work creatively"[224]—ideal traits for legal researchers.

Analytical Thinking

When legal answers are not obvious, or the facts or rules seemingly disfavor a client, the best lawyers think harder: further good news for introverts. As Tanner points out, "The introvert, then, is a wrestler. That is what happens in the quiet place. Here is pondering and noticing, processing and formulating, wondering and delight . . . This is introvert practice and with care it is a great gift, both in the fruit and the process that is shared with others."[225] Introverts go deeper than surface analysis; they "live deeply and are drawn to wisdom. [They] wrestle and are not easily satisfied with half-answers."[226]

"Groupthink" is defined as "a psychological phenomenon that occurs within a group of people in which the desire for harmony or conformity in the group results in an irrational or dysfunctional decision-making outcome."[227] Introverts resist "groupthink" and instead seek quiet to scrunch up their faces and sort through difficult topics free of outside influence; "[a] loud voice can promote groupthink more than considered critical analysis."[228] Introverts can be the foil to groupthink. Indeed, Dr. Kozak emphasizes that "[s]olitude is a necessary ingredient for the creative process, and solitude helps to avoid the biasing effects of groupthink."[229]

Additionally, an introvert's penchant for privacy to reflect on challenging concepts can have a positive ripple effect on others who have not yet learned how to cleave a quiet refuge. Tanner suggests, "The internal process of reflection and engagement needs space, which means that introverts also are able to curate space for others."[230]

Creative Problem-Solving

Law is about solving conundrums, frequently tough ones with no obvious answer. Introverts can demonstrate remarkable creativity, not only in legal research, but in developing solutions to seemingly insurmountable challenges. Experts opine that introverts—by curtaining off external distractions—effectively tap into innovation, resourcefulness, and ingenuity. Undeniably, "[c]reative expression takes undistracted time,"[231] and introverts excel at carving out quiet reflective space and blocks of uninterrupted time for concentration. Dr. Kozak notes that quiet can spark "imagination,"[232] a spirit of inspiration and inventiveness. Cain concurs, "[*I]ntroverts prefer to work independently, and solitude can be a catalyst to innovation.*"[233]

Cain invokes a vivid image of Sir Isaac Newton when she describes the introvert's creative process: "[T]he most spectacularly creative people in many fields are often introverted. . . [A] person sitting quietly under a tree in the backyard, while everyone else is clinking glasses on the patio, is more likely to have an apple land on his head."[234] Similarly, Dr. Helgoe advises, "An introvert who sits back in a meeting, taking in the arguments, dreamily reflecting on the big picture, may be seen as not contributing—that is, until he works out the solution that all the contributors missed."[235] Some experts contend that introverts "are better at critical thinking and solving problems that require insight,"[236] and "the more creative people tend to be socially poised introverts."[237]

I have worked with lawyers—on both my side of a case and the opposing side—who approach every new client matter the same way: Take an aggressive stance on each issue, fight about even the most inconsequential discovery matter, bury the opposing party with discovery requests and motions, write briefs that accuse the other side of nefarious behavior at every turn, constantly threaten sanctions, etc. This type of case strategy is usually uncreative. The team doesn't invest the time to get to know the individuals and personalities involved. The mantra is: Fight, fight, fight, fight, win . . . or sometimes lose, and lose big. I am not suggesting that an aggressive litigation stance is wrong; I take hardline positions frequently in my legal writing, and I always prefer to be on offense rather than defense. However, experts suggest that empathy for others, and a good dose of intellectual humility,[238] can stimulate creativity,[239] especially in the area of problem-solving. Exiting our narrowly focused personal world to step into the universe of another can spark new ideas or alternative approaches to conflict resolution in the law.

Legal Writing

Lawyers write. Every day. Whether through emails, internal legal research and strategy memoranda, communications with clients or opposing counsel, transactional agreement term sheets, proposed contract language, litigation-oriented pleadings, discovery requests, or briefs, lawyers transform every client matter through the written word. For litigators and transactional lawyers alike, legal writing is a potent weapon in the advocacy arsenal, and an essential lawyering competency perfectly suited to the introvert temperament.

Cain notes that introverts "often feel as if they express themselves better in writing than in conversation."[240] Dr. Kozak agrees that many introverts favor writing over speaking.[241] Dr. Kahnweiler proffers writing as a formidable tool for introverts; "[b]ecause introverts tend to prefer writing to talking, they often tap into writing as a powerful influencing strength."[242] Authors Anne Tyler, Jessamyn West, and Bernard Cornwell reiterate that writing is a "solitary occupation." Likewise, author John Green once said, "Writing is something you do alone. It's a profession for introverts who want to tell you a story but don't want to make eye contact while telling it."[243] Legal writing offers quiet law students and lawyers the perfect milieu to think, analyze, edit, rephrase, test thoughts, and be choosy with words. An introvert who loves the art and science of legal writing inescapably will play a pivotal role in every client representation.

Professor Gallacher draws a thoughtful connection between writing and empathy, stating, "Writing is an empathetic act, and the goal of persuasive writers is to place themselves in their audience's minds in order to understand how best to influence them while they make their decisions."[244] He explains:

> *Writing, after all, is—or should be—an exercise in applied empathy. In order to persuade a reader of something, whether it be the accuracy of a set of facts, the soundness of a legal interpretation, or the believability of a fictional account, a writer must attempt to place him or herself in the mind of the reader and try to imagine the reader's response to the written material.*[245]

As legal writers, we consider our audience, and what moves our reader. Cultivating empathy makes us more effective legal writers. Quiet law students and lawyers who already are drawn to legal writing over oral advocacy—and who understand the impact of empathy—can use the written word as a powerful vehicle to amplify their authentic voices.

Persuading, and Resolving Conflicts

Whether through writing, or in person through a transactional negotiation or litigation-oriented debate, at some point every introverted lawyer will be called to influence and persuade other human beings. An introvert's capacity for empathy is a valuable endowment in persuasion. Professor Gallacher notes:

> *A lawyer who can project him or herself into the thoughts of another and understand how that person—juror, witness, judge, or other lawyer, for example—is thinking has the ability to calibrate language, posture, and gesture in a manner calculated to persuade the subject to believe whatever argument the lawyer is making. Conversely, a lawyer who fails to make this empathic connection with others will find it much more difficult—perhaps even impossible—to communicate effectively and persuasively, especially with non-lawyers.*[246]

As Dr. Kahnweiler notes, "[I]ntroverts can be highly effective influencers when they stop trying to act like extroverts and instead make the most of their natural, quiet strengths."[247] Dr. Laney highlights the differences in the way introverts and extroverts argue: "Extroverts often argue in a win-lose style. They emphasize being right. Sometimes this leaves the other person (often the introvert) feeling wrong. Many introverts argue in a win-win style. They want each person's ideas to be heard. In general, introverts tend to question more and criticize less."[248] Having a win-win mentality does not make an introvert weak; it makes him smart. Introverted law students and attorneys can use their listening skills, thoughtful analysis, comfort with silence, and careful choice of words to make a persuasive impact when they are ready to speak.

An introvert's empathic nature also is an exceptional asset in negotiation toward conflict resolution. In bargaining for a resolution or settlement of a conflict, "it is important for each side to understand their adversary's needs for the purpose of knowing what will satisfy them."[249] Professor Rosenberg contends that empathy enhances credibility in negotiation: "[I]f one can respond empathetically, that response alone will both generate good will and add to the credibility of the empathic listener. Ultimately, it makes it more likely that the empathic person can get what she wants."[250]

Impactfully Communicating

Eventually, even introverts must speak, which on occasion still can feel like a monumental energy drain. In 2013, NBC's *Today Show* reported a statistic from psychiatrist Louann Brizendine, M.D., who said that "the average woman speaks about 20,000 words a day, while the average man utters about 7,000."[251] It would be interesting to study the number of words spoken, respectively, by extroverts and introverts on an average day. As a female introvert who spends 80 percent of the work week alone, I easily undercut the cited male average.[252]

Choosy speech is an elegant characteristic of introverts. As Tanner notes, introverts "will in a few words pin down a conversation that has been dancing around an issue for much time. To learn to speak does not necessitate learning to be talkative."[253] My dad, an Episcopal minister, is a fellow quiet soul. When the man finally speaks, people listen. He can sum up in one sentence what a politician or policymaker might take an hour to convey.

In the legal context, introverts might struggle to wedge a word into a rapid-fire volley of extroverted advocates or resist the energy depletion required to step into a debate. With the right advance thinking, careful deliberation, and thoughtful writing, an introverted lawyer's ideas revealed through selective speech can be pure magic.

Of course, many extroverts also are skilled in the aforementioned lawyering competencies. Their introverted counterparts, however, if given quiet space to think, might burrow even more deeply into a challenging legal concept or conflict, allowing refreshing solutions to bud, away from the noise of the legal world. Overall, introverts should be more heralded in the profession as effective counselors-at-law. As Dembling encourages, "those who slow down, sit down, and look us in the eye might see that our inner flame burns brightly and puts out some heat."[254] With enhanced self-awareness and the strategic application of techniques described in the second half of this book, quiet individuals can channel their inherent traits—which once might have been perceived as weaknesses in the combative legal world—into mighty strengths.

PART II

A SEVEN-STEP JOURNEY TOWARD AUTHENTICALLY EMPOWERED ADVOCACY

CHAPTER 4

Don't Just Do It . . . Just Be It

The question for an introvert is . . . not why I am such a bad hammer. It is whether I am willing to be happy being an excellent screwdriver . . . and quietly get on with inserting screws while others enthusiastically attack the nails.

Mark Tanner[255]

"Just Do It." The sports apparel company Nike gave us one of the most motivational advertising messages of all time, urging the average American to heave off the couch, lace up a pair of sneakers, and tap into one's dormant inner athlete. Nike is the Greek goddess of victory, "both in war and in peaceful competition."[256] Archaeologists found an *akroterion*, an architectural ornament, of the goddess Nike at the Temple of Apollo, the location of the Seven Sages' inscription: "Know thyself." The sports brand's imperative promotes the empowering message that we can accomplish anything to which we set our minds, simply by "just doing it."

Some well-intentioned mentors prod at introverted, shy, and socially anxious individuals, "Just put yourself out there! Grow a thicker skin! Sell yourself! Just speak up!" Unfortunately, these mantras remind me of the cartoon character from *The Simpsons*, Troy McClure, an infomercial spokesperson who promotes his self-help videos with the tagline, "Hi, I'm Troy McClure. You might remember me from such self-help videos as 'Smoke Yourself Thin,' and 'Get Confident, Stupid.'"[257] Just do it. Get over it. Man up. Get confident, stupid.

We're not stupid. We're smart and we're quiet. We just might need a refreshed perspective on how to amplify our voices authentically when it's time for the legal world to hear our messages. But because "just do it" is not going to work for us in this context, we need an alternate strategy.[258]

NEITHER TOTAL AVOIDANCE NOR MINDLESS MASOCHISM IS A VIABLE HOLISTIC SOLUTION

Regrettably, so many of the coping strategies some of us invoke when we are confronted with interpersonal exchanges in the legal context impede rather than foster our growth. Some quiet law students and lawyers become masters in artful dodging and creative avoidance: wielding laptop screens like invisibility cloaks while hiding in the back row of a classroom, taking a "pass" when on-call in the Socratic Method (even if abstention affects a participation grade), bypassing hard-core Socratic-driven electives, choosing transactional law careers (assuming compulsory extemporaneous debate will be minimized) instead of litigation jobs, or hopscotching from case to case within a law office, demurring deposition and trial opportunities to more outgoing colleagues. Drs. Barbara G. Markway, Cheryl N. Carmin, C. Alec Pollard, and Teresa Flynn explain that avoidance behaviors constitute "maladaptive coping"; indeed, evasion "provides temporary relief" but "can quickly become part of the problem. In the long run, such strategies feed your anxiety and keep your fear of disapproval alive."[259] Flowers echoes this principle: "Unfortunately, the very effort to escape thoughts, or even suppress or control them, usually intensifies them."[260]

Others adopt the opposite tack; they *have* been mechanically "just doing it." They levitate hands in the air to answer Socratic questions while weathering internal punches from thudding hearts. They boldly enroll in trial advocacy courses in a misplaced effort to will the innate resistance or nerves away. They join public speaking groups hoping the rote practice will eliminate natural hesitation or trepidation toward addressing an audience. Despite these admirable and courageous aspirations, this approach still nosedives, and, worse, can trigger or exacerbate interpersonal anxiety. Merely surviving one experience after another, for better or worse, does nothing to address the dissonance between our natural quiet personas and the pressure to orate in the legal arena. Not realizing the potential detrimental repercussions of this brute approach, many teachers, parents, siblings, classmates, significant others, law office mentors, and colleagues continue cheering, "Just do it!"

WHY "JUST DO IT" DOES NOT WORK TO "FIX" QUIET FOLKS

Why exactly don't rousing slogans like "just do it" and "fake it till you make it" work for quiet individuals in the legal context? First, Drs. Markway, Carmin, et al. convey that well-intentioned quips to hesitant speakers like, "Being nervous just means you care," or "Just imagine the audience members in their underwear," can be "trivializing."[261] Telling a quiet law student or lawyer that his or her internal conflict is no big deal demeans the already vulnerable individual and reinforces the feeling of fraudulence: "If this feels so bad to me, and nobody else can relate, maybe I'm not cut out to be a lawyer."

Second, Flowers explains that the "just do it" approach is rational and logical, while much anxiety toward social or professional interaction stems from *emotions* and *feelings* not based in rationality or logic; "[o]ne of the problems with [the 'doing'] approach is that it's linear and goal oriented, whereas feelings are neither."[262] (These types of irrational and illogical feelings are, of course, distinguishable from the introvert's scientifically validated—and rational—resistance toward certain interpersonal scenarios, as described in Chapter 1). Flowers elaborates:

> *Most people attempt to overcome shyness using rational thought, which isn't surprising, as this is the mental orientation in which we generally spend most of our time . . . This is the kind of thinking that enables us to create lifesaving medications or build spacecraft, and it sometimes comes in handy for figuring out where you placed your car keys, but it can cause problems when it's the only approach you use to manage fear or social anxiety.*[263]

For "just do it" folks valiantly trying to "get over it" as advised by mentors and peers, this pursuit soon takes on the character of punishment—which, well, stings. As Drs. Markway and Markway describe, "We think if we punish ourselves enough, we'll change."[264] We hurl ourselves into the scary evaluative fray, hoping that one day, the discomfort, self-criticism, or fear of disapproval will vanish. Yet, as Flowers counsels, "As long as you're looking at yourself from somewhere outside . . . and trying to perform to what you believe to be the standards of others, you will be judging and striving. You'll be trapped in doing mode and out of touch with your more authentic, whole self."[265] Instead of scrapping and hustling to adhere to external standards of extroversion, we need to *still* ourselves and focus inward—where we introverts thrive.

CHANNELING SOCRATES AND THE SEVEN SAGES: GETTING TO KNOW THYSELF

Socrates said, "The unexamined mind is not worth living."[266] Flowers echoes that "[n]othing can cause quite so much trouble as an unexamined mind."[267] Left unexplored, embedded patterns repeat on a loop in our brains, and negative thoughts tighten their grip. Something truly awesome and earth-shattering needs to happen to stop this vicious cycle once and for all, so we can expel our mental detritus.

To tackle introvert discomfort or deeper shame-fueled shyness or social anxiety, we must step back and survey our genetic and environmental landscape. Hesitance toward social engagement in the legal arena likely reflects our personal organic makeup intermingled with our unique combination of life experiences. Many of us have no idea how deeply the roots of our modern-day quietude were seeded through biological facilitators such as "genetics, neurobiology, and temperament," combined with environmental stimuli such as childhood influences, adult-child dynamics, and other formative undercurrents.[268] In addition to our inborn personality trait of introversion, kernels of judgment, criticism, or censorship may have been embedded in some of us ages ago, perhaps inadvertently and naïvely by well-meaning caregivers or mentors, or more nefariously by hurtful critics. We absorbed and internalized these messages. Through repetition, we ossified them into schema of avoidance, self-protection, fear, and doubt. Negative soundbites became part of our mental soundtrack. Now, years later, they replay over and over as we step into our new roles on the legal stage.

Of course, we realize something is off, but we can't feel better until we pinpoint exactly what hurts. Our unhealthy mental, physical, and behavioral responses to stressful scenarios are *automatic* and *inevitable* without thoughtful observance, recognition, reflection, and reframing. That's why "just do it" doesn't *do* anything in this setting. Striding into yet another torturous performance-oriented engagement in the legal arena—without enhanced self-awareness and mindful intent—accomplishes nothing more than repeating the problematic thoughts, feelings, and behaviors, further hardening and fortifying our harmful responses to stress. Dutifully, we throw ourselves into the same fire that we have leapt into many times before, yearning for a different outcome. Albert Einstein is attributed (though writers say the true source cannot be confirmed)[269] as saying, "the definition of insanity is doing the same thing over and over again and expecting different results."

Let's stop this brand of insanity. Let's dismount the treadmill-to-nowhere. Instead, let's study ourselves, become aware of our unhelpful triggers and responses in the legal environment, recognize that our prior habits are malleable, and consciously repurpose our obsolete negative energy into something useful. Let's "just be it." Let's *be* quiet yet transformative advocates. Caveat: "just be it" does not mean we get to loll around like lotuses, expecting instant acceptance from our extroverted family members, professors, classmates, colleagues, bosses, judges, clients, and opposing counsel. Far from it! In marked contrast, this process requires a dogged willingness to examine ourselves from all angles: personality traits, physical habits, preferences when engaging socially, and historical internal messages that might have served a purpose in the past but are no longer helpful or constructive today. We must carve out a space to discover—perhaps for the first time in our lives—the toxic talking heads occupying our internal news feed, officially banish them all, and replace them with one solid, forward-thinking, personal mission statement.

Flowers describes how "human beings have two principle modes of operation: being mode and doing mode."[270] He reveals: "Being mode offers resources for learning, healing, and well-being that doing mode can't access. In being mode there is no judgment or striving, whereas in doing mode it's hard to stop judging and striving."[271] Instead of trying to "do something" about introversion, shyness, or social anxiety in the legal panorama, individuals first need to just *be* quiet, shy, or anxious. Shifting to "being mode" affords us the luxury of observation, so we can actually see and recognize detrimental triggers and responses—like peeling back a hazy film from a glass window to reveal a clear vista.[272] Flowers offers a great quote from Tao philosopher Lao Tzu: "To be, don't do."[273] Likewise, Drs. Markway and Markway advise individuals to "stop working so hard to prevent your anxious reactions."[274] Let the reflexive stress responses happen so they can be "illuminated,"[275] and then repurposed.

It takes a strong person to look behind the curtain, but we have good role models. Socrates is reported to have "worked every day of his life to 'strengthen his soul' in four ways: Self-control, Authenticity, Self-discovery, Self-development."[276] As did Swiss psychiatrist and psychotherapist Carl Jung, who "devoted himself to the soul-work of 'going within' to seek authenticity, self-knowledge, and self-creation."[277] It's time for us quiet folk to shed the mask, the costume, the mantle of trying to be someone else, and *be* real.

THE SEVEN-STEP PLAN

So, how can we just *be* quiet law students or lawyers, capitalize on the positive traits of creativity, sensitivity, and empathy found in many introverted, shy, and socially anxious individuals, and contribute influential advocacy in the most authentic way possible?

Drawing from the advice of many psychology experts whose work is codified in the bibliography of this text, the next half of this book offers introverted, shy, and socially anxious law students and lawyers a seven-step self-study progression. Over the arc of the seven steps, we will examine ourselves as human beings, students, and attorneys, to identify and understand individual personality preferences, stress triggers, and mental and physical manifestations of anxiety in the legal world. Then, we will develop a gradual realistic program to convert perceived weaknesses into strengths, participate authentically in the law school and law practice experience, and become powerhouse advocates. Flowers, in his book, *The Mindful Path Through Shyness*, encourages an attitude toward self-examination that really is the opposite of "just do it"; "[i]t's certainly not a matter of toughing it out or shutting down your emotions and forcing yourself to endure things you hate."[278] Instead, he suggests, "[i]f you can create a little distance between yourself and your thoughts and learn to examine these creative narratives as mental events rather than facts of reality, you can begin to dismantle some of the personal narratives that create so much anxiety."[279] He distinguishes between a rational, analytical, harsh, judgmental "taskmaster" method of change and a non-judgmental, "non-striving," "mindful" approach, focused on enhancing personal "awareness, intuition, acceptance, and compassion."[280]

The following program tailored for quiet law students and lawyers synthesizes the guidance of the many experts referenced herein, and merges their advice into a seven-step sequence built specifically for the legal framework. While specialists use varied terminology to describe the developmental increments along this expedition, consistent themes resonate. For example, Dr. Breggin recommends three tasks to achieve freedom from unproductive emotions: (1) "learn to *identify* the weeds," (2) "*reject* and pull [them] out," (3) "replenish" and "select and cultivate" fresh emotions.[281] In the same vein, the process that actor and public speaking consultant Ivy Naistadt offers for understanding and conquering "stage fright" has four prongs: "(1) discover and acknowledge, (2) release, (3) reframe, and (4) visualize and make real."[282]

Here's our seven-part plan:

- **Step 1—Mental Reflection:** Begin listening carefully to, and then transcribe verbatim, the negative messages that automatically launch and replay in your head in anticipation of, or during, a law-related interpersonal interaction. Get the messages on paper. All of them. Word-for-word. Then, try to identify their original sources. Start to realize and acknowledge that the sources and messages are no longer relevant in the legal context today.

- **Step 2—Physical Reflection:** Start noticing each physical reaction triggered by the anticipation of, or participation in, an interactive law-related event. Describe the physical manifestations as specifically as possible—on paper. Blushing? Sweating? Shortness of breath? Trembling? Stomachache? Migraine? How and when does each physical response begin, crescendo, and eventually subside? Note your default physical protective stance: Hunched shoulders? Crossed legs or arms? Averted gaze? Are you making yourself small or closing inward, trying to go unnoticed or unseen?

- **Step 3—Mental Action:** Begin ejecting unhelpful messages from the past and crafting useful taglines and prompts for the future. Delete the old censorious messages and write motivating new ones.

- **Step 4—Physical Action:** Adopt new physical stances, postures, and movement techniques to better manage and channel excess energy ignited by a law-related interpersonal exchange. An open, well-aligned, physical comportment will help increase blood and oxygen flow, enhance thought clarity, and power voice strength.

- **Step 5—Action Agenda:** Construct a reasonable and practical "exposure" agenda, brainstorming a series of realistic law-based interpersonal interactions and ranking them from least stressful to most anxiety-producing. Through this thoughtfully structured chronology, and with careful planning and mindful intent, we will experiment with modified mental and physical approaches to each agenda event, with the goal of capitalizing on quiet strengths and amplifying our authentic voices.

- **Step 6—Pre-Game and Game-Day Action:** Develop personalized mental and physical pre-game and game-day routines for each law-related exposure agenda item. *Then*, step into each exposure event, consciously integrating the new mental messages and physical adjustments adopted in earlier steps.

- **Step 7—Post-Action Reflection, and Paying It Forward:** Reflect on and acknowledge successes and challenges within each exposure event. Tweak the pre-game and game-day routines for each subsequent exposure agenda item. Continue visualizing your ideal authentic lawyer persona. What does that quiet lawyer look like? How does he/she act, speak, think, write, analyze, communicate, participate, help, listen, or create? Note your impactful moments as a quiet yet magnanimous, altruistic, and empathetic advocate. Share your story and empower others.

By working this process, perhaps even more than once, inevitably you will start to feel calmer throughout the arc of each interactive event. You will note the inevitable rise of mental and physical anxiety symptoms—recognizing that *initial* reticence might always appear instinctively—and the increasingly faster dissipation of those pesky stress feelings and biological reactions. As you grow into your authentic lawyer voice, your impact in the law will solidify and strengthen. Together we will create a happier, healthier profession.

AUTHENTICITY

The goal throughout this seven-step excursion is authenticity. No more "fake it till you make it." Just the opposite. Just be it. Be yourself, enhance self-awareness, make hyper-conscious mental and physical strength adjustments, and you will make it. Not as rhyme-y a catchphrase, but light years more effective. As Naistadt points out: "To be a good communicator, you have to be authentic, which requires finding out what's stopping you from being authentic, an approach [to which] many programs on public speaking give little regard."[283]

NO QUICK "FIX"

This process takes time. Drs. Markway and Markway emphasize its gradual nature: "Don't do too much too soon."[284] There is no overnight, instant, "quick fix" to amplifying our voices or eliminating anxiety in the legal world, and in fact, we do not need to be "fixed." Take your time. Don't just do it. If we scramble to don our sneakers and bungee-jump off the cliff to presumed psychic freedom, we will never notice the crocuses blooming on the precipice, the texture of the sweatpants of the guy strapping on our harnesses, the foamy whitecaps of the river rapids below. We need time to reflect on our histories; let vignettes from childhood, adolescence, and adulthood coalesce in our minds; and recall past human interfaces that might have contributed to the current silencing of our voices—like a hidden optical illusion that suddenly becomes obvious. Our steps forward might be plodding at first, not fleet-footed, but the journey eventually will transform not only us, but our law school communities and legal system.

CHANNELING YOUR INNER PRIVATE INVESTIGATOR

On this expedition, we are going to observe every facet of ourselves. Like detectives on a stakeout, we will study incremental mental and physical nuances. "Hmmm, that professor's questioning of my classmate across the room made me clench my left fist . . . Wow, the mere thought of delivering that oral argument made me pull my baseball hat brim lower over my eyes . . . Interesting, when the partner asked me to defend that deposition, I lost my appetite for the pulled pork barbecue sandwich sitting on my desk."

We must be willing to observe our quiet selves, what makes us tick, what makes us happy, comfortable, angry, uncomfortable, stressed, panicked, freaked out, and relaxed. We must gaze (gently) back as far as we can remember and identify moments when we experienced shame, embarrassment, guilt, or censorship, or felt ignored, invisible, judged, or criticized for being quiet or just for being ourselves. We might need to rappel to sometimes daunting depths, excavate through the mental vines, bushwhack our way through the debris, and churn the desiccated soil.

This is exciting stuff.

DIFFERENT JOURNEYS FOR DISTINCT INDIVIDUALS

As noted in Chapter 1, quietude has many shades. The non-shy introvert's experience along this seven-step path likely will vary from the shy or socially anxious individual's evolution.

For introverts who do not necessarily suffer from shyness or social anxiety but still encounter discomfort and strain in situations mandating spontaneous expression about the law, an enhanced awareness of introvert assets is the initial goal. Dr. Laney validates that "[i]f [introverts] are not helped to understand how their mind works, they can underestimate their own powerful potential."[285] Tanner agrees, "I believe that introverts are a blessing to the world . . . but unless we learn to express this we will not be able to offer the gifts that we bring."[286] In this journey, I recommend that introverts first reflect on their preferences in law school or law practice for studying or researching quietly, having time to reflect before conversing about the law, writing prior to speaking, and working independently (at least at first) rather than in teams or groups. We can acknowledge the effectiveness of these habits in helping us generate quality work product, while at the same time comprehending perhaps for the first time how—and why—certain aspects and characteristics of law school or practice can be challenging for introverts. Then, the introvert's seven-step process will entail identifying any sources of messages suggesting that quietude is out of place in the law, deleting those scripts, and reframing our thinking. With this foundation, introverts can build upon innate strengths, develop tailored plans for mentally and physically tackling initially daunting law-related scenarios, and use introvert traits and preferences in the most effective yet authentic way—ultimately fulfilling, and exceeding, the expectations of law professors, law office bosses, clients, and judges.

Shy and socially anxious individuals who experience a deeper level of angst while roving through the law school experience or piloting their daily lives as lawyers can use the seven-step process slightly differently: going deeper to explore historical catalysts of self-censorship, and expunging psychological and physical barriers to speaking their minds in the legal area. For these folks, Naistadt reiterates the need for more than surface-level Band-Aid quips and tips:

> *Look at it like putting out a fire where there is a lot of billowing smoke. Similar to nervousness, which is just a symptom of what's holding you back, the smoke is just a symptom of the fire. Aiming the hose at the smoke won't put the fire out. You need to identify the source of the fire in order to extinguish it. Without adding this critical component to the mix, no amount of tools, tips, or other how-tos for auditioning, interviewing, speechmaking, or presenting effectively will produce results that last.*[287]

To tackle interpersonal anxiety, we have to be willing to go deep. Naistadt urges: "The key to speaking without fear is exposing the core issues behind your stage fright (issues that can be different for each of us but have common denominators) and rooting them out, then developing a solid technique you can count on for creating and delivering your message."[288] Whittling down to the true core of what is holding us back from finding our lawyer voices is "the overlooked weapon in the communicator's arsenal, and very often the most important one."[289]

Finally, some of you might never have considered yourself to be an introverted, shy, or socially anxious person and are wondering why you suddenly have a blushing problem or recurring migraines at the thought of attending a certain law school class or taking a deposition. Before law school or law practice, you might have been outgoing and gregarious, thrived in social exchanges, acted in plays, reveled on the athletic field, served on the debate team, held a leadership position, or taught classes. But law school or practice has pressed a big red "MUTE" button and you have lost your voice. You might have situational public speaking anxiety activated by the interruptive dynamic of the professor-student or judge-attorney Socratic exchange, or the perceived antagonistic nature of oral arguments or negotiations. Not to worry. Your seven-step process will help you identify past internal messages that currently are impeding your lawyer voice, understand their potential origins, realize their present-day irrelevance, adopt new taglines reflecting your current and future authentic lawyer persona, and mindfully construct a realistic strategy for tackling each public speaking scenario in your own style.

WE CONTROL THE DELETE-AND-RE-RECORD BUTTON

It can be quite revelatory when we discover that troubling cognitive, physical, and behavioral responses accompanying a distressing law-related event are simply knee-jerk automatic reactions from years of reinforcement of outdated messages. Routinely, we meander through life completely unaware of these programmed emotional loops. Usually, unless or until something traumatic happens, we do not investigate and study them, though, as Flowers points out, "they can be extremely predictable and create a great deal of suffering."[290] When we finally halt, listen, and transcribe the negative messages replaying in our heads, recognize disturbing physical manifestations of stress, and note unhealthy reactionary behaviors (avoidance, self-shaming, self-criticism), we can interrupt the noxious spin cycle and launch a whole new sequence. Flowers emphasizes that past patterns might be well ensconced and need tough extraction but they are not permanently fused; "the most troublesome components of shyness are things you can work with: thoughts, emotions, sensations, and behaviors that are impermanent, malleable, and within your personal capacity to change."[291] He reassures that we "can take the whole thing off of automatic pilot."[292]

We proceed from here mindfully and deliberately, as introverts naturally do. Ours is not an issue that can be solved in one, immediate swoop by ripping off a psychological Band-Aid, by ziplining away from a painful past, or by diving into the deep end of emotional confrontation. It is a process that starts slowly and purposefully, and consciously increases momentum with small successes, each incremental step a necessary component part of our overall greater triumph.

So, are you ready for transformation?

Exercise #1

Christopher Phillips, who conducts Q&A gatherings called Socrates Cafés around the world, quoted one of his participants, Wilson from Ecuador, as querying: "[W]hat I really want to know is, is it possible to be silent if everyone else around you is screaming?"[293] I promise, it's possible. Let others scream. But to thrive in our quietude, we first must become hyper aware of our context (our surroundings, cast of characters, and events) in the legal world so we can pinpoint the specific aspects of our environments that trigger unnecessary stress and anxiety. Then, we can disconnect any negative ignition switches and take command of our new impactful role in the field of law.

To get started on your "just be it" journey, go to your favorite stationery store or bookstore and buy a new journal. Or, if you bond better with your electronic device, access your preferred note-taking feature or app. Find a quiet place and contemplate the following questions:

- While in law school or law practice, have you felt overwhelmed around other people in certain situations? If so, what was happening around you? How many people were in the room or occupying the space? Who were they? What sounds do you remember? What other external stimuli do you recall? Lights? Smells? What exactly were you doing, or being asked to do, in that moment? What was your role? What were the roles of the other individuals present?

- Have you experienced anxiety anticipating or participating in an interaction with *one* particular person in the legal world? If so, who was that person? Was this person an acquaintance, a stranger, an authority figure, a peer? Were you afraid of something? Try to be specific. "I was afraid he/she would . . ." "I was afraid I would . . ."

- Have you experienced anxiety anticipating or participating in an interaction with a *few* other people in a law-related scenario (i.e., a small group)? If so, were these people acquaintances, strangers, authority figures, peers? Were you afraid of something? Try to be specific. "I was afraid they would . . ." "I was afraid I would . . ."

- Have you experienced anxiety anticipating or participating in an interaction with a *large group* of other people in the legal environment? If so, were these people acquaintances, strangers, authority figures, peers? Were you afraid of something? Try to be specific. "I was afraid they would . . ." "I was afraid I would . . ."

- Do you experience anxiety toward public speaking in the legal context? If so, is this a new feeling for you or a lifelong struggle? Describe the first instance you felt anxious about a public speaking event in the legal arena. What were you asked to do? (Participate in a Socratic Q&A? Present a case? Give a speech? Deliver an argument? Negotiate?) Who asked you to do it? Who else was present?

- If you experienced public speaking anxiety *before* law school or practice, describe a few of the most memorable episodes. Be specific. What was the event? What was the topic? Who was present? What exactly did you fear? Did you experience physical stress symptoms? What precisely did you feel?

- Do you recall a performance-oriented event from your past (before law school or practice) in which you felt *little* or *no* apprehension or anxiety? What was the scenario? Who was present? What was your role? What went well? What did you enjoy about the experience? How did the circumstances or logistics of this event differ from law-related performance events that trigger anxiety?

- Does delivering a prepared speech (without interruption) give you less anxiety than speaking in front of an audience and being interrupted with questions, or are both scenarios equally anxiety-producing?

- Is there at least one performance-oriented scenario in the *non*-law-related part of your life that you enjoy? Is it leading an exercise class, running in a 5k, playing music for others, guiding a tour, teaching a workshop?

- In what scenario(s) do you feel most confident in your life? Are you taking a test? Participating in a sport? Playing an instrument? Teaching kids? Writing? Traveling? Cooking? Painting? Dating? Hosting a party?

Now, let's take a moment to think about our quiet personas. Which of the following traits or activities do you identify with or enjoy?

- Listening: Do you consider yourself a good listener? *How* do you listen when others are talking? How do you physically position yourself? Where do you focus your attention? Do you maintain eye contact? How do you demonstrate to the speaker that you are listening?

- Data-gathering: Are you a good note-taker? How do you capture the thoughts of others, and your own thoughts, while others are speaking?

- Perceiving: Do you consider yourself a perceptive person? Do you notice details that other friends miss? Sights? Street signs? Landmarks? Facial expressions? Smells? Tastes? Patterns? Textures? Sounds? Other people's emotions?

- Researching: Do you consider yourself a good researcher? How do you go about researching something or trying to figure out the answer to an unknown? What do you do when you get stumped? If you can't easily find an answer, are you comfortable changing tactics and trying new research angles or sources?

- Creative thinking: Do you consider yourself a creative person? This does not necessarily mean artistic, but instead, being innovative in your thinking. Do you come up with interesting or even wild ideas for solving problems?

- Deep thinking: Do you consider yourself a deep thinker? Do you find yourself wrestling with problems or concepts to figure them out?

- Writing: Do you enjoy writing? If so, what type of writing? It doesn't have to be legal writing. Think about what genres of writing you enjoy: Text messaging? Creative Facebook posting? Emails? Poems? Songs? Letters?

- Choosy speech: Are you a person of few words or do words come easily to you? Do you like finding the right word to express a thought? Do you think about how to phrase your ideas before relaying them aloud? When you speak, are people sometimes surprised at the depth of your ideas?

- Negotiating: When you negotiate, do you prefer a win-win effort, or a winner-takes-all competition?

- Tolerating silence: Are you comfortable with silence? Why or why not? If so, with whom?

- Modeling empathy: Do you consider yourself an empathetic person? Are you able to listen to another person describe his or her experiences and understand that person's reactions, feelings, perceptions, and choices—even if they are different from your own? Do you convey to others that you understand their feelings or emotions? If so, how?

Now, try to recall specific situations in which any of the foregoing inherent traits or activities were beneficial in solving a problem, resolving a conflict, achieving progress in a stalled situation, or counseling another person through a difficult circumstance.

Trait/Activity: _____   Scenario:_____

_____

Trait/Activity: _____   Scenario:_____

_____

Trait/Activity: _____   Scenario:_____

_____

Trait/Activity: _____   Scenario:_____

_____

Going forward, we are going to focus on capitalizing on our natural strengths as quiet individuals to amplify our authentic lawyer voices.

CHAPTER 5

Step 1: Mental Reflection

The first task in the "just be it" journey is to quiet down, and then listen to and transcribe—verbatim—the automated, harmful, mental messages from the past that are triggered when we anticipate a law-related interpersonal exchange today. When thrust into nerve-wracking "command performance" scenarios, the brains of many introverted, shy, and socially anxious law students and lawyers immediately generate censorious "cognitive messages." When we sense the first notion of pressure to speak or perform, the negative mental scripts start spewing forth, like paper from a court reporter's stenotype. In a team meeting, an introvert comfortably note-taking and internally problem-solving might observe one participant after another jumping into the conversation pool, and feel an imaginary spotlight switch on, shine brighter, and burn hotter, and the walls of the room begin to close in to highlight her lack of contribution. The internal messages start: "Why won't you speak? Everyone is going to think you have nothing to say! Why are you such a chicken? It's just a meeting! Just do it!" In classroom, conference room, or courtroom exchanges, shy and anxious individuals can sustain repeated cognitive blows through what Flowers characterizes as over-anticipating negative events that have not happened yet,[294] catastrophizing,[295] self-criticizing,[296] self-judging,[297] and overall feeling inadequate.[298] In our heads we hear: "You're turning red. What's wrong with you? Why don't you know the answer? Why aren't you as quick as they are? Why are you even here?" Worst-case scenario thinking commences, and negative mental slogans begin a continuous loop, thwarting healthy reactions and responses.

To be able eventually to reject these messages, first we must *recognize* them. Some of us have been hearing these scripts for so long, they have become mental wallpaper we barely consciously notice. We must listen to their exact words and phrasing, write down the precise language, and then reflect on their original sources. This requires a little self-discovery voyage. Who from our pasts might have planted these untruths in our minds—inadvertently or intentionally? Strap in for the ride; this part could get a little bumpy. But this is an essential first step in the "just be it" process.

Naistadt emphasizes that a huge part of what stokes stage fright is the "[i]nhibitions that plague us on an individual basis, requiring a deeper level of commitment to resolve because they stem from fears we've nurtured as obstacles over time."[299] She urges that "[r]ecognizing and identifying what fuels your particular form (and degree) of stage fright so that you can move beyond or even overcome it is *essential* to being an effective communicator."[300] Dr. Breggin agrees that "[u]nderstanding our negative legacy emotions can help us to triumph over and to transcend them in pursuit of a life based on self-determination; resilience; higher purposes; and love for others . . . ."[301] If fear, anxiety, shame, or guilt cling to us like barnacles from our past, we must mindfully pluck them off, take one last look at them, and affirmatively chuck them away.

It is important (and OK) to recognize that our present-day self-censorship initially might have been sparked and perpetuated by people we care about, including relatives and other key influencers in our formative years.[302] Everyone learns how to handle emotions—positive and negative—early in life, through reinforcement by caregivers.[303] Hilliard explains that, beyond one's genetic makeup, adult quietude, shyness, and social anxiety can germinate from environmental dynamics in childhood such as: (1) how "parents or caretakers soothed or irritated [a child's] nervous system, training it into a state of alertness or cautiousness"; (2) positive or negative messages delivered by family or other authority figures, which either generated and nurtured feelings of "being loved, respected, and safe" or, conversely, of "being flawed, unworthy, unsafe, inhibited, or inadequate"; (3) being labeled as "shy" in a negative way as a child; (4) traumatic experiences; and (5) other life circumstances.[304] When coping with distressing emotions like fear, anger, shame, or guilt, if a child learns from a guardian or caregiver that it is unsafe to express these emotions through normal outlets, the child might self-protect through quietude. For these children, a pattern of "censorship" by authority figures "can 'prime the pump' for social anxiety to develop at a later point."[305] Embarrassing and shaming experiences in childhood—by caregivers, teachers, coaches, siblings, or other authority or influential figures—can be, as Naistadt describes, "tremendous blows to our self-esteem that may leave considerable personal devastation in their wake. The bad news is that if [we] don't work through the fear by pinpointing the source and clearing it away, it will very likely continue to get the better of [us]."[306] As Naistadt emphasizes, this process of identifying critical messengers from our past is not intended to encourage a "blame game,"[307] but it is an essential step in the transformational process to understand where negative messages originated so that they can be deleted and rewritten going forward.

For other quiet law students or lawyers, self-censorship in adulthood might have sparked from a *single* traumatic event rather than a lifelong pattern of repressing hurtful emotions. According to Drs. Markway and Markway, "[a] study conducted in 1985 by Professor Lars-Goran Ost at Stockholm University found that 58 percent of people with social phobia attributed the onset of their disorder to a traumatic experience."[308]

Whatever environmental contributors originally might have forged a law student or lawyer's reticence toward interpersonal engagement, the first step is unearthing and acknowledging these infiltrators, and then understanding and celebrating the fact that their suffocating grip can be released forever. To do so, we try to identify the original historical sources of judgment-oriented messages. We consider how such scripts might have been reinforced by other powerful figures in our lives throughout adolescence, and into adulthood, law school, and eventually law practice. And then we acknowledge that those messages no longer apply in the law context and can be silenced or rewritten. We can press "stop" on this endless loop of internal criticism, and compose fresh new maxims that encourage rather than censor our authentic thoughts, speech, and behavior.[309]

Help Is Available! For some law students and lawyers, this step might require the assistance of professional counseling. Personally, over a 15-year period, I sought assistance from four different professional therapists during various life phases and transitions to help me expunge my negative soundtrack. Many law schools and bar associations provide health and wellness resources and links to counseling services. The website of the American Bar Association offers mental health resources for law students and lawyers: check out www.americanbar.org and the Law Student Division's Mental Health Initiative, the Young Lawyers Division's Health and Wellness Initiative, and the Commission on Lawyer Assistance Programs.

HEARING AND TRANSCRIBING OUR INTERNAL MONOLOGUE

Invest in the time to hear and listen to the literal language of your personal mental scripts, and to reflect on characters in your past who might have relayed to you these particularly negative lines. Naistadt explains that many of us received forcefully detrimental messages "at some point in our lives that we have internalized and nurtured over the years, bestowing upon them a hold over us in the form of inhibitions that, in most cases, they were never intended to have and do not warrant."[310] Naistadt urges us to take out our chisel, "mine" our unique history, and "identify those . . . messages that have become our thorniest—and stickiest—hidden obstacles. Such messages . . . act like red lights, signaling us to STOP! We must change that signal to a green light in order to become powerful, persuasive communicators."[311] Dr. Breggin similarly describes guilt, shame, and anxiety as "invasive weeds and vines in our minds."[312] These emotions are the culprits that are choking off our authentic voices. Let's start bushwhacking our way to these roots so we can clear out our mental debris.

Here's an example of how.

Envision an interpersonal scenario in the legal context that triggers anxiety: A Socratic dialogue? A mandatory oral argument exercise? An upcoming meeting with a law firm partner? A negotiation with opposing counsel?

Choose a realistic event with particular players who have names and faces, and anticipate the real-life encounter. What mental messages do you start to hear about your ability to perform? Can you quiet down and listen to the exact language? No need to act on the messages yet or try to change them. Remember, we are not "just doing it" and glossing over our internal critic to badger ourselves into toughing out an event. Instead, just be in the moment. Listen to the words. Don't ignore them, pretend they don't exist, or try to edit them.[313] The change comes later.

Consider this law student scenario: You arrive at Civil Procedure class, and slink into a seat. You arrange your laptop and your notes from last night's reading on your desk. Your classmates converse around you. You watch the professor stride to the podium. She gazes serenely at the class and says, "OK, let's get started. Today, we're going to discuss diversity jurisdiction in federal court." The class hushes. She scans the clamshell seating chart. The microphone booms your name. You blink. Your brain has vacated the premises. Sweat beads on your neck. The professor queries, "Under what circumstances can a litigant file a claim in federal court based on diversity jurisdiction?" You prepared the answer six different ways in notes, outlines, flash cards: None of the plaintiffs can be citizens of the same state as any of the defendants, and the amount in controversy must exceed $75,000. But instead of the clear legal rule you memorized and fully understand, the following messages might flurry across your brain like a stock ticker: "Hurry up. Answer the question. Everyone will think you are clueless if you don't get on with it. Everyone is staring at you now. You're not as smart as they are. Your professor already seems annoyed. You're going to fail. You're a law school fraud. What are you even doing here? You don't deserve to be here."

Consider this law practice scenario: You arrive at the law office toting your Starbucks tumbler, eager to add the finishing touches to a brief to be filed by the end of the day. You settle into your desk chair, and clack away on your laptop, engrossed in final edits and proofreading. You hear one of the more pugnacious partners stomping down the hallway. He declares, "Everyone on the Penske case, conference room, now!" You grab a legal pad and a pen, and scurry to the conference room. Like a game of musical chairs, your colleagues scramble for seats. You slide into the one closest to the senior partner. He fires questions: "Where are we on document review? Who's drafting the motions *in limine*? How are we doing on expert retention?" Your colleagues answer, interject, get involved. You want to say something, be seen. Everyone has spoken now, except you. You feel the spotlight. You might hear in your head: "Just speak up! He's going to think you are useless! Just talk! Everyone else is contributing. Why can't you?"

Maybe your script sounds like these, or maybe yours is wildly different but equally harsh. The goal of Step 1 in our seven-step process is to start spotting these noxious thoughts as soon as they appear, almost as if they pop up in bright orange "thought bubbles" above your head. *Hear* them. Buy yourself a shiny new journal, or tap open the Notes app on your phone, and *transcribe* them *verbatim*. You might be shocked at the actual words you hear and have been absorbing for years! Mean stuff. Nasty. Unkind. Let it come. Let those vicious voices jabber whatever they want. They're not going to occupy the stage much longer so let them have at it. But write down their exact words. Then, label them: Hazardous.[314] Negative. Unuseful. And, transient, impermanent, and forever deletable, after we identify their original sources and realize that the messages and their messengers are no longer relevant to our present-day lives in the law.

In Step 1, our initial focus is on mentally perceiving each message, and physically writing it down.[315] Flowers encourages: "Noting is a way to build and nourish your ability to observe without attachment or resistance."[316] Hilliard reiterates the effectiveness of "writing these negative messages down on a piece of paper . . . moving them from inside your head to outside on paper, or into the air."[317] Part of the "just be it" process is learning that these toxic messages are "impermanent, very short-term visitors"[318] that we *later* can evict. In anxiety-ridden moments, we often think in extremes and we imagine that the awful mental and physical sensations will persist forever. But they always subside, at least until the next interpersonal event. Our ultimate objective in this seven-step internal recalibration and restoration is to reprogram ourselves to get better at (1) more quickly recognizing the "red alert" messages, emotions, and feelings that normally might initiate a mental tailspin; (2) letting the thoughts flutter in; (3) realizing their transience; and (4) sending them on their way.[319] "Through mindfulness awareness," says Flowers, we "can learn to recognize these thoughts for what they are."[320]

Eventually, we start to appreciate our internal power in "hav[ing] a choice about whether or not to jump on trains of thought."[321] These historically automatic responses to a twinge of anxiety—which, if left unattended, could swirl into an emotional tornado—become a conscious choice. By "just being it," we can linger momentarily when troublesome past slogans reappear,[322] and realize that they are just words that can be edited or deleted. As Flowers emphasizes, "Just finding ways to step outside of your thoughts and investigate them without identifying with them or trying to push them away is a powerful practice that can help break their spell."[323] So, instead of outright rejecting the messages or pretending they do not exist, we first let them show up and begin to run their automatic course. In Step 3, we will break the harmful reactive chain[324] and replace the negativity with positive personal taglines to buoy us through each interpersonal encounter. Only by acknowledging the message first can we expel it, "no longer feeding the fear body with more fear."[325]

Allowing harmful verbal messages from the past to arrive—uninvited as usual—so we can discipline them appropriately like the unruly bullies they are is a much more effective long-term solution than "just doing it." We accomplish nothing by compartmentalizing the messages, by shoving them into mental storage bins, and by repeatedly burying them in order to brave an interpersonal interaction or a public speaking challenge. In "just do it" mode, the baggage lurks, taking up precious intellectual space. Along this new path, we permanently purge our mental rubbish. Flowers encourages:

> [T]he more you try to block, avoid, control, or escape difficult emotions, the more certain they are to revisit you time and time again and become problematic. On the other hand, if you're swept up by each passing emotion, you'll find yourself careening from one overwhelming event to the next. But if you can learn to attend to difficult emotions with clear awareness and acceptance, you may be able to find a middle ground where you can work with your emotional states more skillfully.[326]

This new course of action takes practice. This is not an overnight fix, and this mental maneuvering will not become second nature until we have experienced repeated opportunities of successes and failures, with time for reflection and tweaking. Patience is essential. One of my favorite quotes from the Roman poet Ovid is *Perfer et obdura; dolor hic tibi proderit olim.* It means: Be patient and tough; someday this pain will be useful to you.

IDENTIFYING SOUNDTRACK SOURCES

After hearing and transcribing the messages, the next pivotal step is to reflect on our personal history, and to try to identify the earliest sources of the destructive words and phrasing. Again, we are not engaging in a "blame game"[327] or deflecting personal responsibility. Instead, by seeking to identify the original envoy of the critical text playing on automatic loop in our minds, we can realize that those dialogues took place in the past, are outdated, and therefore, are no longer relevant in our present lives in the law. In Step 3, we'll overwrite that negative language with productive taglines to use in future law-related interpersonal engagements.

SOME OF MY HISTORICAL SOURCES

As the daughter of an introverted Episcopal minister and an extroverted singer and piano teacher, my childhood reflected a peculiar intersection of public display, community-image consciousness, humility, and modesty. Always emphasizing education, my parents enrolled me in an all-girls, private school. I meandered fourth through 12th grades with relatively the same cadre of 49 girls. Scrawny, nerdy, freckly, a year younger than most of my cohorts, and sporting a gap between my front teeth wide enough for a Mack truck, I was not cool by any stretch. My best friend was the daughter of a World Bank executive; being one of few minority students in the late 1980s in our predominantly white suburban private school, she was not in the cool cliques either, but she was a rambunctious extrovert and was unafraid to speak her mind.

I was a straight A student, but generally I tried to duck the limelight outside of academics. I abhorred conflict and I was a pleaser and a rule-follower. The church was our family's solar axis. My parents toted my younger brother and me along to sing with choirs at nursing homes, perform live holiday nativity scenes, and smile at parishioners after Dad's sermons on Sundays. In lulls between church services, my brother and I played "communion" in Dad's office, reverently serving each other dry wafers, viscous grape juice, and Chips Ahoy cookies pilfered from the coffee-hour stash.

In mining my personal history, my earliest memories of losing trust in my voice flash me back to middle school. One new science teacher didn't seem to like my voice. At all. I recall one fall day, our class convened outside on a sliver of the carpool roundabout's blacktop to conduct an experiment with paper, a magnifying glass, and sunlight. I marveled out loud, "Oh! If you catch the sunlight in the glass, the paper catches fire!" I was thrilled at our collective superpowers and unusually verbal about it. My teacher swooped in, hovered over me in a shadow, snatched my magnifying glass, and snapped, "You just ruined the experiment for everyone." Dazed and unaccustomed to being rebuked by teachers, I turned purple and clammed up.

A few months later, as winter break approached, our class engaged in a Secret Santa gift exchange. I arrived in homeroom one morning, elated to discover that the largest polychromatic package under the tree bore my name. Truth be told, I was accustomed to receiving Christmas presents from my frugal and pious grandparents in a gray Hefty trash bag with a stapled nametag, because "giftwrapping is a media conspiracy." (As were greeting cards and cut flowers.) This time, I felt so lucky to be the beneficiary of a preppie classmate's good taste and generosity (I coveted their authentic Guess jeans and Pappagallo purses), and pointed out the enormity of my Secret Santa package to my best friend. The same teacher overheard me and hissed loudly, "The best things in life come in *small* packages." I turned magenta and zipped it.

The year I turned 10, Ronald Reagan ran for president against Jimmy Carter. My conservative parents and grandparents were devoted Republicans. I learned at school, and from my Democrat carpool drivers whom we knew from church, that Mr. Reagan was a dynamic guy and a popular Hollywood actor, but apparently was hell-bent on launching a nuclear war. So, at our weekly Sunday dinner, as my parents and grandparents discussed their upcoming uniform vote, I announced, with all the fervor of my 10 years, that Mr. Reagan was itching for Armageddon and that, if I could vote, I would cast my ballot to re-elect President Carter. My horrified grandmother scolded, "Do not disrespect your family just to be rebellious." Confused and stone-quiet thereafter, I avoided my blueberry pie.

Just as I hit the height of pubescent awkwardness, my father became the chaplain of an Episcopalian boys' boarding school. We moved into a house positioned like a fishbowl in the middle of a sprawling suburban campus. Is it every adolescent girl's dream to be surrounded by 300 boys dressed in seersucker and madras, who were living in dorms, studying in libraries, and playing football and soccer in fields mere steps away from her TV room? Well, not exactly. Puberty was not my friend. I boasted a mouthful of braces to finally close the monstrous gap. My best friend had dubbed me "Stork," thanks to my stick legs and bony knees. Every morning before high school, I donned makeup to appease my fashionable mother before we walked as a family out our front door, across a brick pathway, and into the boarding school dining hall for breakfast of institutional eggs and chipped beef on toast with the 300 boys. Then, on the way to school, I smeared off all traces of blush and eyeliner to avert my best friend's ridicule for pandering to my mother and trying to lure attention from the boarding school boys. Each night, my family reconvened in the boarding school dining hall, sharing our days' events over plates of veal parmesan and Pepperidge Farm three-layer cake. We sat at the other end of the headmaster's table, with different groups of male students rotating through assigned seats each week. A new terrarium of family life. The makeup went back on. At church and at the boarding school, being messy, bored, grumpy, upset, or antisocial wasn't really an option for my brother and me. (It didn't go over great when he got caught smoking and I got caught with pierced ears.)

I longed for a robust gaggle of cheery girlfriends and a high school boy-friend, but daily shuttled between (a) my closest friend who mocked me mercilessly for wearing makeup and knockoff preppie clothes, and (b) an untouchable bonanza of 300 boys, many of whom were either afraid to talk to the chaplain's daughter or pretended I didn't exist. One varsity basketball player approached me in the dining hall after dinner one evening and asked me to "hang out," which I believed for a nanosecond was the turning point in my love life. It wasn't. A week later at school, I overheard the popular field hockey players laughing about how the boy had been restricted to campus for curfew violations and had asked me—the only female teenager available—out solely based on a very public "dare." Rather humiliating.

After graduating from high school with salutatorian and *cum laude* honors, I scampered off to The University of Virginia, double-majoring in foreign affairs, and French language and literature. I pledged a sorority, was voted rush chair, had plenty of friends, and finally, by some miracle, had a gorgeous serious boyfriend. In my French and Italian classes, I spoke loquaciously—to the vast annoyance of my classmates. While speaking in a foreign language felt natural, my regular English-speaking voice faltered. In Foreign Affairs lecture classes about the Middle East conflict and the art of warfare, I hid in the sea of faces, letting eager extroverted classmates carry the debate.

Home on seasonal breaks, though, I still itched to share my blossoming opinions about issues I was studying in national and world affairs with my parents and grandparents. I craved unconditional love from my grandmother, a strong, independent, hard-working woman who taught me to read at the age of three, co-read Judy Blume books with me, and ignited my desire to travel the world someday. I yearned to connect with her during the robust dinner table debates about politics or religion, but suffered stints of isolation when I said the wrong thing. Once, over a rainbow-marbleized pot roast, I gushed about my admiration for two UVA students who had launched a Post-Conviction Assistance Program and were recruiting younger students to do research for defendants facing Virginia's death penalty. My grandmother sent me back to school with a care package of Top Ramen and boxes of macaroni and cheese but avoided eye contact and her usual hug.

I now understand that these and other snippets of what I perceived (whether incorrectly or correctly) as criticism, censorship, or discouragement from weighty influencers—teachers, my best friend, revered caregivers, and eventually long-term boyfriends whose love I desperately feared losing—contributed to internal confusion and a feeling of isolation in an upbringing situated somewhat amidst public scrutiny (a challenging dynamic for self-critical individuals even on a small community scale). Verbalizing nascent views and experimenting in natural adolescent and early adult self-expression often led to public mocking or shaming and private withdrawal of affection or attention. In public, I felt I had to smile and pretend everything was perfect, but my insides hurt and I felt nervous, afraid, and lonely. I certainly realize that none of these experiences equated to childhood trauma; I received a solid upper-middle-class American upbringing from faithful parents and two sets of grandparents grounded within the strongest marriages I've ever witnessed. I thrived in a top-notch education. I loved living at the boarding school and the other wacky housing experiences we had (one was a haunted "mansion" with a rickety elevator, which the church rented from the city for a dollar). But later, studying my introversion and anxiety toward forced public interaction, and further reflecting upon my life vignettes, it makes sense why law school Socratic exchange and my early combative law practice experiences plagued me. Wait, you want *me* to express (and be excited about) an opinion that differs from my professors, peers, and colleagues, and that isn't fully fleshed-out and perfect? The messages I replayed in my head from ages 21 to 40 were: "You're not allowed to be yourself. Your opinions are not valuable. Your opinions are wrong. You should be ashamed of your opinions. Look perfect. Act perfect. Be perfect. Look, act, feel, and think how others want you to look, act, feel, and think. Don't disagree with anyone. Agree with everyone. Don't let anyone down. Don't disappoint." Even today, if I make a mistake, my absolute first knee-jerk thought is, "You're an idiot." No, I'm not an idiot. And please get out of my head.

My science teacher quipped those words, probably without even thinking, around 37 years ago, in a tiny classroom, five states away from where I live now. I have no idea where she is, or if she is even still on this planet. My high school best friend and I completely lost touch 30 years ago when we matriculated in colleges on opposite coasts. My grandmother—whom I adore (and whose personality my own mirrors in countless ways)—passed away. So why does the wounding timbre of their statements ages ago warrant an iota of power over me now? Do these messages and many exceedingly more traumatic ones from other deeply influential characters in my past still sting at times? Yes. But now I understand how useless those ancient scripts are. In Step 1 of my "just be it" journey, I realized it was time to eject the valueless soundtrack whirring in my head.

Exercise #2

In Step 1 of your "just be it" process, it's time to hear and transcribe the negative historical messages replaying in your mind that are hindering your quiet strengths in the present. Your goal is to capture the exact words, write them down, identify their original sources, and hopefully realize that the words no longer have relevance to your lawyer persona today and that the original sources no longer have a grasp on you. Later in Step 3, we will edit or delete the useless scripts and craft priceless new personal lyrics that will empower your authentic lawyer voice.

Grab your new journal, or access your preferred note-taking feature or app on your electronic device. Now, envision an interpersonal interaction, a command performance, or a public speaking scenario in the legal context. Be specific: Is it a classroom dialogue or exercise? A law office presentation? A meeting with opposing counsel? A conference call? A negotiation? An argument or speech?

Imagine you are a detective on a stakeout noting every nuance of your target's behavior.

- What messages do you hear? What are the exact words, language, terminology, or phrases? Do you hear yourself being described in nouns and adjectives? Write them down.

- Do this more than once. In fact, take a few weeks to really notice the negative messages that replay in your head in anticipation of, or during, a law-related interpersonal encounter.

- Later, when you have a quiet half-hour or hour, think about how those words, language, terminology, or phrases make you feel? Agitated, annoyed, nervous, angry, numb?

- Now, try to think back to events in your past when you experienced similar feelings and heard comparable language.

  - Who was there?

  - What was happening?

  - Did anyone in particular make harsh, critical, negative, or judgmental comments to you?

  - What were their exact words, language, terminology, or phrases?

- Make a list of those past messages and their sources. You might have many or you might only be able to remember a few. Try to be specific with your memories.

  - Where were you?

  - What was happening around you?

- Who was present?

- What exactly did the speaker(s) say?

- How did you feel?

- Were you afraid, angry, ashamed, embarrassed?

• Now, when you have another free half-hour or hour, think about how much time has passed since you originally received those messages.

- Are any of those original sources *no longer* in your life?

  • Do those original messengers who are *no longer* in your life have any relevance to your present life *in the law*?

- For those original messengers who *are* still in your life, do they deserve to retain such power over you? Has anything about your relationship changed such that you are now on equal footing? Can you view those messengers in a different light, perhaps with *compassion*, and realize their words might have come from a place of their own *fear*, but have no relevance *to your legal persona* now?

- ◦ If you can, label the messages as no longer useful, and name the original sources as no longer relevant or influential in your current life *in the law*.

- Give yourself permission to let the messages go, delete them, or overwrite them. For now, just give yourself permission. We'll get to the task of officially releasing the old and writing the new messages in Step 3.

- Throughout Step 1, be cautious and compassionate with yourself. If this process triggers emotional pain, acknowledge that. Be open to asking for help. (See the resources referenced on page 69).

- Breathe. Step 1 is the hardest part of this process. And you just did it. Actually, you just *were* it.

CHAPTER 6

Step 2: Physical Reflection

For many introverted, shy, or socially anxious law students or lawyers, the physical manifestations of stress that are triggered by an interpersonal interaction, a command performance, or a public speaking event exacerbate the emotional impacts. Not only does it *feel* unnerving to sweat, flush, blush, shake, or experience a fluttering heart, shortness of breath, or tightening of the throat, some of these biological responses are visible to an audience, aggravating the speaker's embarrassment or shame. Hilliard reports that "[r]oughly twenty to thirty percent of the participants in [her social anxiety support] groups have rated their physical symptoms as their number-one concern," characterizing their outward indicators as "excruciating."[328] Those of us who endure such tricky automatic physical responses worry that when others see our external markers, they judge. We try to fight our instinctive biological reactions, chiding ourselves for being so weak. Why can't we "just do it"?

According to the experts, this type of bodily response to stress is not one of abandonment, although we often feel betrayed by our physicality in those moments. Instead, our bodies react out of self-protection,[329] a battening down of the hatches in anticipation of a storm. Hilliard explains that "[t]hese are the same bodily responses that are activated in an emergency involving some sort of physical threat."[330]

Thus, experts like Hilliard suggest that, instead of being ashamed of or embarrassed by somatic reactions to interactive events, we can embrace these outward symptoms as "life coursing through [the] body."[331] Step 1 of our seven-step process invited us to recognize and consider the sources of the negative *mental* messages that appear in our minds at the onset of an intimidating event in the legal context. In Step 2, we focus on noticing individual *physical* responses to stress, understanding what is happening within our bodies, and letting go of the judgment associated with these behaviors which we previously might have misconstrued as weaknesses. In Step 4, we will make minor physical adjustments to transform our bodies, posture, and stance into pillars to bolster our voices. Flowers encourages that "[t]he body is a place where you can become more grounded and stable in working with difficult emotions like anxiety and fear. It can be an important ally in meeting challenging emotions and dealing with them well."[332]

To illustrate, let's use extreme blushing—my nemesis—as a test case. Serial blushers like me feel as though their introversion, shyness, or social anxiety is being flashed in neon on a colossal Times Square billboard for the world to see. Hilliard validates that blushing "is a topic often ignored or only briefly mentioned in most social anxiety literature."[333]

I blush. I blush in meetings, when teaching, on dates, and even sometimes when a JetBlue flight attendant kindly asks me if I want another ice cube in my water. I can't control it. When I try to stop it, the flush flames more brilliantly—fiery pinks and reds creeping up and around my neck and cheeks like ivy. Inexplicably, many extroverts and non-blushers feel obligated to point out my blushing: "Wow, your face is so red! Why are you turning red? Did you know your face is red? Yikes, your face is red." Nothing makes a woman on a first date feel more sexy, beautiful, and goddess-like than when a man points out, "Geez, your face is so red!" Aestheticians mutter, "Wow, your skin is so sensitive. So sensitive! Why are you so sensitive?" I yearn to scream, "Leave me alone, people. I blush. Deal with it!" But, for years, I felt defective.

Before I started this introversion evolution, during negotiations on behalf of clients, if I tried to float a point I did not really believe in, I blushed. In depositions, if opposing counsel objected to a question and I was not spontaneously certain how to push back or rephrase my question, I blushed. As a professor, if I misspoke during a lecture or needed a moment to ponder an intriguing query posed by an enthusiastic student, I blushed. Each time I sensed the first heat trace of a blush on my cheek, before I knew it, its vines had spiraled around my neck. I routinely began to worry more about the blush than my spoken words. Turtlenecks and scarves dominated my wardrobe.

When I started to study introversion, shyness, and social anxiety, I discovered that blushing can originate from shame. Dr. Breggin explains the link: "Biological evolution has built a kind of lie detector into our bodies. When we experience shame, our skin lights up with a blush that announces, 'You got me! I'm embarrassed, ashamed, and maybe even humiliated.'"[334] He describes "a specific connection between the feeling of shame and the physiological dilation of the blood vessels of the cheeks and sometimes the face, neck, and shoulders. The increased blood flow can produce a sensation of warmth or heat. Many people also experience creepy, crawly, or prickly feelings in their skin during shame."[335] As I forged through my seven steps, I learned that my shame stems from censorious life experiences that whittled away the trust in my voice and in my worthiness of having opinions. My blushing is an instinctive biological response to a perceived attacker or critic, a manifestation of feeling like I have done something wrong—or that I *am* wrong—and therefore am unworthy of my audience. To best manage the blushing reflex with this newfound awareness, I had to accept that I cannot reprogram this aspect of my innate biological and physiological makeup, and I cannot completely erase my past. However, I *can* control how I respond emotionally to the blush, and whether I interpret it as a weakness. For nearly 20 years, to echo Dr. Breggin's words, I felt ashamed, embarrassed, and sometimes even humiliated by my blush. I needed to find a way to cartwheel the message.

The answer appeared when I read Hilliard's book. Hilliard suggests that a die-hard blusher, rather than immediately feeling self-conscious (which of course perpetuates and flares the fiery burn), can try to take "ownership of blushing."[336] *Be* the blush. Hilliard releases the stigma of an embarrassing blush by reframing it in a positive light; "[t]o see a blush is to celebrate life's living . . . fullness, ripeness, color, and flourishing life."[337] She advises life-long blushers to "[t]hink of your blushing as footprints left by the blood surging into the blood vessels under your skin. They symbolize the fact that life is coursing through you."[338] Further, "[b]lushing is a reminder that you are a vibrant human being, complete with a rich array of emotions. It's a package deal. We laugh, we cry, we fume, we flame."[339]

I resolved to "*be* the blush." The next time I felt a blush coming on, I noted the initial flash, and instead of tumbling down the ravine of automatic self-loathing, I paused, and swapped in a new message: "OK, so I'm on a first date with an intelligent guy who speaks three languages, loves to travel, and is interested in my book about the Socratic Method. I met him five minutes ago and I am in full-on blush mode. He probably thinks I'm hideous. Oh, wait, no. This is just life coursing through me. I'm alive. Yay, me. I can't stop the blush so I might as well just let it do its thing and it will go away. Relax and talk to this guy about Socrates." That blush took forever to subside, but eventually it did. (So did that relationship. He never called me again. But, score one for Team Blush! I learned that I could keep calm, be myself, and the adverse physical response would recede.)

I kept "being the blush." Sometimes, while teaching, if a full-on blush smeared across my face, I said out loud, into the microphone, "Wow, tough evidentiary question. Let me ponder that for a second. Geez, I'm turning red right now. Well, there's nothing I can do about it, and it will go away so. . ." A few students laughed—which I chose to perceive as supportive rather than judging—and I forged onward and answered the question. And each blush subsided.

NOTING PHYSICAL RESPONSES TO LAW-RELATED STRESS

Here in Step 2, it is important to take the time to notice individual automatic physical reactions to stressful law-related interactions. These will vary for each one of us. Just as we transcribed the specific words comprising our negative mental messages in Step 1, we must get down to the physical nitty-gritty, cataloguing which physical response occurs first, second, third, etc., and the exact sensations, movements, and progressions within each biological reaction. When you anticipate or participate in an interpersonal exchange, do you feel a rapid heartbeat first, followed by sweating? Or do you experience shortness of breath or lightheadedness? Do your hands or knees start to shake?

After indexing your chronology of physical responses, the next step is to understand their biological cause. Legal communication experts Brian K. Johnson and Marsha Hunter explain, "[f]eelings of anxiety and excitement inevitably trigger the flow of adrenaline, which sends excess energy coursing through your system."[340] They reiterate that adrenaline is both a sword and a shield; it "is a natural hormone released by the adrenal glands. It flows through the body when your instinct signals a need for extra energy, perhaps to defend yourself, run away, or respond to the pressure of performance."[341] Indeed, "[a]drenaline is a natural source of energy while public speaking, but it can be a nuisance unless you understand and channel it."[342] To build upon an analogy propounded by Naistadt, think of adrenaline like a white-water rapid river,[343] and our physical bodies like the shoreline. If we close up and compress our bodies in self-protective mode, perhaps crossing our arms or legs, hunching, bracing for a blow, constricting our airways, and confining our blood and oxygen flow, we limit movement of the tempestuous current inside us. This can cause the pent-up energy to bounce around aimlessly, agitating us, and hindering our peak performance. Naistadt urges, "Nervousness is *not* a sign of weakness! It is a sign of *excess energy* that you must learn to control and redirect."[344] She explains, "[i]f we don't have a way of releasing and channeling that excess energy so that it flows evenly and naturally in a positive, productive direction, it may explode from us, throwing us into overdrive, or implode on us, creating inhibitions."[345]

Once we learn to recognize our instinctive self-protective physical reactions—in posture, stance, pose, breath rhythm, vision focus, and voice intensity[346]—and learn how to tweak and adjust those anatomical and physiological habits, we can harness our energy and use it to help us perform like powerhouse athletes. Johnson and Hunter encourage, "by learning to control your breath as well as the movement of your legs, arms, hands, and eyes, you can channel the power of adrenaline and dictate how your body responds to it."[347] They reassure that "if you learn to recognize the impulses to fight, flee, or freeze, you can counter adrenaline's negative effects by proactively gaining control of specific parts of your body."[348]

So, for now, focus on *recognizing* your individual physical responses to performance-driven scenarios and tag them with new labels; instead of flaws or weaknesses, they have purpose, and with enhanced awareness, can be fine-tuned to support instead of hinder our mental faculties. "OK, now I'm blushing, not because I am an embarrassing wreck, but because life and vibrancy are surging through me. Now my hands are shaking because adrenaline is pumping me up with excess energy that I haven't quite yet learned how to channel. OK, I'm short of breath because I crossed my arms and legs and am hunched down in my chair in self-protective mode; maybe if I open back up, my breath will normalize . . ." We identify and label these reactions, and honor their transience. Sweat evaporates, shakes subside, blushes fade. Step 2 is all about becoming *aware* of the energy inside us. In Step 4, we will construct new physical routines for stepping into law-focused exchanges with command.

Exercise #3

Grab that journal or the notes app on your phone and start cataloguing your individual physical responses to performance-driven events. Do this when you are anticipating a *future* event, when you are actually in a *present* one, and when reflecting as close-in-time as possible *afterward*. Observe and track the chronology of your physical shifts. Pause and take note—in slow motion. If you watched a frame-by-frame videotape of yourself exercising, say jumping rope, you might sense your heart rate increasing, a bead of sweat trickling down your cheek, your breath becoming labored. Stop, take a breath, feel the pound of each heartbeat. Notice your chest rise and fall with each inhalation and exhalation of air. Feel the sweat drip from your chin. Experience both subtle and obvious changes in your body and record each one, as if someone is snapping photographs of each new physical response the instant it appears.

- What part of your body do you feel or sense first?

- When you felt the first emotional kick of stress or anxiety toward or in the interpersonal exchange, did your physical body shift in any way? Are you sitting or standing? Did you subconsciously cross your legs? Fold your arms? Hunch or crouch lower? Grit your teeth? Clench your fists? Grip an object? Avert eye contact?

- Did you feel anything different internally? Did you gulp, take a deep breath, or lose your breath? Is your heart beating faster? Does your stomach hurt? Does your head ache?

- Are you noticing any external clues? Are your hands or knees shaking? Are you blushing? Sweating?

- Do you feel hot? Cold? Numb?

- When/if you speak, does your voice sound different? Is your voice shaking? Is it higher or lower pitched than usual? Are you swallowing more? Or less?

- What else do you physically feel or notice?

Now, assess exactly how and when each of your physical responses abate. What aspect of your body returns to "normal" first? Next? Last? How long does it take to return to a relaxed state? Does one response take longer than others to subside? Finally, which physical symptoms annoy or bother you the most? The least? Why?

CHAPTER 7

Step 3: Mental Action

In Step 1, we listened to the exact language of the messages playing in our heads when confronted with an interpersonal interaction in the classroom, law office, or courtroom, and transcribed the words:

- "Hmmm, every time I'm prepping for Torts class, I hear, 'You'll never speak as smoothly as that college debate team guy who sits in the front row.'"
- "When I think about having to negotiate that settlement agreement, I hear, 'No one cares what you think.'"
- "As I don my business suit to go to court, I hear, 'You look fake.'"
- "When I try to network but feel self-conscious, I hear, 'Grow a thicker skin.'"

We observed, we recorded, we noted. We assessed the original sources of these messages and hopefully realized that the historical messengers no longer have any relevance to, or power over, our lawyer personas. Now, it's time to delete and expunge those messages and draft new positive mental prompts for the future. We will use these freshly crafted taglines as foils, to interrupt the automatic spin cycle that launches at the onset of an uncomfortable or nerve-wracking law-related interaction.

Dr. Breggin reminds us that we have a "personal right to reject communications and actions that threaten or offend [us]."[349] Many of us have been tolerating the annoying static of our destructive mental soundtracks for years. Drs. Markway, Carmin, et al. suggest that "[t]o get rid of self-defeating thoughts . . . [we] must learn to replace them with more adaptive and constructive thoughts, called *coping statements*."[350] Instead of harmful rebukes like, "I'm such a wimp; I can't do this; I'll never cut it as a lawyer," Drs. Markway, Carmin, et al. encourage us to recast those jibes into "realistic" and "brief and simple" affirmations, using formulas like:[351]

"Most people will accept it if _____. I can cope with disapproval. It's not that bad."[352]

Using this template, here are a few law-related taglines:

"Most professors will accept it if I stumble over a word or phrase in explaining a rule from a case. I can cope with a quizzical look. It's not that bad."

"Most of my fellow law students will accept it if I don't know the answer to a confusing Socratic question. I can cope with taking a few minutes to sort out my thoughts. It's not that bad."

"Most of my law office colleagues will accept it if I need time in a meeting to settle in before chiming in with ideas. I can cope with being the last one to speak. It's not that bad."

"Most judges will accept it if my face turns red when I deliver my oral argument. I can cope with knowing it's outwardly obvious that I'm nervous. It's not that bad."

Drs. Markway, Carmin, et al. recommend crafting new "coping statements" to disrupt the "maladaptive thoughts,"[353] and writing out a "coping card"[354] if a physical tangible reminder is necessary to halt the negative loop. Similarly, Hilliard encourages anxious speakers to "listen to the negative messages that you tend to give yourself, and then . . . invent an antidote, a completely opposite message."[355] Dr. Laney concurs: "[R]ealize there is negative talk going on in your head . . . [P]ictur[e] the 'judge' who is criticizing you. First tell him or her to 'put a sock in it.' Next, switch channels to thoughts of something pleasant . . . [R]eplace that critical voice with a kinder, gentler, more supportive one: 'You're doing fine.'"[356] When that disparaging internal bobblehead chimes in with a totally unworkable "you can't do this," we must perform the mental version of the fire safety rule, "stop, drop, and roll," and say, "wait a minute, I *can* actually do this." The voice might press on: "But what if it doesn't go well?" Well, but what if it does?

In the 2016 Summer Olympics in Rio, U.S. gymnast Laurie Hernandez whispered to herself, before mounting the balance beam, "I got this."[357] And she did.

The first year I taught legal writing at New York Law School, I planned an inaugural series of Overcoming Public Speaking Anxiety (OPSA) workshops for students experiencing apprehension toward the spring oral argument assignment, the culmination of our year-long 1L legal writing course. Meanwhile, as part of my own professional development, I had volunteered to present a draft law review article at a Tuesday Faculty Workshop—a somewhat daunting venue in which law professors (mostly tenured or tenure track) present their latest piece of legal scholarship through a 20-minute talk, and then field questions from colleagues to vet the strengths and weaknesses of the draft article's premise. Historically, non-tenure-track folk (including myself at the time) were not typically on the speaker lineup. One of my fellow non-tenure-track colleagues cautioned that he would not want to be an "interloper" on the Tuesday Faculty Workshop stage. Still a bit oblivious to faculty dynamics, I thought, "Well, I respectfully disagree. As new 'scholars,' shouldn't we seek, and be welcomed, to learn how this system works?" I had been slogging on a paper entitled *Converting Benchslaps to Backslaps: Instilling Professional Accountability in New Legal Writers by Teaching and Reinforcing Context*, and I uncharacteristically felt the urge to talk about it. To a cadre of tenured and tenure-track faculty. Most of whom graduated from Harvard Law School or Yale Law School. And who could be a pretty intense and intimidating bunch.

During the five weeks working with my OPSA students to conquer their trepidation toward the oral arguments, I had to practice what I preached. First, I outed myself to my students, told them about the upcoming faculty event, shared my increasing angst, and then set to work to upturn my internal messages. Anytime the looming faculty presentation occupied airtime in my brain, my tired mental messages began to loop: "You're not as smart as they are. They're going to tear your work apart. Who are you to have an opinion about law teaching? Who are you to write a law review article? You went to The University of Virginia School of Law, not Harvard or Yale. Your writing isn't intellectual enough. They're going to think you're wasting their time." Working Step 3 of my personal program, I sat down at my desk, took out a legal pad, and wrote:

1. Be open.
2. You care about what you have to say.
3. You absolutely know what you are talking about.
4. You have something interesting to say and an important perspective grounded in experience.

5. You write for a living.

6. UVA Law is ranked No. 8 in the country.

7. This is only 20 minutes of your life.

8. You're a good, smart human who tries hard.

9. It ultimately really doesn't matter whether they all like you or not.

10. You deadlifted 150 pounds this week; you *are* strong. Go *be* strong.

I made copies of that handwritten sheet of personal messages and distributed it to my OPSA students, encouraging them to craft their own reinvention assertions.

The day of the Tuesday Faculty Workshop, sporting my go-to cheerful bright green knit dress and black cardigan, I marched into the event space armed with a Power-Point, handouts, and the 10 personal taglines tucked in a folder. I plunked in the designated seat at the crest of the horseshoe-shaped table arrangement and inhaled five deep breaths, plastering what I am certain was a deranged-looking smile across my lips. My heart jackhammered. I scanned the room for at least one smiler or nodder, and found three. As faculty trickled in, piled their lunch plates with lasagna I surreptitiously special-ordered from the cafeteria (instead of our usual cold cuts), and occupied their seats, I commenced my talk. Four minutes in, the PowerPoint technology failed. I kept talking for a full minute before I noticed a colleague gesticulating at the blank screen. IT guys swarmed the dais like SWAT, hovering over my laptop, clicking, tapping, jiggling plugs. That demon—my blush—began enveloping my face and neck. This time, instead of letting my automatic physical responses and the routine mental script seep in, I mentally "stopped, dropped, and rolled." I quickly fired up the new taglines, and invoked a few extras: "This is important to you. Keep going," and "You blush. So the heck what."

I waved off the IT guys, brandished a handout, and cracked a joke: "Good thing the public speaking-phobe has two backup plans!" Colleagues chuckled and nodded, I took a deep breath, carried on, and it went great(ish). The PowerPoint even rebooted. Later, I received an email from one of the tougher critics on the faculty, a recognized scholar in criminal law (my worst law school grade): "You have an endearing innocence about your mode of speaking that makes people want to listen. Excellent job." Another 20-year veteran of the law school wrote, "You can teach anything."

It was not perfect, by any stretch. Not my finest intellectual moment. But I got through it by cartwheeling my internal message and refusing to let the automatic negative script invade that space. I followed Dr. Breggin's advice: "[R]eject communications and actions that threaten or offend you."[358] My outdated mental soundtrack was threatening and offensive. At the onset of the heat of panic, I chose to reject it, interrupted the automatic loop, initiated my new positive mental prompts, and kept going. It worked.

My current repertoire of positive and productive slogans includes:

- Perfection is boring; be yourself.
- You care about what you have to say, and you care about people.
- You have a different and interesting perspective to bring to the table.
- Your face is going to turn red, it's life surging through you, and others will just have to deal with it.
- You finally like yourself; not everyone needs to like you.
- You are a good human being.
- If people are not listening to you, or ignore or talk over you, it's their loss; let them be.
- If you feel drained during or after speaking, remember that's normal for you.
- You work on yourself every day; you are putting your best self forward.

Exercise #4

Hopefully, in Step 1, you transcribed your historical messages, reflected on their origins, and started to realize that the one-sided commentary from the past is no longer relevant to your present law student or lawyer persona. Years, months, or weeks have passed, circumstances have changed, and you have evolved. It's time to overwrite those messages and create new ones—helpful, productive, energizing maxims.

At the same time, it's important to keep in mind that because your mental soundtrack has had years, maybe even decades, to lock into place, the knee-jerk messages likely are going to continue to pop up for a while, unannounced and uninvited, like annoying, freeloading houseguests. That is why we must *write down* both the old and new slogans, to enrich our awareness of their wording and phrasing. That way, when the tiresome messages reappear, we recognize them immediately, temporarily let them loiter, consciously acknowledge, "Oh yeah, here they are again," and then, swap in the new slogans. Eventually, our reaction time will shorten; our new soundtrack will kick in almost instantaneously as we mute the old one.

Consider the following prompts, and then contemplate a list of new personal taglines that can help you recalibrate and take control of your thoughts in an upcoming law-related interpersonal encounter:

- I feel strongest and most like a rock star when: _____. [*Note: This could be weightlifting at the gym, playing the guitar, cooking, running, painting a picture, rehabilitating an abused pit bull, whatever. Be specific with the details. The point is to identify an environment in your life where you feel almost invincible. We want to bring some of that swagger into the legal context.*]

- I am really good at: _____. [*Note: This can be completely unrelated to law. Again, we are trying to identify aspects of ourselves that showcase our strengths. Then, we bring some of that swagger into the legal context. For example, some of my law students and law office colleagues were amazing ballet dancers, football players, artists, and singers before law school.*]

- I feel really smart when I: _____.

- I feel really physically capable when I: _____.

- People seem surprised when I: _____.

- My best day was when I: _____.

- My ideal day is when I: _____.

- People listen to me when I talk about: _____.

- I bring something different to the table because I: _____.

- I am not afraid to speak to others when: _____. [*Note: Identify circumstances in your daily life in which interpersonal communication or public speaking is not a problem for you at all. Be specific. Is it with your best friend, a personal trainer, the Starbucks barista, a stranger on the subway, the toll collector, workshop class-mates, fellow churchgoers, etc., . . . We identify our strengths in these circumstances to bring them into the law context.*]

Now that you have reflected on the scenarios in your life in which you feel most powerful, write out at least 10 positive personal slogans. If you need a prompt, or are not sure how to phrase them, try these:

- I am a _____ person.
- I bring _____ to the table.
- I care about _____.
- I deserve to be treated _____.
- Perfection is boring; be _____.
- Who cares if people can see [*insert your individual physical response to stress*]; I will keep talking and it will go away.
- Who cares if I don't express myself perfectly; it is more important in this moment for me to be _____.
- Not everyone needs to like me; _____ likes me.
- This doesn't have to go perfectly; my goal is to get through the experience, while doing the best I can while I am learning, and reminding myself that _____.
- I do not need to be perfect at this; this is just practice in _____.

CHAPTER 8

Step 4: Physical Action

In Step 2, we catalogued our individual physical responses to anxiety ignited by law-related interpersonal exchanges. We learned that when our natural introverted resistance to certain interactive scenarios kicks in, or our brains interpret social interface as potentially threatening (based on past life experiences), our bodies launch protective biological and physiological firewalls. Adrenaline surges. Energy pumps through our extremities, priming us to battle or bolt. Some of us tremble; others perspire. Our hearts thump, voices quiver, stomachs twist. You might feel winded and lightheaded. I turn Rorschach-blotchy. Until now, many of us might not have understood that our body's preparation for a looming interpersonal interaction is a measure of armor, an individualized Department of Homeland Security. Instead, we might have felt body betrayal. Thankfully, if we embrace this positive revelation and make minor adjustments to the way we physically approach each anxiety-producing task, our bodies become a vehicle to bolster our mental strength and amplify our lawyer voices. Seemingly infinitesimal adjustments to the way we sit, stand, move our arms and legs, breathe, gaze, and aim our voices can have a colossal impact on our ability to calm ourselves down and excel in a law-related interface.[359]

PHYSICAL STANCE

Our instinct to self-safeguard is natural and automatic; our bodies indeed might respond protectively in an *initial* flash of panic for a long while, possibly even the rest of our lives. Many of us instinctively react to law-related stress by folding ourselves inward, shrugging shoulders, crossing limbs, making ourselves smaller and less of a target. By caving the skeletal frame inward, however, we do ourselves a disservice, giving our power surge of energy less space to undulate, blocking oxygen, and limiting blood flow. Unfortunately, our bodily origami can trigger or exacerbate many outwardly visible symptoms as we restrict and constrict instead of unfold, unfurl, and expand. In Step 4, we train ourselves to recognize these protective physical reflexes as they occur, and then consciously adjust our frame, opening back up, growing bigger rather than smaller, allowing our energy, breath, and blood to flow unrestrictedly, transforming our body into a supportive stanchion for our voice.

Do you have a favorite athlete or sport? Notice how most athletes stand when preparing to move.[360] Weightlifters approach a deadlift barbell with an upright frame, shoulders back, hands open, toes and knees angled outward. Golfers face the tee in a centered stance, bending knees, adjusting arms and hands, aligning their bodies toward the ball. Tennis players greet the net openly, facilitating the ability to scoot left or right depending on which direction a serve bounces. Football offensive linemen stabilize on two firmly planted legs and one or two hands, a sturdy tripod or quadripod at the line of scrimmage. Of course, tightrope walkers distribute weight evenly to avoid tumbling off the rope! Ballet dancers elongate every vertebrae, angling feet and knees outward, awaiting the first musical note. These stances are a starting point: conscious preparation for subsequent movement. Interestingly, legal communication experts Johnson and Hunter note that "[d]ancers and stage actors are taught to think of good posture as a *direction* to feel and not a *position* to hold."[361] As we begin to consider how best to use our physical bodies to amplify our voices, we can think about how to improve our starting positions to be prepared for and sense *eventual* movement in a positive direction. Finally invoking our inner Nike athletes *here*, let's "just feel it."

As we approach each interpersonal interaction or performance-oriented event, instead of crumpling inward in protective mode, we must broaden our physical stance—uncross our legs and arms, reach the top of our heads to the sky, distribute our weight evenly on feet planted on the ground, whether we are seated or standing. How you are sitting right now? Are your legs crossed? Uncross them. Are your arms overlapping? (Well, one hand is probably holding this book.) Uncross your arms. Position your weight evenly on your glutes, legs, and feet. Elongate your spine. Open your arms and hands for a moment, and inhale a deep breath. That's the beginning of open uninhibited power right there. Once we become accustomed to balancing and grounding our physical frame, we use that aligned strength as a conduit. We channel energy, blood, and oxygen effectively to minimize anxiety, maximize clear thinking, and connect our thoughts to our voices. As Naistadt explains, "[i]n public speaking situations, as pressure builds and you feel the surge of excess energy it creates, you must be able to physically control the movement of this energy so that it is released outwardly, through the communication—thereby adding to the communication's strength—and not inwardly, jeopardizing the communication."[362]

Amy Cuddy, a social psychologist and Associate Professor of Business Administration at Harvard Business School, delivered an engaging TED Talk about body power dynamics. She champions the message, "our bodies change our minds."[363] Professor Cuddy does, in part, endorse the concept of "fake it till you make it," although she modifies this mantra to "fake it till you become it." Many introverted, shy, and socially anxious folks have been urged their entire lives to "fake" their way through interpersonal scenarios—without success in reducing related stress. Therefore, while I respectfully disagree with the "fake it" approach, I wholeheartedly subscribe to Professor Cuddy's theorem that a person's physical stance and confidence level are linked. In her TED Talk, she asks, "what do we do when we feel powerless . . . we close up . . . we wrap ourselves up . . . we make ourselves small." We "collapse." To counteract this crumpling effect, she recommends adopting a "high-power pose" for a period of time *before* a "stressful evaluative situation." Professor Cuddy's high-power poses entail adopting a wide-open stance, adjusting legs into a balanced position (sitting or standing), placing arms on hips or clasping hands behind the head—for two minutes. Her scientific studies reveal that individuals who assume a potent physical bearing like this can increase the sense of internal power and externally project confidence.

As introverted, shy, and socially anxious law students and lawyers, if we consciously adjust our physical bodies into this recommended balanced, open, stabilized yet flexible position, we can breathe with purpose and begin channeling energy, oxygen, and blood in constructive manners.

BREATH

We all know our brains need oxygen to function, yet sometimes, we forget to breathe.

Last year, feeling that my fitness regimen had reached a plateau, I enrolled in a lesson at an authentic boxing gym called Trinity Boxing in Lower Manhattan. I already work out almost daily—lifting weights, climbing the treadmill on a steep incline, spinning at SoulCycle—so I figured, how hard could boxing be? Plus, I'm a fan of the sport.

At my lesson, I started off strong, dancing through jump-rope drills, listening for a two-minute bell to signal my stops and starts. Then, my trainer, Butch, wrapped my hands in bright yellow gauzy tape and slid on my first pair of boxing gloves. Through more two-minute drills, he taught me how to jab, cross, hook, and upper-cut. He adjusted my stance, coaching me to pivot my foot with each punch, "like squashing a lit cigarette." He reminded me, "Keep your hands up to protect your face. Stop overthinking. Relax." And then he put me in the ring. For another two minutes, he directed: "Jab, cross, hook, duck, swish, shuffle . . ." while he skipped around the ring and I followed. I felt great, and powerful. At first. The bell rang. We stopped. A twinge of dizziness washed over me, but I managed to lift my smartwater bottle with the bulbous boxing gloves and pour water down my throat. The bell clanged and we started anew. I made it through the next round but when the stop bell pinged, I stumbled. I tried to hang onto the ropes but my gloved hands felt like giant mushy pillows. The room orbited. "Stick her in a chair underneath the fan and grab her a Gatorade!" I heard the gym owner John yell to Butch. That neon blue Gatorade tasted like nectar of the gods. As I regained coherence, John and Butch summed it up, "You forgot to breathe." They were right. I was so worried about failing. About looking foolish, punching "like a girl" in a predominantly male gym, seeming like I didn't belong. All that brain chatter. Not enough air. I needed to breathe, and remind myself that punching like a girl involves *authentic* inherent power. *You are a girl; punch hard like one.*

Legal communication experts Johnson and Hunter advise: "Once you learn to mindfully control your breathing, it will help you calm down, project your voice, and oxygenate your brain."[364] When we feel out of place, get nervous, obsess, or intensely concentrate, we lose control of our breath. Now that we know this fact, we can learn to recognize when that phenomenon starts happening, stop, and consciously focus on air. Inhale, exhale. Count to 5 or 10 breaths if we need to, but we must respire. Take a deep breath right now. It feels good. Do it again. Even one giant deep breath recalibrates our system and gives our brain a power surge. Add breath onto the physical open stance: plant your feet, open your frame, elongate each vertebra, flip back your shoulders, breathe deeply.

APPENDAGES

Legs, arms, and hands can be bothersome tattletales of nervous energy: Knees shake, feet bounce, arms jitter, hands tremble. Instead of letting our appendages get the best of us in stressful interpersonal interactions, let's employ them as instruments to channel the excess energy in the direction we want it to go. By grounding our feet in a balanced stance, we propel superfluous energy into the floor. Our hands can drive extraneous energy into physical objects:[365] a hidden totem, a stress ball, or a desk. These objects are resilient; they can take it. Further, Johnson and Hunter suggest offering "away nervousness with the *give* gesture"[366]—outstretching our arms and hands when making a point. Experiment with appendages, non-distracting physical objects, and gestures and consider which energy-dispersing maneuvers work best for you.

EYE CONTACT

When a professor commences a Socratic exchange or an aggressive lawyer lobs a challenging salvo in a negotiation, a quiet law student or lawyer instinctively might look away. When not quite ready for interpersonal exchange, or anxious toward it, we naturally sever eye contact with the speaker. *Mayyyybe if I look away, or down, or sideways, or up, he won't see me and will move on to someone else.* However, eye contact is another effective way to thrust extraneous energy *out* of our bodies toward our audience, like a laser beam (but not as scary).

In preparing for 1L oral arguments, I advise law students to scan the panel of three judges for a friendly face, a nodder, or a smiler. Hopefully, there will be at least one. As a professor, I love noticing a nodder, the student who bobs in sync with a lecture, offering positive reinforcement to the teacher. When we engage in an interpersonal encounter, instead of averting our gaze in self-protective mode, we must consciously forge eye contact, hopefully with a nodder or smiler, and then, after a few moments, shift our visual connection to another person. We can use this conscious eye contact and movement to channel energy outward and around the room, first to the nodder/smiler (if there is one), then to the less friendlies, returning to the nodder/smiler when we need a boost.

If there is no nodder or smiler, consider imagining one (or more), just to power you through the event. Apologies for another *Ally McBeal* reference, but . . . when lead actor Calista Flockhart's character, Ally, a lawyer, needed encouragement in a stressful situation, she imagined three backup singers, The Pips, at her flank. Think about it: who would be your Pips? If there is no nodder in the room to help bridge natural eye contact, it's perfectly fine to imagine your biggest fan or cadre of backup singers nodding and snapping right along to everything you say.

VOICE MAGNIFICATION

Just like we try to make ourselves invisible by constricting our bodies and averting our gaze, many hesitant speakers lower their voices, so as not to be heard. *If they can't hear me, maybe they will forget I'm here.* Even for a not-so-nervous introvert, voice projection—without conscious awareness and intention—can seem energy-depleting and so we instinctively try to avoid it. (I need a nap even thinking about conversing in a multi-party conference call or a group brainstorming meeting.)

However, Naistadt points out that "[v]oice projection is a key ingredient in releasing repressed nervous energy and relieving your tension immediately."[367] She explains that "as you must physically exert yourself to up your volume to any level, you automatically release any nervous tension you may be feeling, and make yourself relax."[368] She recommends that the simplest way to project one's voice in a group setting is to "pick a person in the audience who is farthest away from you and start by speaking to that person."[369] We can combine this maneuver with eye contact for a double-energy-projection whammy.

Likewise, on a conference call, Dr. Kahnweiler suggests, "Don't sit, *stand.* Yes, even though people can't see you, they will hear more energy in your voice. Standing up is proven to make your voice more robust as your diaphragm opens and you breathe in more oxygen."[370] This works. When I read Dr. Kahnweiler's book, I realized that every time I begin to speak on a law-related conference call in the privacy of my home office, I instinctively stand up. I pace the room. The moment the call concludes, I plunk down on the couch, depleted. But the standing and pacing enable me to boost and then channel my energy for the duration of the call, articulating my words more clearly and projecting assertiveness.

HANDLING BLUSHING AND SWEATING

As an epic blusher and sweater, I can vouch that these can be two of the more frustrating external manifestations of nervousness toward social interaction, especially in legal contexts where vulnerability feels scary. Obviously, other people can see blushing and sweating. And while these visceral reactions absolutely can be managed, unfortunately—in the moment—they take a little longer than some of the other physical manifestations to abate.

According to the National Health Service in the United Kingdom, blushing occurs when "[a] sudden and strong emotion—such as embarrassment or stress—causes your sympathetic nervous system to widen the blood vessels in your face. This increases the blood flow to your skin, producing the redness associated with blushing."[371] Sweating likewise reflects a mind-body connection. Our nerves naturally generate energy, which triggers body heat, stimulates sweat glands, and releases perspiration as a form of regulating body temperature; as sweat evaporates, water absorbs the heat from our skin. We cannot stop these natural chains of events, but we can set ourselves up to stay as cool as possible—mentally and physically—and control how we react to the blush and sweat. First, it's likely we are harboring useless historical messages about our blush or sweat, which we can identify and discard. It's time to reprogram our attitudes toward these physical responses. This is not easy to do, I know. I still initially get annoyed with myself when I blush, which happens often, in the most inopportune times, around the worst possible audiences, often when I'm not even nervous. But now, more quickly, I catch the self-shaming, and replace the negative judgmental messages with reprogrammed positive statements. If your body reacts to interpersonal interaction by sending a red-hot flush to your face, to not let this annoyance derail you, you must, as Hilliard urges, assume "ownership"[372] of the blush. You know it's coming. It's impossible to stop it. Remember Hilliard's view: "To see a blush is to celebrate life's living . . . fullness, ripeness, color, and flourishing life."[373] It's up to us to swap the script: "OK, I'm blushing again. Whatever. It's part of me. I'm alive and fully of energy and power. It will go away in a few minutes. Just keep talking."

I once was the turtleneck and scarf queen, trying to hide my blush and sweat. But the more layers I wore just exacerbated the overheating, which also aggravated the sweating. Now I just own it. I plan ahead and wear clothes in which I will not feel overheated (and I keep a cool-looking bandana or handkerchief handy just in case). And then, if it happens, I go full-on-blush. Just be it. If non-blushers feel the need to point out the blush, "Are you OK?? You look overheated? Why is your face so red?" I respond, "I blush. My face gets red. It's annoying, but I'm fine." And in 5 to 10 minutes, the blush disappears, my body cools down, the sweat stops, and I feel all right again.

FORTIFYING YOUR MACHINE

If you already enjoy exercise, or at least engage in it, consider your fitness regimen as another integral part of this mental and physical strength training process. Alternatively, if the idea of hitting the gym makes you shudder, try to reframe your mindset. Beyond aesthetics, your exercise routine can be about fortifying your mental strength through your physique, aligning your posture, getting in touch with your breathing, and enriching your stamina: all to help you power through law-related interpersonal exchanges.

Thankfully, I cherish exercise, but I never really appreciated how much working out drives my endurance and strength to forge through, and even triumph within, stressful interactive scenarios until the semester I taught 130 students in an Evidence class. In my smaller legal writing courses with 20 students, I move a lot during each class period, straying from the podium, sitting on a table when engaging in more casual banter with students, or meandering around the classroom during collaborative exercises—so I am constantly recalibrating my energy level. However, the Evidence course—a traditional lecture class—tethered me to a podium for an hour and 15 minutes, narrating PowerPoint slides with rule-based patter, responding to students' challenging questions about civil and criminal evidentiary rules. Often around the 60-minute mark, my energy waned. I blushed, sweated, and eyed the clock. Handling that many vibrant voices, the harsh glare of the fluorescent lighting, and what felt like a stadium-sized classroom was an introvert challenge to say the least. A year prior, I had become obsessed with an indoor cycling class (SoulCycle). During each 45-minute stint, the spinning teachers choreograph rhythmic movements on stationary bikes, chiming instructions about posture, alignment, and frame: "Shoulders back! Heart open! Eyes up! You didn't walk in this room today to quit! We're all in this together! Let's stride out of here stronger than when we came in. 15 more minutes. Let's go!" At the 60-minute mark in my Evidence class, when weariness and a strong urge to seek solitude crept in, I recalled my upbeat spinning instructors' voices. I remembered that I didn't die when I felt short of breath on the bike; instead, I realized I hadn't really been breathing. Behind the podium, I subtly adjusted my stance: I unslouched, stopped leaning, stood up a tad taller, shifted my shoulders back a smidge, and opened my frame. Small movements helped me breathe and reenergize to push through to the end of each class session, giving my students the enthusiasm and attention they deserve.

Last year, I began working with a 27-year-old female trainer who competes in Strongman competitions and converts even her daintiest personal training clients to heavy lifting. Me, deadlifting and bench pressing? I watch as she loads 105 pounds of metal plates onto a 45-pound barbell intended for me and think, "Yeah, no way." But I do it. Repeatedly. Each time I work with her, I leave the gym and strut back to the subway with borderline obnoxious swagger. Later, in a law school meeting, if a kernel of self-doubt pops in my brain, I hearken back to the 150-pound deadlift and think, "You're strong and you try hard. Say what's on your mind."

I recently attended a conference about the future of legal education and met a female law school dean. When asked to share a "fun fact" about herself, she said, "I just competed in a powerlifting competition." Perhaps we need a catchphrase: #lawprofswholift. Physical conditioning absolutely can enhance our mental strength.

Overall, if we anticipate and approach each interpersonal encounter by opening up and balancing our physical stance, consciously breathing, channeling extraneous energy through our appendages, forging eye contact, projecting our voices, and reprogramming our attitude toward habits like blushing and sweating, we can facilitate oxygen, blood, and energy flow to transform our bodies into an instrument for clear thinking, empowered communication, and human connection.

Exercise #5

Use this chart as a guide to reflect on the physical stress responses you identified in Step 2, and consider conscious adjustments you can make when preparing for, and stepping into, an interpersonal exchange in the legal context:

Physical Characteristic	Your Personal Physical Reaction to Stress Identified in Step 2	Physical Adjustments You Can Make in Approaching, and Participating in, an Interpersonal Encounter
Stance and Posture (Seated and Standing)		
Breath		
Appendages		
Eye Contact		
Voice Projection		
Blushing		
Sweating		

CHAPTER 9

Step 5: Action Agenda

Newly armed with fortified mental and physical instruments to handle inter-actions in the legal context more productively and with less reticence, it's time to begin stepping into the legal community as our refreshed authentic selves. But instead of "just doing it" and jumping in full-throttle, we need a consciously crafted plan. To reconfigure our mental, physical, and emotional approaches to interpersonal, performance-driven, and public speaking chal-lenges, psychology experts recommend developing a measured "exposure" agenda: a thoughtfully designed gradual sequence of interactive scenarios chronologically ordered from least stressful to increasingly more high-stakes. Our transformation into our more empowered quiet selves is not an over-night makeover, but a reconditioning process. In this chapter, we will become acquainted with the "exposure" concept and design a pragmatic exposure agenda. In Chapter 10, we will construct personal pre-game and game-day routines for each genre of exposure event and tackle the anticipated scenar-ios one at a time.

WHAT IS "EXPOSURE"?

Flowers describes the notion of "exposure" as follows:

> *Sometimes, the very things that hurt and scare us also offer a healing balm. In regard to shyness and social anxiety, this means finding healing by turning toward and looking within interpersonal relationships. In the parlance of psy-chology, this is called* exposure, *and it's an important part of cognitive behav-ioral therapy for the treatment of shyness.*[374]

Drs. Markway, Carmin, et al. define exposure as "the process of facing your fears, rather than avoiding situations that engender them."[375] Now, before you face-scrunch and say, "Um, exposure sounds to me like a twisted version of 'just do it.' I'm out of here . . . ," let me reassure you. This exposure process will not even remotely compare to past external pressure to barrel into public interaction, push through anxiety, and gloss over mental and physical discomfort, feigning triumph. The approach is quite the opposite.

There is a critical distinction between confronting one's resistance in a measured, consciously aware manner versus all-out "just do it" anarchy. An effective exposure involves mindfully stepping into a law-related interpersonal interaction (for example, a Socratic questioning, a negotiation, or an oral argument), noticing the automatic swell of the often scary mental and physical responses, purposefully making subtle changes in mental, physical, and behavioral reactions, lingering in the episode long enough for the undesirable reflexive reactions to at least begin to recede, and ideally completing the event in a calmer state. Flowers explains that, within each exposure event, individuals "approach and stay near the edge of [the] social anxiety and fear deliberately."[376] The goal is to shape a new connection with challenging emotions and their triggers.[377]

What differentiates this process from the "just do it" mentality is the individual's level of personal awareness, intention, and reflection throughout, and the strategic gradual nature of, the experiences. We no longer are cavalierly donning our favorite neon sneakers and zip-lining across a ravine to prove our grit to ourselves and everyone else. Additionally, we flip the power dynamic; instead of these events happening *to* us, we deliberately enter into them with refreshed resolve. These scenarios now serve *our* purpose, not someone else's. Each episode is an experiment in our personal power amplification process.

Flowers describes the incremental slope of the process as follows:

First you come up with a list of social situations that are likely to elicit anxiety or shyness, and rate the severity of the anxiety, fear, or avoidance they're likely to provoke. Then you arrange the situations in a hierarchy from least to most distressing and begin to intentionally expose yourself to these situations to build tolerance, beginning with a low-ranked item.[378]

The ideal exposure agenda reflects a thoughtfully constructed stair-step-like progression, rather than a haphazard series of abrupt confrontations of all shapes and sizes foisted upon us. We start with the least daunting law-focused interpersonal exchanges and progressively work up to more intimidating ones.[379] Experts emphasize that "gradual practice [is] clearly superior to taking on the most frightening tasks early on . . . [Individuals] want to be challenged, not overwhelmed."[380]

Regardless of the exposure type, the critical ingredient is staying in the exercise long enough "to feel the rise and fall of anxiety symptoms."[381] Flowers notes: "[I]n most cases, once a strong reaction has happened, it can take fifteen or twenty minutes for the body to physically assimilate all of the self-calming hormones and chemicals it has produced and once again find its steady state."[382] For each exposure to contribute to a long-term holistic mitigation of anxiety toward performance scenarios in the legal arena—rather than undermine this aspiration—we must dwell in the temporary discomfort, and implement the planned mental and physical adjustments (designed in Steps 2 and 4) until our anxiety begins to dissipate to a manageable degree.[383] If we exit the event at DEFCON 1 stress levels, unfortunately our trepidation toward these experiences can be exacerbated, rather than mitigated.[384] Hilliard agrees: "If you quit while your sympathetic nervous system is on full blast, with your heart racing and your breath speeding, you don't get to experience the relief of anxiety reduction. You don't have the opportunity to develop the trust that things will work out."[385] This principle is why many attempts at "just do it" fail and can have further detrimental effects on introverted, shy, and socially anxious law students and lawyers. Instead, here we cultivate self-awareness *before* the event, pay attention to mental and physical nuances *in* the moment, make conscious adjustments to power us *through* the experience, and self-reflect *afterward*.

Drs. Markway and Markway reassure individuals that "[f]acing your fears can be powerful, especially when you stay in the situation long enough to learn that you *can* cope with it and that a catastrophe isn't likely to occur."[386] Law students and lawyers who embrace this process will start to realize that the unpleasant mental and physical reactions always subside.[387] Fortified with a well-planned exposure agenda, we learn to trust our system. Gradually, we become more comfortable lingering in the experience, recognizing (and riding) the rise and fall of the automatic mental and physical responses, replacing past negative messages with new prompts, adjusting our physical stance to traffic energy productively, and noticing the welcome retreat of the pulse of anxiety and the restoration to a calmer state.

In psychology terms, the end result is "habituation" and "desensitization." Habituation is the lessening of the natural or innate response to a given trigger,[388] or in other words, the "diminishing of a physiological or emotional response to a frequently repeated stimulus."[389] Desensitization is the "extinguish[ing] of an emotional response (as of fear, anxiety, or guilt) to stimuli that formerly induced it."[390] My wonderful former therapist, Barbara Roberts, described habituation as "controlled exposure" and desensitization as "reduced reactivity." Drs. Markway, Carmin, et al. explain that "[w]ith repeated, properly executed exposures, your body begins to react more calmly in a situation that used to make you nervous."[391] This mindful incremental approach is distinguishable from the "just do it and you'll get over it" mentality.

Regarding habituation and desensitization, I do not endorse that we extinguish *all* emotional responses—only the personally harmful ones. Author on public speaking anxiety M. F. Fensholt reminds us that "[c]reativity and emotional sensitivity are two positive traits often shared by people who experience anxiety."[392] The legal profession needs more creative and empathetic law students and lawyers who feel. Rather than numbing ourselves, by exercising mindful awareness, we can channel our emotional sensitivity in a healthy direction to interact within the legal community with clarity, insightfulness, and impact.

CRAFTING A GRADUAL EXPOSURE ITINERARY

For an exposure agenda to succeed, experts consistently highlight the importance of conscientiously calculated increments. Drs. Markway and Markway emphasize that the "key to successful exposure treatment is to go slowly and don't take on more than you can handle."[393] After a series of successful exposures (and recovery from occasional ghastly ones), we become more adept at the cycle: noting the arrival of the intense thoughts and feelings, addressing them with awareness and authority, making mental and physical adjustments, pressing onward, and completing the scenario. With each success, we reframe our attitude. We shift our mindset: Wow, yes, I *can* be an impactful quiet lawyer. Likewise, with each speedbump, we hone and sculpt the exposure plan further. The profound beauty of this process is that we redirect all the negative and destructive energy we formerly expended resisting, avoiding, reacting, and self-shaming into positive and constructive power; "[e]nergy and attention that formerly had no place to go can now be channeled."[394]

Exercise #6

Start listing the kinds of interpersonal interactions in the legal context that spark reticence or anxiety in you, at mild, intermediate, and intense levels. Don't worry about organizing them in any order yet. First, simply call to mind a variety of law-related situations that stoke internal discomfort. For example, for a law student, one might be: "Getting called on in a law school class and questioned in a Socratic Q&A." For a lawyer, a stressful event might include: "Arranging and participating in a conference call with opposing counsel to negotiate a discovery plan for a case."

Next, after you have identified general scenarios, envision three situations *within* that type of interaction, with varying degrees of pressure, stress, or stakes. Be specific in your descriptions of each potential event: name the professor, lawyer, colleague, client, or judge; state the location; identify the members of the audience; note the subject matter; describe the forum and format.

For instance, for a law student, three scenarios that involve the Socratic Method, offering varying degrees of associated hesitation or anxiety, might include:

1. Getting called on in Torts class (with a smart and firm but compassionate professor, and a subject I understand the best out of all my law school subjects) on a day I know I will be on-call so I can mentally prepare and maybe even talk to the professor in advance [*still scary, but less so than No. 2 and No. 3*].

2. Getting called on in Contracts class (with an intimidating professor, and I don't understand the subject matter as well as Torts) on a day I know I will be on-call so I can prepare [*scarier than No. 1, but less so than No. 3*].

3. Getting *cold-called* in Criminal Law class (with an extremely intimidating professor, and I don't understand Criminal Law yet at all), with no advance notice [*scarier than No. 1 and No. 2*].

Or, in the law office context, consider these three alternative versions of the conference call scenario:

1. Arranging and participating in a conference call to discuss changes to discovery deadlines with reasonable opposing counsel on a case that is running smoothly [*still intimidating, because you need to change some agreed-upon dates, but less scary than No. 2 and No. 3*];

2. Arranging and participating in a conference call to negotiate a discovery plan with uncooperative opposing counsel who has a habit of fighting over everything [*more intimidating than No. 1, but less so than No. 3*];

3. Arranging and participating in a group conference call with more than one challenging opposing counsel [*more intimidating than No. 1 and No. 2*].

Overall, list at least five exposure categories and two or three different scenarios within each category. If you are not sure where to start, try these prompts:

One-on-One Interactions That Trigger Anxiety

1.

2.

3.

Group Interactions That Trigger Anxiety

1.

2.

3.

Scenarios Involving Socratic-Style Q&A

1.

2.

3.

Scenarios Involving Negotiation or Participation in a Potentially Adversarial Exchange

    1.

    2.

    3.

Oral Argument or a Law-Related Presentation

    1.

    2.

    3.

Scenarios in Which You Must Be the Center of Attention (e.g., a job interview or client interview)

    1.

    2.

    3.

Set the list aside. When you return to the list later, organize the items into a chronological progression from least anxiety-producing, to medium stressful, to most daunting. Consider writing each scenario on a flash card and then moving the cards around, shuffling and repositioning them into a logical escalating order. Envision a stair-step progression. After we start the exposure journey, we can always adjust, swap, and modify the events in the chronology. In fact, we might need to undertake several exposure agendas before fully tapping into our authentic lawyer voices. With each milestone we surpass, we amplify.

Here are three sample exposure agendas to get your wheels turning.

Sample Law Student Exposure Agenda
(for Students Interested in, or Leaning Toward,
a Career in Litigation)

1. Make an appointment with an approachable teaching assistant to engage in a one-on-one discourse about a legal topic of your choice.

2. Make an appointment with an approachable law professor during office hours to engage in a one-on-one discourse about a legal topic relevant to that professor's course.

3. Make an appointment with a more intimidating law professor during office hours to engage in a one-on-one discourse about a legal topic relevant to that professor's course.

4. Raise your hand in a class taught by an approachable professor, to voluntarily answer a single question.

5. Volunteer to be on-call on a specific date in a class taught by an approachable law professor.

6. Prepare for and deliver a two-minute oral argument before a classmate or teaching assistant about any topic (legal or otherwise) you are interested in (with no judgment, interruptions, or feedback).

7. Prepare for and deliver a two-minute oral argument before a single professor about a legal topic you are interested in (with no judgment, interruptions, or feedback).

8. Prepare for and deliver a two-minute oral argument before a single professor and an opponent, about a legal topic you are interested in (with no judgment, interruptions, or feedback).

9. Prepare for and deliver a three-minute oral argument before a single professor and opponent, about a legal topic you are interested in (with intermittent questions and feedback).

10. Prepare for and deliver a five-minute oral argument before a panel of three judges and an opponent, about a topic you selected and briefed (with intermittent questions and feedback).

Sample Law Student Exposure Agenda
(for Students Interested in, or Leaning Toward,
a Career in Transactional Law)

For a law student who is more interested in transactional work than litigation, the second half of the exposure agenda above could be replaced with a mock client interview, a mock client counseling session, a presentation to a mock client about deal terms, a mock negotiation with a teammate, and a mock solo negotiation with opposing counsel—each with time limits.

Sample Lawyer Exposure Agenda

1. Make an appointment with an approachable supervising attorney to engage in a one-on-one discourse about a legal topic related to a client's case.
2. Make an appointment with a more intimidating supervising attorney to report the results of an assigned research project.
3. Participate in, and speak at least once in, a group meeting within the law office.
4. Interview, or gather case or transactional facts, from a client on the phone.
5. Interview, or gather case or transactional facts, from a client in person.
6. Provide an advisory opinion on a legal matter to a client on the phone.
7. Provide an advisory opinion on a legal matter to a client in person.
8. Participate in a conference call with cooperative opposing counsel.
9. Participate in a conference call with more difficult opposing counsel.
10. Conduct a deposition or a negotiation in-person.
11. Perform an oral argument in court, or if you are a transactional attorney, perform an oral presentation concerning a transaction.

CHAPTER 10

Step 6: Pre-Game and Game-Day Action

Our aspiration in our "just be it" journey is to fortify our brains, bodies, and minds beforehand, and then to navigate each exposure event with the following conscious intentions: (1) notice the initial surge of any automatic emotional and physical responses; (2) linger in the moment, not panicking; (3) remind ourselves that the reflex emotions and biological reactions are transitory; (4) swap negative mental messages with new positive taglines; (5) adjust our physical stances to channel blood, oxygen, and energy for effective breathing, clear thinking, and empowered speaking; (6) trek forward through the duration of the event, noticing shifts in our mental and physical strength; and (7) ride out the eventual descent of the intensity, ideally ending and recovering from the interpersonal encounter in a more relaxed state. Because this process—which could span mere minutes to an hour or longer—involves myriad mental and physical maneuvers that might be hard to remember and put in motion when our nerves kick in, it helps to combine all the work we have done thus far into tangible mental and physical checklists.

Legal communication experts Johnson and Hunter advise lawyers to develop mental and physical pre-game sequences in preparation for interpersonal interactions:

> *Sports psychologists teach that if you want to perform at a high level, you need a consistent mental and physical ritual on which to base your performance. This is to enable the mind, through repetition and practice, to control the body, and to enable the body to control the mind. Together, body and mind help control emotion.*[395]

Just like athletes, actors, and dancers train, rehearse, warm up, and perform repetitive rituals—like listening to a rabble-rousing song through headphones or touching a baseball bat reverently to the plate—before starting every performance, we can do the same, to quash self-doubt and ignite strength.

PRE-GAME PLANNING

Naistadt recommends three sequences of pre-event prep: (1) a verbal rehearsal; (2) a physical/technical rehearsal; and (3) a mental rehearsal.[396] Before you start to twitch at the idea of rehearsing once, let alone three times, these are not like traditional run-throughs that often exacerbate rather than reduce anxiety for us quiet folks. I would sooner leap off a moving Amtrak train than dry-run (or in lawyer terms, "moot") a presentation before my academic or law office peers. My law faculty colleagues eagerly moot one another before conference presentations, and many lawyers do the same before oral arguments. Anytime anyone broaches the idea of mooting me, my response now is, "Um, thank you so much for the kind offer, but that's not part of my process." If you have a choice in how to prepare for a performance event, it's 100 percent OK for you to do it *your* way.

The three pre-game sequences suggested here differ from "just do it" rehearsals around our friends or peers, and vary from the traditional advice to "practice in front of the mirror," which for us can feel inauthentic. Building on Naistadt's rehearsal sequence, we will construct three pre-game routines tailored to the law context: (1) **brain** pre-game (preparing our substantive material and then forging links in a chain between our thoughts and our voice, through thinking, writing, and speaking); (2) **body** pre-game; and (3) **mind** pre-game. While the brain and the mind might at first glance sound like the same thing, in this context the brain does the functional hard work of legal analysis and organization of law-related concepts, while the mind emotionally fortifies to best handle each interpersonal exchange.

Brain Pre-Game

The brain pre-game starts with our normal substantive preparation for a law-related event: reading research sources, extracting key information, analyzing the legal issues, vetting strengths and weaknesses of theories, and anticipating questions and challenges. Then, we deliberately create brain-body-mind links, first through writing, and then through speaking aloud (in solitude). We organize and write out our thoughts, and then read our notes aloud—connecting thoughts to written words to speech, consciously solidifying the concepts into our memory banks for faster retrieval later in the heat of the performance moment.

The writing process is an instrumental medium for quiet law students and lawyers to think through tough problems, test possible solutions, and formulate clear answers. In a tribute to U.S. Supreme Court Chief Justice Warren E. Burger, the Honorable Kenneth F. Ripple, a judge for the U.S. Court of

Appeals for the Seventh Circuit and former clerk of Justice Burger's, described how the Chief Justice used legal writing practice as a conduit for critical thinking and problem-solving:

> *For the Chief Justice, writing was not just a means of communication. It was a necessary tool for thinking through the most difficult problems. For him, tough analytical thought and precise legal reasoning were not the product of oral disputation. Rather, the fundamental intellectual process of lawyering and judging occurred when the validity of an initial hunch or intuitive flash was tested by pen meeting legal pad. As the pen met paper, private musings and oral dialogue were transformed into solid analysis or discarded as useless as he searched for the appropriate outline of the opinion, the "best" phrase, the "right" words to convey a thought. After reading briefs, studying cases, and listening to oral arguments, he would often say, "Let's see how it writes out."*[397]

Building on the Chief Justice's problem-solving process, we can use the mantra "write it out" in preparing for interpersonal encounters in the legal arena. We write as part of our brain pre-game for two reasons. First, scientists indicate that the act of writing (rather than just thinking) helps us remember concepts better, especially if we hand-write instead of type. Stanislas Dehaene, a psychologist at the Collège de France in Paris, indicates that "[w]hen we write, a unique neural circuit is automatically activated."[398] Likewise, writer Lizette Borreli describes a study by two psychology scientists, Pam Mueller of Princeton University and Daniel Oppenheimer of the University of California, Los Angeles, confirming that "[t]he old fashioned note taking method of pen and paper boosts memory and the ability to understand concepts and facts."[399] The act of writing by hand "is a better strategy to store and internalize ideas in the long haul. Writing by hand strengthens the learning process."[400] Although this method might seem time-consuming, it's worth it; consider first handwriting your prep notes, and then typing them up into useable performance tools—a double-whammy for entrenching those thoughts and ideas into your brain for faster recall later in the interactive exchange. Second, because we already know that nerves can derail our breathing and thinking, our written prompts—for our eyes only—will serve as cues to help us course-correct in the moment. People might declare that the best speakers converse without notes (they quip, "it's all up here!," tapping their vast noggins), but the peak performance of us quiet individuals absolutely necessitates the artful use of written prompts.

Let's envision a brain pre-game plan for a potential Socratic dialogue:[401] either a one-on-one meeting with a professor or a supervising attorney, a

Socratic questioning in class, or an oral argument in court. You likely already know the topic of the anticipated conversation: a particular case or group of cases, a statute, a legal issue affecting a client, or all of the above. To prepare for a Socratic dialogue, start by situating the conversation within a context and overall framework: "This case is about _____. This statute is about _____. This conflict is about _____." Then, write down bite-size pieces of information. For instance, if the dialogue will focus on a precedent case, note: (1) the parties, (2) the governing jurisdiction, (3) the date, (4) the basic facts of the legal matter, (5) the legal issue sparking the conflict, (6) the governing rule, (7) the court's holding on the legal issue, and (8) two or three reasons for the court's decision. For a statute, break down the rule components into a checklist of required elements or a list of factors the decision-maker will weigh.

Embrace the tried-and-true "IRAC" (Issue, Rule, Application/Analysis, Conclusion) structure to prepare for more challenging queries. Some professors might pronounce, "I don't use IRAC!" They likely *do* use some form or variation of it; they just might call it something else. That's OK. Regardless, let's use IRAC *here* because it absolutely works as a starting point to organize your legal analysis. Target the *issues* in the case or transaction, the *rule* governing the legal issues, the *application* of the rule to the circumstances of the case or transaction, and the likely result or desired *conclusion*. Use IRAC to anticipate questions you might be asked on each part of the legal analysis, and craft responses. Prepare notes in IRAC structure (with headings for each component) to rely on during your exposure event.

At some point in a Socratic exchange, you will be asked a question that stumps you. This does not make you incapable or unqualified. It's the law, not you. The law stumps. That is precisely what makes it so enticing as an intellectual endeavor. Knowing this eventuality in advance, first contemplate categories of inquiries the questioner might pose, and tailor your preparation accordingly. Study the questioner in advance, if possible. Examine the types of questions he or she asks others. Listen to the language and terminology embedded in the questions. Try to discern a pattern, or words or phrases that help you glean what categories, themes, or types of information the inquisitor typically seeks.

The trickiest Socratic questions ask you to apply the rule(s) to alternate hypothetical scenarios. This exchange requires you to dance intellectually a bit more, executing quick mental twists, turns, and sidesteps—a challenging feat for introverts who need time within conversations to problem-solve. Planning ahead, consider alternate factual circumstances, apply the rule(s) to those situations, and assess whether the result shifts. Write these down and assign them easily recognizable labels: "Insurance Hypo." "Landlord-Tenant Hypo." "Offshore Investor Hypo." "Good Samaritan Hypo."

In rehearsing for the flummoxing moments, think in advance about each party's "theory" of the case or transaction. What contentions or claims does each side assert? Craft a "theme" of the case or transaction. Is there a "public policy" underlying the parties' relationship or conflict? Is the legal opportunity or dispute really about a societal concept like ethics, equality, freedom from discrimination, order, reliability and predictability in the law, economy, fairness, resource conservation, morality, etc.? Is it really about a broken promise, bias, fear, greed, or closed-mindedness? If you struggle to brainstorm a "theme," think about what concepts, ideas, or imagery might comprise a 30-second movie trailer, an anthem, a commercial jingle, a slogan, a car bumper sticker, or a hashtag for the case or transactional relationship: when the questioner poses a query that momentarily stymies you, you can invoke this motif to answer the question. For example, if a Socratic questioner asks you to apply a rule to a confusing hypothetical you had not previously considered, you can refer to your "theme" notes and respond, "Well, the theme or purpose of the rule is to create an even playing field, so to promote equality among the players in the hypothetical, we would need to. . ."

When you finish contemplating, thinking through, and writing down your substantive analysis in a useful format (ideally, writing the concepts by hand first, for a deeper brain-body connection, and then typing them into a useful, readable format), grab a cup of coffee, find a comfortable, private, low-stakes environment, and begin reading your notes out loud. Keep it informal. You do not need to pretend you are in the moment, with the Socratic questioner sitting across the desk, table, classroom, or courtroom from you. Right now, you are planting the words in your brain, getting comfortable saying them aloud, owning them. Your writing forged the first links in the brain chain: from thought, to hand, to memory. Now, the reading continues the linkage: eyes recognizing words, brain processing their meaning, and voice expressing the concepts aloud, further entrenching the ideas in your brain. Later, in the real exposure event, the words already will feel like yours. Read your notes aloud several times. Hear and feel their vowels and consonants. Right now, you are not being mooted or peer-reviewed. You are not rehearsing in front of the mirror. You simply are fusing a deeper mental bond between the thoughts in your head, captured in the words on the pages in your hands, recognized by your eyes, reinforced by your brain, and transmitted outwardly through your voice.

Body Pre-Game

In anticipating an interpersonal interaction, for many of us, physical avoidance mode kicks into high gear. We self-protect by steering a wide berth around the event locale until the last possible second. However, the more we know what the exposure space looks like, what physical objects occupy the room, what sounds, lighting, and smells are present, the better we control our personal positioning and movement within that environment—which will bolster our thought process.

The body pre-game involves taking a field trip to the event space if possible, putting your body in the room, or at least close to it. For a meeting, do a reconnaissance mission to survey the professor's or supervising attorney's office and take a peek inside—how many chairs are present? Are there windows? Is the desk piled high? Where will you sit? How far away from the professor or the supervising attorney will you be? For a presentation, negotiation, or argument, travel to the classroom, the conference room, or the courtroom, if feasible. Scout. Investigate. Is there a podium? A microphone? Is there a platform for your notes and materials? How far away from the other participants will you be?

In the body pre-game, think about how you will enter the space, what direction you will walk, where you will sit or stand, how you will position your physical frame, and where you will place your written materials. Consider the most appropriate physical objects to bring into the event that will make you feel comfortable and supported but which will not weigh you down or hinder your movement. Once, I had an intern who consistently arrived at my office for assignments, laden down by a cornucopia of bags: a purse, a laptop bag, a lunch tote, and a book bag, all in a rainbow of patterns and textures. She also juggled a Starbucks tumbler, an iPhone, and sunglasses. Every time she entered my office, items clattered to the floor. She fumbled with her belongings, and took a solid 10 minutes to calm down and engage in conversation. Each encounter commenced with jitters on both sides of the desk; we both had to work to settle down and focus. We certainly need particular physical items to buoy us through the experience but also should ensure they will not overburden us or distract our audience. Transport notes in an easily accessible folder or binder. Even if a laptop is appropriate for the particular interpersonal engagement (which, often, it is not), you don't want the booting-up process or dreaded screen freeze to rattle you. Print paper copies of your notes, and make sure they are easy to read, with large typeface and organized by quick recall headings, such as Issue, Rule, and Holding.

The next part of the body pre-game is to practice the physical adjustments you will make to your frame that will channel energy, blood flow, and air in the most effective way, paving the way for a calm heart, clear thinking, and poised expression. Experiment with different stances—seated and standing. Summon your inner athlete. Sit in a chair—like it's a throne—or stand behind that podium and think: "power, strength, elongated vertical alignment, horizontal openness." Balanced, planted feet; shoulders back; head high; arms and hands open. Eyes up. Breathe. Do an Amy Cuddy power pose. Imagine forging eye contact with a nodder and smiler. Project your voice, just once, to the farthest spot in the room. Invoke Laurie Hernandez: "I got this."

Further, think about how to treat your body in advance of each event. How can you make it stronger, fortifying your machine?

Mind Pre-Game

In the mind pre-game, return to your comfortable private zone, relax, and walk through the exposure scenario in your head, step-by-step, from the instant you enter the room, until the moment you complete the event and return to quietude. Envision again where you will sit or stand. Imagine the touch and feel of the chair, the desk, and/or the podium. Breathe. Anticipate the arrival of those old negative messages and physical reactions. Remember that they are "short-term visitors."[402] Invoke your fresh taglines. Say them out loud. Tweak your stance and posture. Visualize moving through the event, referring to your notes and prompts as needed. Remind yourself that any uncomfortable mental and physical reflexes that pop up will subside; they always do. This is just one exposure event on a gradual agenda to help you become your most authentic lawyer self. You can do this. One event at a time.

TREAT EACH EXPOSURE LIKE A DIALOGUE INSTEAD OF A PERFORMANCE

Many exposure events simply constitute a *conversation* about the law between you and another human being—someone whose job or role is to help you learn or develop in a new way, or to collaborate with you to solve a legal problem. These individuals might be nice, compassionate, and nurturing about it, or they might not be. As in any other dialogue you engage in throughout the day, if you do not understand a question, say so.

For example, "I'm not sure I understand your question; could you please restate it?" If you ran into a professor, a supervising attorney, or even a judge on the street or in the park, and you did not grasp the phrasing of a query about the weather, sports, or a news event, you might simply say, "Pardon me?" or "Hmm, what do you mean exactly?" In legal scenarios, we can, and should, *respectfully* seek clarity in communications. Ultimately, if you cannot answer a question, it is not the demise of your legal career; it is a learning moment full of opportunity—not only substantively, but mentally and emotionally. Be honest. Focus on your "theme" of the conversation referenced in your notes: "Respectfully, I'm not sure exactly what you mean but the purpose of this rule is to foster an even playing field, and thus in these circumstances . . ." If you absolutely cannot fathom an answer, simply say, "Respectfully, I'm not sure precisely how to respond to that question, but I will promptly investigate." How can anyone fault you for being honest and willing to seek knowledge? Not every lawyer knows the answer to every legal question without research and thought: it's law *practice*, not law *perfection*.

CHANNEL YOUR NON-LEGAL ROCK STAR MOMENTS

Remind yourself how adept and formidable you are at interpersonal interaction in non-legal environments. Maybe you feel most studly on the softball field, jamming guitar riffs on stage with your band, conquering a yoga move no one else in your class has mastered, or soothing a bullied child on the playground. Invite that swagger into your legal persona.

FOCUS ON REALITY, NOT CATASTROPHE

If you enrolled in medical school instead of law school, your professors would not assign you to perform open-heart surgery on Day One; you'd likely step into anatomy class to experiment within and learn from a remarkably less dramatic and more incremental assignment. Similarly, in your law-related scenarios, you likely are not arguing before the U.S. Supreme Court (yet) or testifying before Congress (yet). However, as introverted, shy, or socially anxious law students and lawyers, we often catastrophize, building up performance-oriented events in our minds as if they are opening ceremonies of the Olympic

Games and the world is watching. Let's replace catastrophe with reality. We are not performing the lawyer equivalent of open-heart surgery. More like dissecting a frog (a computer-animated one—no animals will be injured in these experiments!): a low-stakes learning or developmental experience. Just one of a multitude in your career. Not even Super Bowl halftime shows or stadium concerts go perfectly. Madonna, Lady Gaga, U2's The Edge, and Beyoncé have all fallen on, and in The Edge's case fallen completely *off*, the stage. Get up and keep jamming.

WRITE PERSONAL TAGLINES TAILORED TO SPECIFIC EXPOSURE EVENTS

In Step 3, you drafted new mental messages to replace your outdated soundtrack. During the first few exposure events, or perhaps throughout your entire first exposure agenda, consider drafting one or two more taglines tailored specifically to each type of scenario. Write these mental prompts on a cheerful index card in colorful ink. Tape the card to your laptop, slip it into your binder or legal pad, or insert individual prompts into your phone calendar alerts. Here are some suggestions:

- This is not open-heart surgery, the State of the Union Address, the Super Bowl, or the Olympics. This is just a conversation with another human about the law.
- I engage in smart dialogue with others in my non-legal life all day long.
- Many legal questions are confusingly phrased; there is nothing wrong with stating that I don't understand a question; law is about collaboratively seeking clarity.
- If I don't know the answer to a question, I can invoke my "theme" to help me think through, and get to, an answer.
- This interaction is only a short (probably less than an hour) flicker in my multiple-decades-long legal career. It will end and I will be fine.
- I am intelligent.
- I work hard.
- I care about what I am doing and what I have to say.
- I will be a transformational and impactful lawyer, because I have empathy and understanding for quiet individuals like me.

When negative messages creep in, mindfully set them aside. You can do that for a few seconds. And then, a few more seconds. And a few more, to power you through the experience.

GAME-DAY PLANNING

Formidable athletes, actors, singers, and dancers conduct a wide variety of game-day or show-day rituals as they gear up to take the playing field or the stage, and as they commence their first movement or speak or sing their first word. Chris Martin, lead singer of the British rock band Coldplay, shared, "[T]here are about 18 things I have to do before I can go out to perform—most of them are too ridiculous to repeat!"[403] From vocal or stretching exercises to yoga, or consuming particular foods, performers figure out what works best to put them in the right physical and mental zone and stick with it. Major league baseball players display plentiful at-bat rituals—touching the bat to the plate, yanking a shirt sleeve, hiking up a knee, adjusting batting gloves, tapping the bat to their cleats—every single time they anticipate a pitch.[404] Golfers approach the tee, settling their Softspikes into the turf, gripping the driver, taking practice swings. Actors tarry in the eaves of the stage, practicing diaphragmatic breathing, stretching mouth muscles in anticipation of the curtain lift. To prepare our bodies and minds to perform at optimal levels, even in the face of nerves and anxiety, we must develop similar game-day rituals. We move through the steps of our tailor-made rituals intentionally as we approach each exposure event, aligning our physical frames and settling our minds, channeling our oxygen, blood, and energy to enhance our clarity and strengthen our voices.

Socrates seized private time during his game-day ritual: "[He] would often *prepare* . . . by 'centering' before engaging in a dialogue . . . At the start of [a] party at the home of the playwright Agathon, Socrates, the eagerly awaited guest of honor, [was] conspicuously absent."[405] Jason Connell, creator of "Change the World 101" and a leadership consultant, describes his routine: "Ten minutes before a speech I start listening to one of Girl Talk's [an American deejay] albums (I'm superstitious about listening [to] Girl Talk before a speech). After a few minutes, I start jumping around to raise my energy levels. Two minutes [before] the speech, I turn off my iPod and review my notes one last time. As I'm being introduced I tell myself, 'you're going to be f****ing awesome,' start smiling, and step on stage."[406] Naistadt, an actor and public speaking consultant, also spends time alone in the few minutes before she takes the stage.[407] Her warmup routine before every public speaking event involves "15 minutes of physical exercise, 15 minutes of meditation, 5 minutes of just talking out loud; [she] may even throw in a tongue twister or two."[408]

I learned the hard way that I need a game-day routine like Socrates', Connell's, and Naistadt's. One summer, I taught a new law school course on civil discovery. The first day of the session, I entered the classroom toting my materials, began setting up, and overheard that one of my students had forgotten his laptop cord. I knew I had an extra one in my office. I raced down the hall, grabbed the cord from my desk drawer, jogged back to the classroom, handed him the cord, approached the podium, smiled at my new crew of students, and began to speak. Except I couldn't. I had no air. My nerves frazzled. My heart beat like Morse code . . . again. I could not believe this was happening after all the work on my introversion and social anxiety I thought I already had accomplished. I croaked, "Sorry, I think . . . I need to sit down. I guess I'm a little nervous." A wonderful student—a veteran of Yale School of Drama who wrote for the *L.A. Times* and worked in Hollywood as a writer-producer—countered, "Of course you're out of breath, Professor, you just ran a half mile to and from your office." She was right. What horrible game-day behavior! I sat down, caught my breath, and started again. Whew.

From that debacle, I learned that no matter how hyped-up, adrenalin-pumped, or rock star–prepared I feel before a class, I must NEVER race to get there. My pre-game ritual for teaching a new class or group of students involves a **brain** prep (writing out my notes, typing them up, and reading them aloud several times), **body** prep (scoping out my classroom in advance, testing equipment, and practicing my stance behind the podium), and a full **mind** rehearsal a few days beforehand—chilling on my couch in a library-like space I created in my apartment, surrounded by my books, graffiti photos from my travels, and pictures of my dogs. Then, I completely stop preparing 24 hours before the first class. I discovered that my former habit of overpreparing for every speaking event often backfired and undermined my natural strength. Now, on game day, I allow myself to read my substantive notes aloud one more time in solitude, and then I slow-walk to the teaching location. If weather prevents a walking commute, I at least circle the building once or twice before entering. I avoid people (even if I have to pretend to be engrossed deeply in a cell phone conversation and can only communicate through a nod, a smile, and a wave). I try to dodge conversation on my journey to the classroom. I stay in my head, in my personal zone. Before entering the room, I stand outside the door and take five full breaths (pretending to be checking something in my bag if I must). I enter the room. I smile at somebody. I walk to the podium, and arrange my props. I take a dry-erase marker, face the board, and write an agenda in the upper left corner. Breathe five more breaths while writing. Listen to what the students are chatting about: the dorm, something funny that happened in Torts earlier that day, what they ate for lunch. I turn around and ask one of them a question about lunch, Torts, the dorm. Non-legal conversation to ease the moment, laugh, calm the beating heart. One more deep breath. I approach the podium, ground my feet, balance my stance, shift shoulders back, make eye contact with a nodder or smiler, tell myself, "You love legal writing and teaching. Focus on the love," project my voice to the person farthest away. "OK, let's get started. Today we're going to talk about . . ."

PRE-GAME AND GAME-DAY PLANNING ADVICE FOR SPECIFIC LAW-RELATED EXPOSURE EVENTS

If you are not sure how to begin, take a look at the following suggestions for pre-game and game-day planning for a variety of realistic exposure events in the law school and law office environments.

ADVICE FOR LAW STUDENT SCENARIOS

Law School Meeting with a Professor

- **Brain Preparation:** Prepare a discussion agenda. Write it down, type it up, and print it out so you can take it to the meeting in hard-copy—not on a laptop. You want the encounter to go smoothly and efficiently, so it's best to avoid fumbling around with technology. Paper allows you to maximize eye contact and minimize technological glitches. Prepare specific questions and write them down: the more you can use your written notes as talking points to guide and drive the conversation, the more you forge momentum, calming any rapid breathing and heart rate and maintaining a connection with the professor. In preparation, read your agenda and questions out loud a few times. Review the professor's website biography (for information and possible interesting conversation-starter material only; do not be intimidated by the professional pedigree; instead, look for interesting bonding nuggets: hometown, areas of interest, life experiences). Also, consider scanning the professor's teaching evaluations (prior students might have described personality quirks that provide keen insights—focus on the positive).

- **Body Preparation:** Do a scouting mission to the professor's office so you know where it is, and, if possible get a glimpse inside, observing the physical layout (chairs, desk, windows, lighting, etc.). Practice how you will adjust your physical stance while waiting in the hallway, entering the room, and taking a seat. Think through how you will manage your physical possessions and props to minimize fumbling.

- **Mind Preparation:** Remember that the professor might seem intimidating but he or she is just a human being who is eager to share knowledge with you about the law. Resolve to show the professor that you care about the subject and are excited to learn (nothing makes a professor happier). Review your new taglines.

- **Game Day:** On game day, find a quiet place and do a two-minute Amy Cuddy power pose. Slow-walk to the professor's office, and take five deep breaths before entering, balancing your stance and opening your frame to get that oxygen, blood, and energy flowing constructively. Remember your new taglines and even read them off a notecard before you enter the office if you need to remind yourself of their power and might.

  ◦ When you enter the professor's office, notice any physical objects that you could mention to establish rapport (pet photos, artwork, sculptures, quirky desk items).

  ◦ Look the professor in the eye.

  ◦ Sit down, adopt your balanced seated stance, and breathe.

  ◦ Use your notes, and take notes too.

  ◦ Limit the meeting to 20–30 minutes (unless the professor seems engrossed), respect the professor's time limitations (office hours and student meetings can be tiring for introverted professors especially), and model respect for other students awaiting their turn for office hours.

  ◦ Say thank you, make eye contact, and smile as you leave.

Socratic Classroom Experience

- **Brain Preparation:** In anticipating a Socratic classroom experience, for as many weeks as possible beforehand, observe the professor's pattern of questioning other students (he/she likely has a rhythm of inquiry; instead of taking class notes on other students' *answers*, transcribe the professor's *questions* word-for-word and use them as prompts in your own preparation).

  ◦ **Prepare Props:** It is impossible for us introverted, shy, or socially anxious folks to remember all our brilliant thoughts in those stressful moments. Write them all down. Again, I recommend hard-copy notes (it is hard to find information quickly on a laptop, and, inevitably, in an inopportune moment, the laptop will freeze). Use the IRAC formula (Issue, Rule, Application, Conclusion) to organize the legal concepts within the day's assigned reading. Consider alternate hypotheticals and possible questions, and write out a few sentences to address each. Use color-coding and one- or two-word prompts if they help you retrieve information quickly ("Rule," "Counter-Argument," "Public Policy"). Make a list of any new words/terminology and their definitions. In preparation, read your notes aloud a few times.

- Work on a "theme" of the subject matter in that day's reading, and plan to invoke your theme if you do not know the answer to the professor's question: "Well, this case seems to be about a fair playing field," "Well, this case boils down to freedom of contract," "Well, this case involves the competing concerns of public safety and the right to be free from discrimination . . ."

- See the general discussion under the heading of Brain Pre-Game earlier in this chapter for additional tips on substantive preparation for a Socratic experience.

- **Body Preparation:** You likely are already familiar with your law classroom, but you can rehearse your physical adjustments, sitting with legs uncrossed, feet firmly planted on the ground, shoulders back, spine elongated, arms uncrossed. Practice maneuvering your reading notes on the desk, and decide if making changes in formatting or printing would help you access information more quickly during a Q&A. Make a notecard with your tagline reminders and tuck it into your class prep notes for easy access.

- **Mind Preparation:** Stay focused on reality, not catastrophe. Much of our internal drama toward the Socratic classroom orbits around our fear that peers scrutinize our every word with critical judgment. In the week or two leading up to this exposure event, look around; many of your peers are—much to the professor's chagrin!—multitasking. Others will root for you because, if your Socratic questioning proceeds swimmingly, the professor might stay focused on you for a while instead of shifting to a new questionee. Yes, there might be a few of your peers who judge, but who cares—you don't need everyone in the room to like you. Laser-focus on your one-on-one conversation with the professor, and tune everyone else out for the 10–45 minutes you might be on-call.

  - If you know the date that you are on-call, consider visiting the professor during office hours beforehand to create a human connection. Candidly share that you are a bit nervous about class participation and want to do the most effective preparatory work possible and contribute well. Have a few substantive questions handy about the subject matter of the course (see suggestions above for how to handle office hours). Also indicate that you have paid attention to the professor's pattern of questions in class by asking, for example, "I've noticed that you ask questions about X. In preparing for class, should I be looking for _____?" Use the dialogue during office hours to practice having a normal conversation with the professor. Later, visualize the classroom dialogue as a similar follow-up conversation rather than a performance for an audience. Some professors still might give advice like "just do it," "fake it till you make it," or "get over your fears." Remember, we already know that type of advice doesn't work for us. That's OK. You're doing the work you need to do to be *your* authentic self.

○ If your professor cold-calls (so you do not have a scheduled on-call date), also consider visiting the professor during office hours as early in the semester as possible. Honestly share that you are a bit nervous but determined to prepare, participate, and contribute. *Consider requesting that he/she assign you a specific day to be on-call for the first time* in that class so you can manage your reticence toward the event a bit more effectively. Explain that you do not want special treatment but you would like to conquer your trepidation by preparing for the Socratic questioning on a known date (Note: Some professors might bristle at this; not your fault; it's worth a try!).

• **Game Day:** Take some time alone before the class. Do a two-minute Amy Cuddy power pose. Slow-walk to the classroom. When you settle into your seat, adopt your balanced seated stance. Breathe. Look at the professor: he or she is just a human being who wants to teach you. Be open. When your Socratic dialogue starts:

○ Recalibrate your balanced seated stance.

○ Breathe.

○ Make eye contact with the professor.

○ Project your voice to the person farthest away in the room (or at least to the professor).

○ Pause when you need to think (It's OK to say, "Hmm, let me think. [*breathe; check your notes; invoke your case themes*] . . . OK, the governing rule here has four parts . . . This case is about . . .").

○ Use your IRAC notes.

○ Listen to the words in the questions. Use your terminology list and break challenging or confusing questions down: "You mentioned the word *intent* which is defined as . . ." "OK, well *reasonableness* is defined as . . ."

○ If you start to falter, remember your personal taglines (keep the reminder notecard handy if you need it).

○ Refer back to your theme.

○ Breathe. Remember, you are trying your best, and you do not need to be perfect; this is a real conversation, not a scripted Hollywood movie.

Law School Group Meeting

Personally, I dreaded law school group work; I didn't realize that, as an introvert among extroverts, my resistance stemmed from the peer pressure to speak before I was ready and the sense that something was wrong with me because I didn't readily jump into collective brainstorming mode . . . Here's some advice I wished I had known.

- **Brain Preparation:** As an introverted or quiet thinker who solves problems through contemplative writing, you actually might be more prepared for a group meeting than others. Channel that advance work into a role for yourself. Perhaps prepare a proposed meeting agenda (on paper or via email) for the group. When the more dominant voices take charge in the actual meeting, you can use your written agenda to establish your voice. Craft a statement or two that will help you intervene or interrupt when extroverted or dominant members of the group take over: "Guys, I want to make sure we don't forget about X; can we focus on that for a minute or two?" "Gang, I had a question about Y; can we focus on that for a moment?" "Hey, I also think it's important that we address Z; can we shift to that for a second?" In preparation, read your notes aloud a few times.

- **Body Preparation:** Determine the location of the group meeting, and assess where within the space you want to sit that will make you feel most comfortable. Practice your physical adjustments, sitting with legs and arms uncrossed, feet firmly planted on the ground, shoulders back, spine elongated. Breathe.

- **Mind Preparation:** This is an *ideal* exposure event to champion your introvert strengths. In a small audience of your peers rather than a professor and a large lecture class, it's the perfect opportunity to showcase your thoughtful planning, active listening, problem-solving, and contemplative writing. Resist feeling pressure to conform to the talkers in the group; assert yourself in your authentic way, contributing through the written word (agenda-crafting, note-taking, follow-up summarizing). On occasion, use your written props to empower you to interrupt the fray and keep the meeting on track. In preparation, review your taglines.

- **Game Day:** Find a quiet space and do a two-minute Amy Cuddy power pose. Head to the meeting location early. Slow-walk to the room. As you enter, find the seat that best works for you. Adopt your balanced seated stance. Breathe. Circulate your agenda. Volunteer to be the note-taker. Use your rehearsed interrupting statement. At the end of the meeting, employ your notes as an excuse to intervene or interrupt again: "Guys, I just want to make sure I've captured our plan accurately; let me read through our meeting highlights . . ." After the meeting, edit your notes, and use them as a vehicle to communicate with the group in writing: "Thank you for a productive meeting. Attached please find our agenda notes . . ."

Law School Presentation

Perhaps your legal writing professor has asked you to report to the class on facts gathered from a hypothetical client, or a seminar professor has assigned you to deliver a presentation on a research topic. These are also prime exposure events and probably the *most effective* interim steps on an exposure journey because they afford you the most control! A law school presentation is more manageable for us introverted, shy, or socially anxious humans than a Socratic dialogue, groupwork, or an oral argument; we don't have to anticipate and manage unpredictable substantive interruptions!

- **Brain Preparation:** As you draft the presentation, construct an engaging beginning (an anecdote, a vivid example, or a captivating image—invoking a law-related *theme*), a middle (with three to five concrete points), and a conclusion, reiterating your theme. Write out the entire presentation by hand (to commence the brain-body-mind connection). Then, type it up in outline form and read it aloud several times, forging deeper connections between your thoughts, words, and voice. Also, consider creating helpful physical props to jog your memory during the presentation and engage with the audience.

  - **Handouts:** I love a good handout. Handouts help reduce public speaking anxiety by giving us an excuse to move around the room before a presentation, to connect with people through a physical object rather than talking, and to demonstrate intellectual creativity in written form. Plus, people focus on the handout and give us a chance to get comfortable until we are ready to make eye contact.

  - **PowerPoint (or Keynote or Prezi):** Accompanying spoken words with engaging visuals and tasteful humorous images can relax the audience and connect different types of learners with the material. As a lawyer, I never understood or used PowerPoint. But, as I developed as a teacher, I began accompanying my lectures with slides highlighting key rules, interspersed with colorful and amusing imagery to enliven the presentation of legal principles. Students chuckle at some of the visual depictions, and their smiles help everyone relax.

(Note: Obviously always be professional and tasteful in your image choices.)

- ○ **Physical objects:** Does the subject matter of your presentation involve a material object you could bring into the room and pass around? When I create legal writing assignments, I try to incorporate a tangible object into each hypothetical fact pattern: a Peruvian ceramic candlestick, a wine bottle with an artistic label, a CD cover. People like to touch things. Seeing audience members' faces light up or scrunch up inquisitively at the tactile sensation will help you connect with their humanity and realize that they are just curious folk who want to learn from you.

- • **Body Preparation:** Before your presentation, take a field trip to the event location, if possible. Sit in the chair or stand at the podium. Absorb the space. Do a two-minute Amy Cuddy power pose. Breathe in the air.

- ○ **Feel Your Props:** Take a professional-looking folder containing your presentation outline in a readable font, other mental prompts you need, and a non-distracting writing instrument to the event site. Practice opening and closing the folder on the podium a few times.

- ○ **Practice with the Technology in Advance:** If you plan to use a PowerPoint or any audio-visual equipment, do a dry-run boot-up during your scouting mission. Does the computer require a password or a few minutes to boot up? Do you need to bring your own laptop or flash drive? What if the Internet doesn't work? Do you know how to dim the lights? Do you need a microphone? If the equipment bothers you, do you know how to turn it off? Are there a telephone and an emergency hotline in case you need to call the IT team?

- ○ **Have a Backup Plan in Case of Technology Failure:** In my Tuesday Faculty Workshop discussed in Chapter 7, my PowerPoint failed. What a relief that I had a backup plan. I had two backup plans. When the technology crashed, I cracked a joke (with IT guys hovering over me) and kept going with my printed hard-copy notes in hand. Prepare a backup plan and a transitional joke!

- ○ **Plan for Technical Interruptions:** No matter how prepared you are, there might be an interruption, or two. People will arrive late. Cell phones will gyrate. Fire alarms or sirens might wail. The power might fail. None of these events are your fault and you cannot control them. All you can dictate is how you respond to them. Make a joke (have one prepared; mine is "Leave it to someone with public speaking anxiety to have a power failure during a speech!") and keep going if you can. Or if you need to stop (e.g., if firefighters appear, or emergency personnel are ordering you to evacuate), just stop. It's the universe saying, "Nice job, soldier! One more exposure event accomplished!"

- **Mind Preparation:** Because it is distinct from a Socratic dialogue or oral argument, a law school presentation is a wonderful opportunity to experiment with your quiet strengths on this "just be it" journey. You have control over the content and the delivery. Capitalize on your research and writing skills and creativity. Instead of trying to be like everyone else, this is a chance to be 100% you: in subject matter, examples, visuals, and delivery. You likely will know more about this topic than anyone in the room. Let your passion and innovation shine. Review your mental taglines.

- **Game Day:**

  - **Attire:** Wear something that makes you feel like a rock star (but is still legal-esque). Suits do not make me feel powerful; they suffocate me. I prefer a bright-colored yet tasteful power dress that somehow cloaks me in Superhero strength, and shoes that make me feel tall. Find something appropriate that makes *you* feel fantastic for *your* own reasons: a tie, a shirt, a dress, a skirt, a suit, a piece of jewelry, or a killer pair of power shoes.

    - Word of Caution: Not everyone is going to agree with, understand, or relate to your fashion choices, especially in the legal world (not exactly known for its couture). One of my A+ legal writing students was nervous about her oral argument, although impeccably substantively prepared. She wore a pair of stylish and sophisticated high-heeled shoes to the argument and gracefully delivered a stunning line of reasoning. A male attorney sat on our judges' panel, completely ignored the substance of her argument, and during the feedback portion, criticized her shoes. Sexist, yes. Realistic, also yes. Nonetheless, in my opinion, our exposure agenda is all about getting through each experience, coming out the other side, and building our authentic lawyer personas through each success so eventually we can go out and stun the world. Thus, I strongly feel that WHATEVER personally authentic tools work to power *you* through these incremental learning experiences, use them. You can make adjustments later, for the office and the courtroom. For now, wear the shoes.

  - On game day, slow-walk to the classroom, and take five deep breaths before entering, balancing your stance and opening your frame to get that oxygen, blood, and energy flowing constructively. As you sit and await the commencement of your presentation, continue recalibrating, breathing, and reminding yourself of your new taglines.

○ **Stand When You Can:** When offered the option to sit or stand in a presentation, I once believed sitting would feel safer; behind a desk or a conference room table, I felt less visible. But through my introversion journey, I learned that the physical act of standing better channels my nervous energy. Instead of energy bouncing around inside me, increasing my agitation, it flows outward through my appendages when I stand. Google the lyrics to the R.E.M. song, "Stand," and watch the music video. In preparation, do the movements! In the real exposure moment, stand. Balance your stance. Use the podium as an energy recipient, and hang onto it (gently) sending all that excess energy into it. Standing also helps with voice projection. Preach to the populace poised to hear what you have to say!

Law School Oral Argument[409]

• **Brain Preparation:** When preparing for oral arguments, we sometimes get ahead of ourselves and jump to worrying about the judges' questions without first thinking through and crafting the arc of an uninterrupted argument. Understandably, the anticipation of the judges' questions is the most nerve-wracking part of oral arguments for introverted, shy, and socially anxious students, as the pattern and subject matter of the queries may seem unpredictable and their timing can interrupt the argument's flow. However, strategic preparation can arm us with the right tools to stay in control during those moments when it seems that we are being pulled away from our plan. Start by using your brief (and your opponent's brief, if available) to outline the substance of an unimpeded argument. Follow your professor's instructions for drafting a "roadmap" introduction. Mine entails something like this: "May it please the court, my name is _____ and I represent _____. This case concerns [*insert case theme*]. The issue before the court today is _____. The rule governing this issue is _____. We respectfully submit that ____ should prevail for three reasons. First, . . . Second, . . . Third, . . . Accordingly, we ask the court to _____." Use the headings from your brief to identify three (to five) key points to frame the reasons why your client should prevail. Identify the specific result requested of the court. Next, you can flesh out the rest of the argument outline, weaving in facts and case law to support each key point. Then, craft an engaging conclusion, perhaps reiterating the case theme you introduced in the roadmap. *After* you have written out the entire argument from start to finish (ideally by hand first, to start making those brain-body-mind connections), set it aside, and *then* use the brief(s) to anticipate judges' questions. In planning for questions, focus on addressing the perceived weaknesses of your client's case. Write out possible answers to judges' questions about those weaknesses. Create two documents in preparation of handling the judges' questions: (1) a case "prompt sheet" with case summaries (in alphabetical order) of the name, citation, jurisdiction, date, facts, holding, and rationale of the key cases cited in both sides' briefs; and (2) a judges' question "prompt sheet" with one- or two-word prompts like "Public Policy" or "Rule Exception" (in alphabetical order, for ready access) and your draft responses. Next, step away from your "prompt sheets" and go back to your written argument. Rewrite the argument in outline form, further creating links between the ideas in your brain, the words on the page, and the concepts in your memory for faster retrieval in the performance moment. Read all your prep materials aloud a few times, to further solidify the links between your brain, words, and voice.

- **Additional Brain Prep:** Who will the judges be? Try to find out in advance who comprises your judges panel. Are they 2L or 3L students? Alumni? School administrators? Professors? Will they wear robes (an added air of formality)? Where will the judges sit? Do you know the judges' personalities or questioning style? Are you familiar with your opponent? Do you know your opponent's personality or argument style?

- **Rebuttal:** Find out in advance whether you or your opponent will argue first. If you are the initial arguer and plan to reserve a few minutes for rebuttal to your opponent's argument, you'll need to quickly scribble notes while your opponent is speaking. Many reticent advocates experience such joy and relief when they complete their initial argument and retreat to their chairs that they forget to listen to their opponents. Instead, resolve to focus, use your quiet active listening skills, and extract two or three points raised in your opponent's argument that warrant a rejoinder. In advance, however, you certainly can anticipate and prepare rebuttal points; by drafting your brief and reading your opponent's brief (if allowed), you will know the weaknesses of your client's position and the strengths of your opponent's. Prepare a rebuttal outline that lists your opponent's strongest arguments, write out responses or counter-arguments, and then, during your opponent's argument, plan to use that piece of paper as a guide, circling the two or three issues that most merit a response.

- **Body Preparation:** If possible, find out in advance where the argument will take place: In a classroom? In a conference room? In a mock or real courtroom? Go there and absorb the space. Is there a podium? A microphone? A platform for your written materials? How large is the room? What is the distance between you and the judges? Where will you sit while you await your argument?

  o Prepare your props and get comfortable using them. Create a professional-looking easy-to-maneuver folder containing your substantive preparation items: (1) the argument outline in large enough font that you can see it without having to squint; (2) the case "prompt sheet"; (3) the judges' question "prompt sheet"; and (4) a rebuttal sheet (if applicable to you). Consider attaching the argument outline to the inside flaps of the folder, and appending the case and question sheets to the two outer parts of the folder. During the argument, you can gently open and close the folder to retrieve the information you need without distracting paper shuffling. Plan on taking a writing instrument to the argument that you will not be tempted to click or twirl; you will need a pen, pencil, or highlighter to mark your spot in the outline when you are interrupted by a judge's question, so after responding, you can smoothly return to the flow of your argument.

- **Mind Preparation:** Remember, this experience occupies only 10 or 15 minutes of your life. You certainly have endured many things more annoying, stressful, or painful in your life for a longer period of time and have come through the other side. Just 10 or 15 minutes. And the time will zoom by. Judges will interrupt you—and their questions will absorb seconds and minutes of your allotted time. If you are the initial arguer, you might reserve two minutes for rebuttal, which means the first foray is even shorter. You can do this.

  o **Use Your Notes:** Some mentors, teachers, and public speaking gurus advise orators not to depend on written notes, declaring, "The most effective speakers memorize!" Yes, we know. But we also know that that such advice often does not work for us introverted, shy, or anxious folks. Our nerves kick in, our minds shift into overdrive as we process multiple bytes of information at once, our bodies go into protective mode, and sometimes we lose our trains of thought. Remember, the goal in the exposure agenda is not to win oratory awards (although, I will tell you that many of my incredibly nervous students have been so substantively, mentally, and physically prepared, and worked so hard to model strength in the moment, they ultimately were selected for moot court or trial teams without even setting out to do so!). Your primary objective for purposes of this "just be it" journey is to navigate the event with the least amount of anxiety possible, and learn from the incremental experience. Your first (or second, or third) oral argument does not need to be, and probably will not be, perfect. Get through it. When the nerves hit, guess what? You might need to *read* your "roadmap" introduction, to keep yourself talking. That's why you took the time to write it down. And because you wrote it out, read it over, and probably edited it numerous times, it is already perfect. So, plan to take a deep breath, balance your stance, make eye contact. You might even write these physical steps into your outline: (1) approach podium; (2) arrange folder; (3) balance stance; (4) take a deep breath; (5) make eye contact with judges; (6) wait for judge (or bailiff, if any) to announce the case or somehow indicate it is time to start; (7) take another deep breath, and . . . recite the first line of the roadmap introduction, "May it please the court, my name is . . ." Gaze up periodically, forge eye contact with a judge or two, and soldier ahead . . . Breathe, balance your stance, and continue powering through the experience.

○ **Intermittent Missteps:** You might stumble on your words. Your next thought might evaporate into the ether. So what. Normal and human. Keep going. Look at the judges, hopefully find a friendly nodder or smiler (and if not, imagine one), pause, find your place, and keep going. Pausing is your friend. Who cares if you have 5–10 seconds of silence? Find your place, take a breath, balance your stance, and keep going.

○ **Judges' Questions:** The judges are going to interrupt you. Try to focus on the judges as human beings. Some law school oral argument judges enjoy the opportunity to step away from their normal daily routine, don a robe, be referred to as "Justice," and play the role of questioner. While the robes, the name placards, the time cards, and the air of authority can seem intimidating, stick to your plan and remember that the judges are just people: facilitators in a short exposure event on your "just be it" journey. Your whole part in this experience will take 10 or 15 minutes, maximum. The more the judges talk, the less you do. Welcome judges' queries and interruptions because you already anticipated this eventuality. You invested the time to craft your judges' questions "prompt sheet." Reap the benefits of it. Now, when a judge poses a question you do not understand, or to which you are unsure how to respond, you have several options. If your misunderstanding stems from simply an "inartfully" phrased or compound question (which happens all the time in law school oral arguments), you could offer, "I apologize, Your Honor, I'm not sure I understand the question. Could you please repeat it?" An empathic judge will rephrase it more clearly or break it down. Or, to respond to a question of which you are not 100% sure of the answer, you could invoke your "themes," stating, "Your Honor, it seems the court is focusing on [*insert a key term/rule/policy*]. That is a pivotal point here because . . . [*insert discussion of the theme of your case.*]" If the judge is not quelled, he or she will ask another question. Apply the same techniques for each question and forge onward. After you respond to each question the best you can, return to your marked spot in your argument outline, and trudge ahead. You do not need to await a signal from the judge to continue each time you finish answering a question. Monitor your allotted time, and endeavor to address your 3–5 primary arguments before time expires.

- **Momentary Pausing:** Give yourself permission to pause briefly to collect your thoughts before you shift to a new issue, or to ponder before you react to a judge's query. Use the pause to breathe.

- **Dialogue:** When nerves creep in, remind yourself that this is not a performance; it is a dialogue with three humans. "Your Honor, yes, that is true because . . ." "Your Honor, no, I respectfully disagree because . . ."

- Review your new mental taglines.

- **Game Day:**

  - **Attire:** (see Law School Presentation advice above).

  - On game day, find a quiet place to do a two-minute Amy Cuddy power pose. During oral argument season, there tends to be a lot of nervous energy floating around the law school; be cognizant of whether other students' energy is affecting yours, and if so, find a place where you can be alone before your argument. Slow-walk to the argument location, and take five deep breaths before entering, balancing your stance and opening your frame to get that oxygen, blood, and energy flowing constructively. As you sit and await the commencement of your argument, continue rebalancing, breathing, and reminding yourself of your new taglines.

○ As you take the podium, balance, breathe, pause, make eye contact, wait for the signal to begin, and then project that voice. Speak your opening sentence, even if you have to read it: "Your Honors, may it please the court, my name is ___, and I represent ____." If the nerves sneak in, recalibrate your stance, and remind yourself that this is just 10 or 15 minutes of your life. You have prepared. You have something to say. Say it in your way.

○ If you are delivering a rebuttal after your opponent's argument, use your rebuttal outline while your opponent is speaking to identify two or three points to assert in response. During your reserved rebuttal time, stand up, take the podium, balance your stance, breathe, make eye contact with the judges, wait for the signal to begin, and deliver your first line (even if you have to read it): "Your Honors, there are two/three points I will address on rebuttal. First, . . ."

○ At the end, say thank you. Breathe. And then smile. Shake your opponent's hand. That is one of the hardest exposures you will do as a law student. And you did it!

Job Interview

Job interviews for legal employment can be stressful for introverted, shy, and socially anxious law students and lawyers because of our perception that law offices seek extroverted, confident, smooth speakers. Plus, the interview process is inherently judgment-oriented. Nonetheless, with the right advance research and focused strategy, we can shine in this type of one-on-one encounter.

- **Brain Preparation:** Before the interview, research the legal employer and, if possible, the interviewers. Find out the logistics of the interview in advance: With how many people are you interviewing? Are they junior or senior attorneys, or both? Will you be eating lunch with them as well? How long will the interview day be? Make a list of substantive questions and write them out; then, type them up. Avoid questions that can be answered through simple research, but instead consider questions about the substance of the work you would be doing in the law office. On what types of cases or transactions do the junior attorneys typically work? What types of tasks do they perform? Research and writing? Do the junior attorneys perform document reviews? Interact with clients? Conduct client interviews? Depositions? Do the junior attorneys work on several legal matters at the same time? How long do the cases typically take to go to trial? How long does it typically take to negotiate and execute a transactional agreement for a client? In what jurisdiction do most of the law office's client matters take place? What types of research and writing projects do junior associates typically perform? Find out where the interviewers went to school, how long they have been practicing law, what type of clients they represent. Reread your résumé. Highlight three to five interesting aspects of your résumé you could discuss if asked an open-ended question, such as "What should I know about you?" Reread your writing sample, and remind yourself of the facts, the legal issue, the governing rule, and the arguments—in case the interviewer asks you about the substance. Before the interview day, read your list of questions aloud a few times, forging those brain-words-voice-memory links.

- **Body Preparation:** Find out in advance where and when the interview will take place. Consider taking a field trip to the office location so you can anticipate transportation, traffic, parking, or building security glitches. Plan your attire: wear a business suit. Organize your physical props in a professional-looking folder: extra copies of your résumé and writing sample, names of the interviewers if provided, your list of questions, an extra legal pad, and a pen. You also might need to bring identification to gain access to the office building. Practice your balanced seated stance.

- **Mind Preparation:** Focus on reality, not catastrophe. Sometimes we build up interviews in our mind as our one and only opportunity in our entire lifetime to gain employment! This interview is just a single conversation between you and one or more human being(s) in hopes of a mutual fit. You know the subject matter of the conversation better than anyone: YOU! All you have to do is exhibit genuine interest in the people you meet and what they do for a living, through asking thoughtful questions and answering queries about yourself, your legal (and probably other) interests, and your abilities. This is not the time to talk about what the law office can do for you and your career; instead, focus on all the amazing things you can do for the lawyers interviewing you, based on your strengths of active listening, deep thinking, researching, and writing. Try to regard the people you meet not as intimidating authority figures dangling a salary and future financial stability before you, but as busy human beings whose jobs you can make easier through hard work and dedication. Review your new taglines: you have an immense amount of impact to offer the legal profession. This is just one of many opportunities to find the right fit. Be your strong self.

- **Game Day:** Travel to the interview location early so you are not stressed about transportation, traffic, parking, or building security issues. Find a quiet place and do a two-minute Amy Cuddy power pose. Slow-walk to the interview venue. Adopt a balanced seated stance while you await your first interviewer. Breathe. Invoke your taglines. When the first interviewer greets you, smile, shake hands firmly, and make great eye contact. Start by thanking the interviewer for taking the time to meet with you, and try to forge an immediate connection by mentioning an aspect of his/her life, education, or practice that you noticed during your advance research. When you sit in the interview chair, adopt your balanced seated stance and breathe. Smile and make eye contact again. Hopefully the interviewer will guide the meeting with questions that you can answer conversationally, but if not, step into the dialogue by asking *your* questions. Use your notes. Listen to the responses; take notes (on paper), which might spark follow-up questions. Be yourself. At the end of each individual interview, smile, shake hands, make eye contact, and say thank you again. Use your writing to amplify your voice through follow-up thank you emails or handwritten notes.

ADVICE FOR LAW PRACTICE SCENARIOS

Law Office Meeting with a Supervising Attorney

I've worked with numerous law firm partners in the tough construction law industry. A few of them have *not* been nice people. Others have been wonderful, caring mentors. Many of them have been intimidating to some degree, because of their status, intellect, quick minds, experience, temper, physicality, gruffness, or short attention span. As a junior associate, my one-on-one meetings with some partners were fraught with anxiety. Here's some advice on how to handle these encounters as an authentic quiet lawyer.

- **Consider two different exposure scenarios with a supervising attorney:** One you control, and one you do not. In the first, make a 10-minute appointment with a busy attorney to "get clarity on a few issues before moving forward with an assignment." In the latter, you might be called *without* notice into the supervising attorney's office to report results on an assignment or case. Either way, the preparation is somewhat similar.

- **Brain Preparation:**
  - ○ If *you* scheduled the meeting, prepare an agenda, and write it down on a legal pad—not on a computer. No matter how cool the gadget or technology-friendly your office is, I do not recommend relying on an electronic device for this conversation. Busy supervising attorneys understandably can get annoyed if they have to wait for your technology to boot up. Plus, you're probably going to need to write a few things down quickly. It's important to maintain eye contact as much as possible while conversing and taking notes. Use pen and paper. Construct four or five specific well-phrased genuine questions about the assignment, such as:
    - "I have exhausted my research in our jurisdiction. Would it be OK to broaden my search for analogous cases in other jurisdictions, or should I stick with *X* law?"
    - "I have completed my research and analysis. Would you prefer a full analytical memorandum or a bullet-point set of talking points for your meeting with the client?"
    - "I feel I have a good handle on the law but wanted to cross-check the elements of the rules against the facts. Can I review the issue file on *X* and incorporate additional facts into my analysis, or would you rather I stick to the universe of facts you originally gave me?"
    - "The weakness of our client's case is *X*. However, I came across a potential counter-argument in one of the cases. Can I go ahead and research that angle further, or would you prefer I stick with the assignment you gave me?"
    - Write out your questions and read them aloud so your brain takes ownership of the words.
  - ○ If the lawyer called you into the office, brainstorm a quick agenda around the subject matter of your assignment:
    - Facts (perhaps Strengths and Weaknesses)
    - Legal Issue
    - Rule
    - Favorable Case Law or Strengths
    - Unfavorable Case Law or Weaknesses
    - Proposed Solutions or Next Steps

- **Body Preparation:** If possible, find out in advance what the attorney's office looks like. Do a scouting mission when he or she is not in the room. Determine how the seating is arranged, how cluttered or clean the space is, what items are on the desk or the walls. Learn whether you need to go through the lawyer's assistant to book an appointment, or whether you can email the attorney directly to schedule a time to talk for 10 minutes. Think about what you will carry into the room (definitely bring a legal pad and a pen, and your outline or list of questions), where you will sit, and what the first sentence out of your mouth will be. Envision adopting your balanced seated stance in the room.

- **Mind Preparation:** No matter how intimidating the supervising attorney seems (and hopefully you will be dealing with a nice, smart, kind, good listener bent on serving as a mentor), that lawyer is human and has personal strengths and weaknesses. Use that great trait of empathy that introverted, shy, and socially anxious individuals offer. Think about the attorney as a human being—with stressors, relationship challenges, life balance issues, financial pressures, and maybe even emotional or physical pains. Any potential gruffness or curtness has nothing to do with you. Model empathy and view your role as trying to make that lawyer's job easier just for 10 minutes, an hour, a day, or a week. Go in there, do your job, be the best authentic lawyer you can be, say thank you, and get out. You are not there to be his or her best friend. You are there to develop as a lawyer and do the best job for your client. Prepare by reviewing your new taglines.

- **Game Day:** On game day, find a quiet place to do a two-minute Amy Cuddy power pose. Slow-walk to the supervising attorney's office, and take five deep breaths before entering, balancing your stance and opening your frame to get that oxygen, blood, and energy flowing constructively. As you sit down, rebalance, breathe, and remind yourself of your mental taglines. Ask your questions. Take notes on the answers. Answer any questions posed the best you can. When you answer, make eye contact. If you do not know the answer to a question, say, "I need to investigate that and I will get back to you by tonight." Do not fake an answer, although you could say, "I believe the answer is ____ but I need to investigate and confirm that and will get back to you tonight." Once the questioning ends and you have your questions answered, do not linger. You are a busy worker too. Say thank you, give a timeline for your next steps, and leave.

Law Office Group Meeting

Law office group meetings can be challenging for introverted, shy, or socially anxious lawyers because often the room seems to have an extrovert-to-introvert ratio slanted in favor of the "Es." Through strategic preparation, you can make an impactful imprint in each meeting.

- **Brain Preparation:** Do not just walk into the room with a blank legal pad and a pen (and again, resist bringing a laptop unless you absolutely know the meeting leader will ask you to access something on it). Instead, think in advance about the subject matter of the meeting and your role in it. Plan an agenda of items that you could discuss or volunteer. Write out the agenda with bullet points about the status of each item, or strengths, weaknesses, or concerns relevant for discussion. Under no circumstances do you need to talk for the sake of talking. However, you probably do have something pertinent to contribute about the client matter, so prepare at least one or more soundbites—write them out and have them ready. In meetings, if I have something to say but feel anxious about saying it, I write . . . it . . . out. I glance down at my scrawl and use that script to get the words off the paper, back into my head, and out of my mouth when my brain starts to do its fuzzy thing . . . Remember, we are good writers, so it is a smart move to use our gift of writing to bolster our speaking. Before the meeting, read your notes aloud a few times to connect your thoughts to the written words to your voice.

- **Body Preparation:** Go check out all the conference rooms where these meetings might take place. Know the seating configuration and decide in advance where you want to sit. Personally, I like to be *near* the end of a table, but not *at* the end (the meeting leader likely will sit at the end, so if that is not you, leave that seat empty). In exercise classes, I choose bikes, equipment, or mats in the front and closest to a wall, to minimize the number of people in my personal space but still connect to the teacher. In conference rooms, I prefer the corner of a rectangular table or the side-end of an oval one. Sit near the leader if you can—being seen taking notes and nodding sometimes can be as effective as speaking, and infinitely more valuable than talking just for the sake of talking. As much as you might want to hide, sit near the leader and be seen. Practice your balanced seated stance in the meeting room chairs.

- **Mind Preparation:** Remember that we introverted, shy, and socially anxious people process information, interact with others, and gain energy in disparate ways from extroverts. The extroverts in the law office conference room (and the not yet self-aware introverts) might never have studied themselves or others as deeply as you are; they are behaving in their everyday normal state. We cannot control them. We *can* control how we react to them. They might agitate us and stress us out, but it's probably (hopefully) not intentional. Therefore, it's up to us to focus on our strengths, recognize the automatic reflexes (mental and physical) that bring us discomfort in a meeting, notice them, recalibrate, and stick to our plans. We do not need to change who we are to be successful in a meeting. We *can* tweak how we react to our innate responses, corralling our thoughts, energy, blood flow, and oxygen in a positive direction.

- ○ **Handling Tough Personalities in Meetings:** In one of my law firm jobs, I attended team meetings led by a partner—a smart, emotionally abusive, un-self-aware introvert who spent at least 10 hours a day in the office forcing a combative extrovert persona. In meetings, he simply would not look me in the eye. He dictated assignments and engaged in conversation with others at the table, but not me. I used to take it personally and worry he considered me useless or incompetent, although occasionally he would backhandedly compliment my writing in front of the team and he often assigned me the most complex briefs to write. I never figured out what his problem was/is, but one day I realized: it's completely not *my* problem. I took detailed notes during each team strategy meeting, and endeavored to ask one intelligent clarifying question—directed to the group, not to him—before the meeting ended, in an assertive voice: "Have we received any follow-up from the experts about the timing of their report drafts?" "Are we planning to run a parallel deposition schedule?" "Do we have any indication from the court on when we might get a ruling on *X*?" Sometimes, I left the meeting saying nothing, and that was fine too.

- • **Game Day:** Before you enter the meeting room, do an Amy Cuddy power pose in your office for two minutes. Plan on getting to the meeting room a few minutes early to choose the seat you want. Slow-walk to the meeting room, breathing intentionally. When you arrive at the room, choose your seat, sit down, adopt a balanced stance, shift your shoulders back, and breathe. Make eye contact with meeting participants as they enter the room: be seen. Use the strategies described above to participate, and when the meeting ends, look the leader in the eye, say thank you, and leave with purpose.

Conference Call

For introverted, shy, and socially anxious individuals, law-related conference calls can be the pits. Several loud, confident, assertive lawyers interrupting one another through crackling speakerphones, cell phone signals fading in and out, and background noise injecting additional interference? It is enough to make every introvert sigh, grit teeth, and mutter, "Why can't we just do this over email?" Nonetheless, we shall overcome.

- **Brain Preparation:** If you are the conference call leader, that's the best-case scenario. Draft an agenda and run the show; circulate the agenda in advance, establish a start time and a hard stop, and then plan to walk through each point seriatim on the phone call. If you are a participant, you can plan to settle in first by listening and letting the others battle it out while you get your bearings; just know that there will rarely, if ever, be a lull for you to interject your voice. If you have something to say, unfortunately you are going to have to interrupt someone. Write out in advance what you want to say. If you know others on the call will dispute your points, have your counterpoints written out, and plan to simply read them. No one will be able to see you. You can stand up and read away. Before the conference call, read your preparatory notes aloud a few times, connecting your ideas to your voice.

- **Body Preparation:** Because no one can see you on a conference call (unless obviously someone else is in the room with you), the technical/physical preparation for this exposure event is less rigorous. I recommend conducting all conference calls on a landline rather than a cell phone. On a landline, there is less of a likelihood of you getting dropped from the call, which can add unnecessary stress to the event. Use the speakerphone and mute buttons if needed so you have more flexibility to stand up and the freedom to flip through your notes/script. In case you get dropped from the call, have the numbers handy to rejoin the conference, and plan to state your name again loudly when you rejoin, even if you are interrupting someone. You can say, "Hi all, this is ____. I was dropped from the call but I'm back on."

- **Mind Preparation:** Prepare yourself that the call might not be fun, but flip the dread into an affirming message: "This is a low stakes experiment because no one can see me." "I can write out my script, stand up, and read verbatim." Review your mental taglines.

- **Game Day:** Stand up in your office before the call and do a two-minute Amy Cuddy power pose. Stand up throughout the call and move around, letting your excess energy dissipate outside your body. If you have something to say, knowing that you are going to have to interrupt someone, stand up or stay standing and project your voice. If someone is still talking, keep talking. Someone will back down, and try not to let it be you. Get your voice on the record. Say your name to remind your audience who is speaking: "Hi everyone, this is ___. On the point about X, we need to make sure we've considered the issue of insurance." If someone is disputing something you wrote in a letter or in a draft of an agreement, step right in and say, "Hi everyone, this is ___. On the contract indemnity provision, the reasons why the language needs to be adjusted are: (1) . . . , (2) . . . , and (3) . . . " Get on the record. Take notes throughout the call. At the end of the call, before everyone hangs up, you could interject one more time, use your notes, and say, "Everyone, this is ___ again. Just to wrap up, we discussed that our next three steps will be: (1) . . . , (2) . . . , and (3) . . . Did I leave anything out?" If appropriate for the context of the call, use the written word as your voice and circulate a recap email to the conference call participants.

Negotiation

Negotiation involves two or more lawyers discussing points of a deal and hopefully coming to terms on a final agreement, through give-and-take, points and counterpoints, bargaining, and perhaps compromise. As a junior associate, I thought I had to pretend to be tough, intense, or demanding in every face-to-face negotiation. I was wrong. Once I realized that my strength really lay in being thoughtful, calm, well-prepared, and measured, negotiations started going my way.

- **Brain Preparation:** To prepare substantively for a negotiation, outline all the key objectives you aspire to achieve for the client, with itemized reasons why you believe the client is entitled to each one—based on applicable law, facts, and/or policy. Craft a confidential list of bargaining ranges and/or alternate positions on each point, prioritizing agenda items from most important to least critical to the client (or vice versa). For an anxious attorney, a key step in preparing for a potentially challenging negotiation is to write out the valid reasons why your client is entitled to each deal point sought. Introverted, shy, and socially anxious lawyers struggle with arguing for the sake of arguing, or posturing, or digging in— without a genuine straight-faced justification for the client's position. We do not like to be inauthentic, and bluffing makes us feel fraudulent.

You have valid legal, factual, and policy bases for your contentions; write them down. Before the negotiation, read your notes aloud a few times to shape those links between ideas, words, and voice. Also, use your writing skills to amplify your voice; offer to take the lead on drafting the first version of the agreement for use as a starting point in the negotiation.

- **Body Preparation:** In advance of the event, try to see the conference room or other location where the negotiation will take place. Try to control your positioning and placement in the scene. Decide in advance where you will sit and where ideally you will direct the opposing party or parties to sit. Figure out which side or end of the table makes you the most/least comfortable. Get a sense of the glare from the windows, the overhead lighting, the doorway, and access to electrical outlets. Plan in advance which props and prompts you will take into the room: outlines, notebooks, legal pads, backup documentation, etc. Practice your balanced seated stance.

- **Mind Preparation:** Envision yourself in charge of the room. This is *your* negotiation. Even if it is not taking place in your office, consider the other side's team to be your invited guests. Advance preparation will help you stay in control. Be your quiet, calm, measured self. You have negotiation talking points to support you if you feel shaky. Stick to the plan. If an opposing lawyer raises his voice or becomes combative or antagonistic, let him stomp his feet, or jump up and down. You do not need to react or respond. He is a human being and perhaps having a bad day. Or perhaps this is his usual mode of communication or the tack he believes he needs to take in a negotiation. Not your problem. You don't need to mirror his acts or tone. You have a job to do and you are doing it—your way. Calm, measured, thoughtful. Be yourself. Give yourself permission to read from your script. This is not a show or a performance. Get your points across. If the other side does not agree with your substantive approach in a negotiation, you might walk away without a final agreement that day. So what. There will be another day. Stick to the plan, and do the best you can. You cannot control other people in the room. You are getting through it being your best, authentic, quiet, calm self. To prepare, review your mental taglines.

- **Game Day:** Get to the site early and decide where you will sit. Organize and arrange your materials, and then find a quiet space for a few minutes. Do an Amy Cuddy power pose, and breathe. Before the negotiation starts, take your seat, balance your stance, shift your shoulders back, breathe, and remind yourself of your taglines. Use your good negotiation outline to step into the conversation. Make eye contact. Smile. The outline and your calm, measured persona will help you deal with any disruptions or arguments. Use your outline to respond steadily to challenges from other lawyers. If they will not budge or they invite debate, repeat your points. Assert yourself as the participant who will capture the interim agreements in writing; consider using a white board or overhead screen to identify such incremental mutual decisions and pare down remaining differences in position, showing the two sides. If a final agreement cannot be reached at the meeting, you might just need to (check with your client and then) walk away for the day. At the end of the event, shake hands, make eye contact, say thank you, smile, and leave.

Deposition

In a deposition, a lawyer questions a witness under oath in the presence of a court reporter, with a defending attorney objecting to questions he or she believes are improperly phrased or that encroach on applicable privileges or other protections. Client representatives and more than one lawyer might be present in a deposition. Deposition dynamics can be stressful for quiet folks because of frequent interruptions to the flow of the dialogue between the deposing attorney and the deponent by objections, which also sometimes devolve into debate. Here is some advice on how to stay calm and controlled throughout the arc of a deposition.

- **Brain Preparation:** As the deposing attorney, you best can control the dynamic in the room by investing significant time in preparing a deposition outline. Review the case pleadings and documentary record, consider your client's "theory" or "theme" of the case, and draft a deposition outline of questions, topics, and documents to explore with the witness. Write out a series of introductory questions to delve into the deponent's background and experience, leaving space beneath each question to take notes, which might spark follow-up questions. You can use your introductory questions as a *script* as you begin the deposition, catching your breath, calming your heart rate, and easing into a rhythm of conversation with the deponent. Who cares if it sounds robotic at first? The transcript generated by the court reporter only shows the words on the page—there is no annotation of, "Oooh, the lawyer is reading robotically from a script." You can read all you want, at first, balancing intermittent eye contact with the deponent to establish a rapport. Eventually, in your outline, transition from the introductory questions to legal substance, exploring case-relevant topics, issues, themes, and exhibits.

Plan enough questions and topics so your outline can serve as a roadmap during the deposition if tense moments ensue or you simply become tired and are not sure what issue to tackle next. After you complete your deposition outline, read the first several pages aloud a few times, getting your brain and voice accustomed to the words on the page.

- ○ **Defending a Deposition:** Senior attorneys and law office supervisors often assign junior attorneys the task of *defending* depositions. Defending a deposition means that you accompany a deponent—the client or witness being deposed—to the deposition, sit next to him or her, and interject objections to questions posed by the deposing attorney that are improperly formed or infringe upon the attorney-client privilege or other confidentiality protections. This might sound like an easier task than serving as the deposing attorney, but for quiet lawyers, defending a deposition can present a greater challenge. In that role, we must think on our feet more, *interrupt* the other players' conversation with objections, and extemporaneously debate the propriety of such objections. Nonetheless, with the following strategic preparation, we can excel as defending attorneys: (1) have a list of standard evidentiary objections handy for quick reference;[410] (2) plan to flex your active listening skills and pay attention to the wording of the deposing attorney's questions; (3) instruct your deponent in advance that when you lift your hand off the table, he or she should stop talking or wait to answer a pending question, creating a natural pause for you to state your objection on the court reporter's record without competing voices interrupting each other. Typically, unless the deposing attorney asks questions that infringe upon the attorney-client privilege or some other confidentiality protection, you simply will be objecting to the *form* of the question: "Objection: Asked and answered. Objection: Compound question. Objection: Vague." You will not need to, or really be allowed to, engage in long-winded "speaking objections," elaborating on your reasons. Plan to tackle the deposition this way: If you hear an objectionable question, lift your hand off the table to signal to your deponent to stay quiet or stop talking; then, say "Objection: Calls for speculation" or some other appropriate objection from your printed list. You might assert more than one objection at the same time: "Objection: Compound question; vague." Plan to ask for breaks when you or the deponent need them, so you can stay alert and focused.

- • **Body Preparation:** In advance of the event, try to see the conference room or other location where the deposition will take place. Try to control your positioning and placement in the scene. Decide in advance where you will sit and where ideally you will direct the witness and other attorneys to sit. Usually, the court reporter sits at the end of the table, the deposing attorney sits next to the court reporter on one side, and the deponent and the defending attorney sit on the other. Figure out which side of the table makes you the most/least comfortable. Get a sense of the glare from the windows, the overhead lighting, the doorway, and access to electrical outlets. Plan in advance which props and prompts you will take into the room: deposition outlines, notebooks, legal pads, boxes of documents or exhibits, tabs, etc. (If you are the defending attorney, simply bring your list of objections, a notepad, and a pen.) Practice your balanced seated stance.

- **Mind Preparation:** Envision yourself in charge of the room. This is *your* deposition. Even if it is not taking place in your office, consider the other side's team to be your invited guests. As the deposing attorney, your outline will help you stay in control. Be your calm, measured self. If an opposing lawyer raises his voice or becomes combative or antagonistic, let him stomp his feet or jump up and down. Again, you do not need to react to it or respond to it. He is a human being and perhaps having a bad day. Or perhaps this is his normal style of handling a deposition. Not your problem. You do not need to mirror this approach. You have a job to do and you are doing it—your way. Calm, measured, thoughtful. Be yourself. As the deposing attorney, give yourself permission to read the questions from your script. This is not a show or a performance. If you cannot get all the information you need from a deposition, despite your strategic preparation and best efforts, so what. There are other forms of discovery in the case. As the defending attorney, if your witness is a bit too loquacious, do your best to object appropriately and preserve the record. Stick to the plan, and do the best you can. Remember, you cannot control other people in the room. You are getting through it being your best, authentic, calm self. Review your mental taglines in advance of the deposition.

- **Game Day:** Get to the deposition site early and decide where you will sit. Organize and arrange your materials, and then find a quiet space for a few minutes. Do an Amy Cuddy power pose, and breathe. Take your seat, balance your stance, shift your shoulders back, breathe, and remind yourself of your taglines. Introduce yourself to the participants, especially the court reporter (a key player in every deposition). If you are the deposing attorney, use your deposition outline to step into the conversation. Make eye contact. Smile. Ask each well-crafted question, look at the deponent, listen to his or her answer (using your good listening skills), and take notes. Use your notes as prompts for follow-up questions. The outline and your calm, measured persona will help you deal with difficult objections or interruptions. Just because opposing counsel objects to a deposition question (or many of your questions) does not necessarily mean there is anything actually wrong with your question. The lawyer could be simply preserving the record or strategically trying to interrupt your flow. You can try to rephrase the question, but if that is not working for you, just re-ask it. Break any compound questions into shorter, more concise questions addressing one topic at a time. The defending lawyer may repeat the objection; that is fine. Keep eye contact with the deponent, not the lawyer. If there is no privilege objection, simply look at the deponent after the objection and say, "If you understand the question, you may answer." If you get rattled, replace any critical messages in your head with positive ones, and keep going. Check your outline, ask the next question, take notes, pause, listen. Take breaks. Breathe. Keep using your outline. Read from it if you have to; this is not a show. Ignore the lawyer if he or she is bugging you. Be nice and respectful to the court reporter. And the deponent. At the end of the deposition, shake hands, make eye contact, say thank you, smile, and leave.

Some seasoned attorneys sense nervousness in new lawyers, and adopt intimidation tactics during depositions. My former law firm boss assigned me a lengthy series of depositions in New Orleans that lasted nearly a year. My gruff opposing counsel—who clearly sensed, and tried to capitalize on, my apprehension—defended his numerous witnesses while chewing on a large unlit cigar and staring me down during my questioning. During one of my depositions, he rolled a television set into the conference room so he and his fellow defending attorneys could watch a high-school baseball championship (on mute). When it was his turn to depose my witnesses, and I asserted objections to his questions, he constantly snapped, "What was wrong with that one?" It took every ounce of my resolve to stick to my plan in each encounter, asserting my questions or objections (from my outlines and list) and not backing down, even though my face burned with a persistent blush. Ultimately, the plan prevailed; I garnered important nuggets of information in each sequential deposition, which I eventually summarized in a summary judgment motion. At oral argument (handled by my boss), the judge asked opposing counsel, "Sir, you didn't really think you were going to skate on this one, did you?" The case ended well, but that was a year of unnecessary and palpably memorable anxiety I could have gone without.

Courtroom Appearance

The unpredictability of courtrooms can stoke anxiety in introverted, shy, and socially anxious lawyers. The environment is chock-full of stress triggers: over-stimulating chaos, crowds, bustle, authority figures, metal detectors, competition, countless situations calling out for empathy . . . In preparing for a courtroom experience, we must reframe the situation in our minds. We must tune out the pandemonium and prepare with singular focus—all we need to do is convey a clear message to a small but impactful audience. The advice here will focus on the oral argument experience in open court, not a full trial.

- **Brain Preparation:** The substantive preparation for a courtroom oral argument experience is similar to the advice provided above for a law school oral argument assignment. Now you are going to court because you want or need something for a live client, or the other side wants or needs something for its client and you are disinclined to give it to them. Oral arguments in real courtrooms move quickly; plan a simple and direct message. Write out an introduction—your name, whom you represent, the nature of the case, the specific issue before the court, the governing rule, the result you seek, and the 3–5 reasons why the judge should grant your request. Choose analogous cases and/or policy statements to support your reasoning. Develop a "theme" for your client's position, and use that as a home base to return to if the judge's questioning takes you down a meandering path. Write the argument out word-for-word first (ideally by hand—to supercharge those neural circuits in the brain as discussed earlier in this chapter). Then, type it up and read it aloud several times, forging chain links between your thoughts, words, and voice. Next, condense the argument to an outline containing enough information to trigger your thoughts if nerves freeze your brain in the moment. Take both your outline and the full argument to court though, just in case.
  - **Judges' Questions:** Use the opposing party's brief(s) to anticipate judges' questions about the perceived weaknesses of your case, and write out answers to address each potential question and weakness—justifying the result you seek. Create short headings or labels to identify the topics of the anticipated questions and answers for quick retrieval during the actual argument. Read your answers aloud several times.
  - **Rebuttal:** After the opposing party speaks, the judge might turn back to you for a response. Try to prepare rebuttal points in advance; you

will know the strengths of the opposing argument, having read the briefs and the cases. Write out some anticipated rebuttal sentences: "Your Honor, in response to counsel's statement about the *Evans* case . . ." Read those sentences aloud several times in preparation.

- **Body Preparation:** The best advice I can give for logistical preparation for a real courtroom experience is: *go* there and watch. Invest this time and it will pay dividends you would not believe. Find out in advance when your trial judge or appellate panel is hearing oral arguments on other cases and whether the courtroom is open to the public. Research how to get there, take a legal pad and a pen, and go watch three hours of arguments. Notice the room. How many people are present? Where do the attorneys for each side sit or stand? Is there a podium? Is there a microphone? How big is the room? What is the spatial distance between the judge and the attorneys? Where will you sit until the judge calls your case? Who is assisting the judge? Is there a bailiff? A court reporter? A clerk? What is the judge's demeanor? Write down the pattern of questions. How long does each attorney typically speak? Does the judge interrupt the speaker mid-sentence or fold questions into attorney pauses? Does the judge rule on the legal issue from the bench, or reserve decision until issuing a written opinion later? Watch the attorneys. Notice any imperfections? I bet you will see a lot of them; these are human beings simply engaged in conversation about complicated topics. Each attorney has a different style and various strengths and weaknesses. I once thought all courtroom orators would be masterful; they are not. You will feel much better about being your authentic self if you go spend three hours watching others in action.

  - **Prepare Your Tools:** Create a professional-looking easy-to-maneuver folder with three items: (1) the argument outline in large enough font that you can see it without having to squint; (2) a case "prompt sheet" with case summaries (in alphabetical order) of the name, citation, jurisdiction, date, facts, holding, and rationale of the key cases cited in both parties' briefs; (3) a judges' question "prompt sheet" with one- or two-word prompts like "Public Policy" or "Exception to Rule" (in alphabetical order) and your draft responses. Take a writing instrument that you will not be tempted to click or twirl, but that you can use to mark your place when you are interrupted by a judge's question, and to help you seamlessly return to your argument flow. When lugging physical items to the courtroom, less is more. Do not bog yourself down with myriad documents, books, files, or binders.

Pare down what you need into the easy-to-maneuver folder and practice opening and closing it as you step to the podium. Know where necessary information is located within your preparation materials.

- Practice your balanced seated stance as you await your argument, and then your grounded standing position when you take the podium.

- **Mind Preparation:** Think about the argument as a conversation between you and the judge rather than a performance. You know the substantive material from writing the brief(s). If you sat in your living room on a weekend and had a casual dialogue with the judge over coffee about your client's case, you probably would not be nervous. Remember that for introverted, shy, and socially anxious folks, it is the dynamic of the authoritarian nature of the courthouse and the pressure for spontaneous banter before an audience that spark our nerves. You have something to say, and are entitled to say it in your way. Stand your ground, use your notes, invoke your new personal taglines, and do the best job you can.

- **Game Day:**
  - **Attire:** Earlier in this chapter, I recommended that students preparing for a *law school* presentation or oral argument exposure event should wear something that makes them feel rock star–esque, to ignite inner power. However, when you go to court, wear a professional-looking suit. Judges expect it, and it is a sign of respect for the court. You can wear a non-distracting rock star watch or other piece of jewelry (or your favorite t-shirt emblazoned with an empowering message hidden beneath your suit!) but this is one scenario when you *must* sport that lawyer uniform.

  - Get to the courthouse early. Getting through security and finding the correct courtroom can be anxiety-producing. Find a quiet place and do a two-minute Amy Cuddy power pose. Choose a seat in the courtroom, adopt your balanced seated stance, and breathe. Try not to absorb the stress of what is going on around you. Look at the judge when he or she enters the courtroom: he or she is a person. You are about to engage in a short dialogue with a human being on a topic that you studied, wrote about, understand, and care about—that's it. You did the substantive, mental, and physical preparatory work you needed to do. When it comes time for you to take the podium, walk slowly, breathe, adopt your balanced standing position, make eye contact, settle in, breathe again, smile.

o **Use Your Notes:** Yes, it would be ideal if we could deliver an oral argument in open court without referring to notes, but being realistic, that often does not work for us introverted, shy, or socially anxious people, at least not in most public speaking scenarios. No worries. Let's be our genuine selves. When the nerves hit, guess what? *Read* your introduction. That's why you took the time to write it down. And because you wrote it out, read it over, and edited it numerous times, it is already perfect. It will get you talking and connecting with the judge. Take a deep breath, balance your stance, make eye contact. Write these physical steps down in your outline: (1) approach podium; (2) arrange folder; (3) balance stance; (4) take a deep breath; (5) make eye contact with judge; (6) wait for judge (or bailiff, if any) to announce the case or somehow indicate it is time to start; (7) take another deep breath, and . . . recite the first line of the introduction, "Your Honor, my name is . . . and I represent . . ." Gaze up periodically, forge eye contact with the judge, and soldier ahead . . . Breathe, balance your stance, and continue powering through the experience.

o **Intermittent Missteps:** You might stumble on your words. Your next thought might disappear into the stratosphere. So what. Keep going. Look at the judge, pause when you need to, find your place in your notes, and then keep going. Take a breath, balance your stance, and keep going.

o **Judges' Questions:** The judge (or panel of judges in an appellate case) likely will interrupt you. Hopefully, he or she already devoured all the briefs and really only wants to use oral argument to ask questions and dig a bit at the weaknesses of your client's position, to vet the strength of the court's ultimate decision. Welcome judges' queries and interruptions because you already anticipated this eventuality. You invested the time to craft your judges' questions "prompt sheet." Reap the benefits of it. When a judge poses a question you do not understand, or to which you are unsure how to respond, you have several options. Your misunderstanding could stem simply from an "inartfully" phrased or compound question—which happens all the time in legal dialogue. If so, you could offer, "I apologize, Your Honor, I'm not sure I understand the question. Could you please repeat it?" An empathic judge might rephrase it more clearly or break it down. Or, in response to a question of which you are not 100% sure of the answer, you could invoke your "themes," stating, "Your Honor, it seems the court is focusing on [*insert a key term/rule/policy*]. That is a pivotal point here because . . . [*insert discussion of the theme of your case.*]" If you absolutely do not know how to answer the question, say, "Your Honor, respectfully, to be honest I need to give that question a bit more investigation but I would be happy to follow up with an answer in writing." (Sometimes, judges may allow, or order, counsel for all parties to submit supplemental filings to clarify an issue that arises, and is not resolved, in oral argument). After you respond to each question the best you can, return to your marked spot in your argument outline, and trudge ahead. You do not need to await a signal from the judge to continue each time you finish answering a question. Monitor your allotted time, and endeavor to address your 3–5 primary arguments before time expires.

- **Pausing:** Give yourself permission to pause *briefly* to collect your thoughts and breathe before you shift to a new issue, or to ponder before you react to a judge's query.

- At the end, say thank you. Breathe. And then smile. That is one of the hardest exposures you will do as an introverted, shy, or socially anxious lawyer. Shake opposing counsel's hand, and go celebrate.

As you prepare to step into your first exposure agenda, consider this reminder from Dr. Kozak: "Introversion is a gift. Don't be afraid to be different. Don't be afraid to stand out . . . amid the wild extroverting around you."[411]

Exercise #7

You already thoughtfully crafted your realistic exposure agenda in Step 5. Now, let's plan your pre-game and game-day routines.

Developing Your Pre-Game Routine

- **General Endurance Training:** What physical exercise do you already, or can you begin to, engage in to build your physical strength and stamina to carry you through your exposure agenda? Even if exercise is not (yet) your favorite activity, consider one type of daily or weekly movement that will add a spring to your step, strengthen your frame, and give you that extra spark of swagger when you step into tough law-related exposure moments.

- **Brain Pre-Game:**

  - What substantive preparation is necessary for your first exposure event?

  - Would it be helpful to create outlines? Case charts? Lists of questions and answers?

  - Would any physical props be useful or appropriate? Handouts? Visuals?

  - Schedule time to write out notes, type them up, and read them aloud enough times to forge brain chain links between thoughts, words, and voice and enhance memory recall within the actual event.

- **Body Pre-Game:**

  - What adjustments can you make to your physical stance and comportment in the performance moment to channel your energy, oxygen, and blood flow in a constructive manner?

  - Can you visit the exposure event location in advance?

  - Will you be sitting or standing? Where exactly?

  - How will you best manage your documents, physical props, and any technical equipment?

  - Do you need to practice using available technology?

- **Mind Pre-Game:**

  - Be realistic about the stakes of the exposure event—it's just one short experience in a long line of interactive opportunities across the arc of a lifetime legal career.

- Be realistic about your audience and viewers—they're just human beings. It is a dialogue, not a performance. (And not everyone around us is paying attention to us.)

- Have you written out and reread your positive personal taglines?

- Have you crafted any additional taglines for this particular event?

- What will you do the night before the event to minimize anxiety?

- What will you do the morning of the event to minimize anxiety?

- What will you do in the half hour leading up to the event?

- What will you do right before you enter the room?

○ Visualize the exposure event space.

- Imagine your entry into the room, and the chronological steps leading up to the moment you begin speaking.

- Anticipate the potential influx of the negative thoughts and physical responses.

- Rehearse halting the negative soundtrack and replacing it with your positive mental taglines.

- Envision physically adjusting your stance, enhancing blood, oxygen, and energy flow.

○ Your goal is to make it through the event and experience the ultimate joy and relief when the anxiety subsides, knowing that you navigated the scenario authentically. Remember, perfection is dull.

Developing Your Exposure Game-Day Routine

- What will you wear to the event that will make you feel like the rock-star (yet still professional) version of you?

- What items will you take with you as substantive prompts or props?

- How early will you arrive at the event location?

- What calming physical exercise can you do a half-hour before the event? Walk around the block? Around the building?

- Can you take some alone time before you enter the room?

- Five minutes beforehand, what can you do to calm your breathing and your heartbeat?

- When you enter the room, what can you do to calm your breathing and your heartbeat? Do you talk to anyone? Or focus on an object?

- How will you situate yourself in the room?

- How will you stand/sit? Where?

- How will you adjust your physical stance as you begin the event?

- What positive internal messages will you invoke as you begin and during the event?

- How will you start speaking? What are your first spoken words?

CHAPTER 11

Step 7: Post-Action Reflection and Paying It Forward

Instead of running for the hills after each exposure event—which, of course, would feel liberating—we have follow-up work to do. To give each agenda item closure and maximize its learnings, we must reflect upon and capture its play-by-play. Have you ever watched the Winter Olympics and observed a skier rehearsing the turns and twists of the slope *before* launching a downhill run? We are going to perform a similar exercise but *after* each exposure episode, recording each gradient of the rise and fall of our thoughts and feelings, emotional and physical. As contemporaneously with the event as possible, grab your reflection notebook or journal, or if you still prefer the technological approach, open a new file on your computer, tablet, or phone. Note, however, that, as we discussed in Chapter 10, the physical act of writing—transporting thoughts from brain to hand to pen to paper—can be more internally impactful than typing.

For each type of exposure event, note the following:

- How did I feel **mentally** and **emotionally** as I **prepared** for this event? [*Be specific. What thoughts and feelings were in your head? Be as raw and forthcoming as you can. No one will read this but you.*]

- How did I feel **physically** as I **prepared** for this event? [*Be specific. What sensations did you feel in your body? Any physical manifestations of anxiety?*]

- How did I feel **mentally** and **emotionally the night before** the event?

- How did I feel **physically the night before** the event?

- How did I feel **mentally** and **emotionally the morning of** the event?

- How did I feel **physically the morning of** the event?

- How did I feel **mentally** and **emotionally** when I **arrived** at the event?

- How did I feel **physically** when I **arrived** at the event?

- How did I initiate the exposure event? What happened first—to commence the interpersonal interaction?

- Did any negative **mental** messages appear automatically? If so, what words did I hear? [*Try to remember and write down the exact language.*]

- Did any uncomfortable **physical** reactions occur in my body? [*What exactly did you feel or notice about your body?*]

- Did I recognize the uncomfortable **mental** or **physical** reflexes when and while they occurred, and remember that these are my normal reactions to anxiety?

- Did I try to replace the negative messages with my positive taglines? If so, which positive slogans did I use for this event?

- Did I make any conscious adjustments to my stance, alignment, or posture, or do anything else **physically** to manage the biological responses?

- What were the three best moments of the exposure event? [*These can be as basic as "I paused and then the answer came to me," or "One of the judges smiled when I said X," or "The professor nodded and said 'Good' when I answered the question about Y" or "I didn't faint."*]

- What were the three moments of the exposure event that "could have used more love"?[412] [*As much as you might not want to relive a moment of challenge, this is exactly the thick of the experience that we want to reflect upon, so we can make tweaks and adjustments for the next event. These can be as basic as, "I confused the states of Washington and Oregon when talking about diversity jurisdiction." Or, "I turned beet red when opposing counsel accused me of misstating the holding of the X case." Or, "I lost my train of thought and paused for a good 30 seconds before I started talking again. Super awkward."*]

- How did I feel **mentally** or **emotionally** the moment the exposure event concluded? [*Don't just say "fine" or "awful." Try to be more specific: Accomplished? Proud? Frustrated? Strong? Weak? Motivated? Annoyed? Exhausted? Judged?*]

- How did I feel **physically** the moment the exposure event concluded? [*Don't just say "fine" or "awful." Try to be more specific: Sweaty? Hot? Shaky? Freezing? Exhausted? Energetic? Jittery? Numb? List the physical sensations you felt throughout your body: breath, body temperature, limbs, stomach, etc.*]

- How long did it take after the exposure event to feel like my "normal" **mental** and **physical** self? [*Note: The goal with each exposure is to feel the crescendo and note the eventual dissipation of the anxiety symptoms. The more we realize that our unpleasant mental and physical manifestations of anxiety are transient and will ultimately disappear, the more comfortable we will get with*]

*their automatic instinctive arrival, and the faster we will become at counteract-
ing them with our positive personal taglines and adjustments in physical stance.
Try to note exactly the moment within or after the exposure event when you felt
relaxed again.*]

- Is there anything I could have done differently in my pre-game to enhance my **brain** (substantive) preparation?

- Is there anything I could have done differently in my pre-game to enhance my **body** (physical) preparation?

- Is there anything I could have done differently in my pre-game to enhance my **mind** (mental or emotional) preparation?

- Is there anything I could have changed in my **game-day** approach (the morning of, the half-hour before, approaching the room, walking into the room, settling into the room) to enhance my state of mind before initiating the exposure event?

For the first several exposure events, or maybe throughout your entire first exposure agenda, the subsidence of the mental and physical stress manifestations might not occur until you settle into this reflection period, escaping the watching eyes of the classroom, the office, or the courtroom. This is fine. Remember that the difference between "just do it" and "just be it" is intention, awareness, and reflection. Naturally, anxiety or adrenalin still might loiter while you are in the presence of your audience, so the return to a calm mindset might need to occur in a different geographical location: the privacy of your library carrel, law office, home, or car. Give yourself the gift of some time to reflect after each event before rushing off to the next class, appointment, meeting, or social interaction. Notice how and when your mind and body return to a relaxed state.

In this reflection period, you are not making judgments about overall success or failure; you simply are considering what aspects of your pre-game and game-day plans are working and what could use more fine-tuning. Remember, this "just be it" process is not an overnight quick fix, but it *does* work—with patience and determination. It took me two years of background research, and then doggedly working through the self-study of a *few* exposure agendas to finally feel authentic when I give a speech, negotiate a contract, teach a class, or debate a legal issue. I still experience setbacks, such as extreme blushing even in the absence of anxiety, and must remind myself of the mission: "just be it." As you work your exposure agenda, examine each incremental step, adjust the program as needed, and celebrate achievements along the way. Acknowledge what aspects of interpersonal interaction start to feel more comfortable, and be honest about what facets do not. Once you finish each event, rejoice! Reward yourself: a great meal, a gift or talisman, a concert, new shoes, an adventure. At the end of your first exposure agenda, design your next one!

CONTINUE TO REINVENT AND CULTIVATE YOUR AUTHENTIC LAWYER PERSONA

After you conquer each exposure agenda, reflect on the type of law student or lawyer you already have become and who you want to be in the future. Continuously craft and hone your individual lawyer persona. Yours will differ from mine. Be you. Bosses, mentors, peers, and family might persist in advising you to change who you fundamentally are or "fake it till you make it." Be mindful that, despite their best intentions for you, they likely have not done this work. They might not know the science. They often confuse the labels. I met up with a long-time friend—a quintessential extrovert—for spaghetti in Little Italy in New York City and exuberantly shared my passion for championing introversion in the law. He responded, "But you're not an introvert." Sigh. Seriously?

When two law firm partners I have known for a long time recently told me—with zero empathy—that I needed to "stop being so academic" in my analytical process (even though I had been researching and writing briefs professionally—and successfully—in a non-academic setting for two decades), schmooze more at networking conferences, and "grow a thicker skin," I finally thought, "Actually, I don't." I'm a thinker. I'm a writer. I'm a teacher. I try to be thoughtful, and mindful of others. I care about people: my students, my colleagues, my clients, my friends, people in other countries I don't know, you. I respect the power of the law, and the written word. Just because I resist fighting with opposing counsel for the sole sake of fighting does not mean I won't write a strong advocacy piece and win. Just because I endeavor to see the human side of my clients and adversaries does not make me weak. As you know by now, in my law practice, my clients built physical structures—bridges, tunnels, assisted-living facilities, hospitals, apartment complexes, malls, power plants. If I could help my clients focus on constructing, creating, and developing rather than fighting, tearing down, and embattling, that was the type of litigator I wanted to be. We can be *both* strong advocates *and* thoughtful, mindful, ethical analysts and counselors, actively listening to clients (and opponents) and collaboratively developing creative legal and non-legal solutions to problems. In doing so, we just might save all parties thousands of dollars, months or years of unnecessary stress, or further loss.

There will be many people in the legal profession who will not understand our quietude, and who will think—based on stereotypes—that there is no role for people like us in the law. Let's prove them wrong. Work your exposure agenda. Then, work another one. Make nips, tucks, and adjustments in your plan. Use your quiet lawyering skills at every opportunity. Continue to envision yourself as an effective advocate *because* of your quietude, *because* of your ability to listen, think, problem-solve, and test the strengths and weaknesses of ideas before sharing your thoughts through the power of legal writing or your mindful spoken voice. Be authentic in law school—in lecture classes, small seminar courses, group work, study sessions, and oral arguments. Be yourself in law offices—interacting with senior and junior attorneys, with tough and gentle clients, with difficult and cooperative opposing counsel, with challenging and even-keeled judges, and before juries. As you imagine your life and career as a quiet lawyer, remember Tanner's advice: "To learn to speak does not necessitate learning to be talkative."[413] Be quiet when you want or need to be. Close your office door to work, and then open it again when you are ready to share. Be a thinker. Be a writer. When you're overstimulated and crave downtime, replenish. Your hard work and integrity will shine bright. Most importantly, your legal career will be more personally enjoyable in the long run. The greater number of quiet lawyers whom we encourage to set an example of living authentic lives, the healthier our legal profession will become. Be you. Change the profession, and impact our legal system, nation, and world.

ASK FOR HELP WHEN YOU NEED IT

It is important to honor the reality that anxiety tied to introversion, shyness, or social anxiety in the legal context can be overwhelming, and tackling it might at times require the assistance of a professional counselor. As I previously mentioned in Chapter 5, my painful bouts of introvert-triggered and shyness-driven anxiety toward interpersonal interaction in academia, law practice, and my personal life prompted me to seek therapy from four different licensed counselors during particularly harrowing phases and traumatic life transitions over a 15-year period. These experts helped me confront personal challenges— relationship, family, and professional seismic shifts—many rooted or steeped in shame. Simultaneously, I invested a substantial amount of time on my own, reading piles of books about introversion, shyness, and social anxiety, all listed in this book's bibliography. Having gotten nowhere by "just doing it"— beating myself up within high-level academic and professional performance events and expecting supreme Nietzsche-esque results ("That which does not kill us makes us stronger")[414]—instead, I finally allowed myself to "just be it."

Integrating and synthesizing the advice of my therapists and the many expert authors referenced herein, I undertook the hard and sometimes scary work of identifying the historical messages I absorbed, assumed were true, and then replayed on a loop in my head for two decades. I jettisoned those falsities, crafted new forward-thinking messages, embraced my blushing as part of me, and adopted a plethora of exercise programs to strengthen my physique and mind. I quit high-paying and lower-paying jobs that were either toxic or undermining my self-worth. I stepped away from unhealthy relationships with friends, colleagues, and bosses that reinforced internal messages that my natural tendencies toward quiet, solitude, and reflection are wrong. Every day, I continue to strive to honor who I am and not feel pressure to morph into someone else's idea of whom or what I should be. It's not a perfect life, but it often is wildly fabulous.

SHARE YOUR STORY AND HELP OTHERS

If you are an introverted, shy, or socially anxious law student or lawyer, hopefully by now, you realize you are not alone, and in fact, there are possibly thousands of us across the country, and probably the world. We must help each other. In the competitive, often-antagonistic, and adversarial but potentially transformational legal environment, we can foster a community of collaborative empowerment and inclusion. As you grow through your exposure agendas incrementally, amplifying your authentic lawyer voice, keep track of what worked for you. Each of our personal voyages will be different. If we construct a network to share tools and techniques for serving the legal industry as quiet but effective counselors-at-law, we can embolden others who have not yet discovered their gifts. In your legal arena, keep an eye out for quiet individuals who struggle. Encourage them to be themselves. Reassure them that they have the right to quietude, and yes, they do deserve to be in law school or law practice. We need them. Validate that they have something to say, and should express it in their own way, when they are ready.

If you meet college students who are considering law school but confide concerns about being introverted, shy, or socially anxious, relay your story. Mentor a law student, or a junior attorney. Peel away one layer of their worry. Start a small group of quiet lawyers to share ideas and techniques for overcoming trepidation toward interpersonal interactions, command performances, or public speaking scenarios in the legal context. Share your exposure agenda and what you learned along the way. Blog about your experiences. Write about your personal expedition in bar association journals. We can improve our world by being vulnerable, admitting to others that we have grappled with this goliath, and serving as an example that we can do anything to which we aspire. I would love to hear about your odyssey as I continue along mine, achieve triumphs, and encounter hurdles and unexpected detours. Please share your story at heidi@theintrovertedlawyer.com. Together, we can change the legal profession forever.

When you become quiet, it just dawns on you.

Thomas Edison

Appendix A
Key Takeaways from *The Introverted Lawyer* for Law Professors and Law Practice Mentors

The following takeaways are summarized from the data and sources provided and cited throughout this book.

PREMISES

- Studies indicate that approximately 60 percent of the "gifted" population is introverted.
- About 13 percent of the general population in America struggles with social anxiety—an often-debilitating fear of *judgment-based* social interaction.
- Law school promotes unnecessary stress. Matriculating law students exhibit psychological markers that are reflective of the general population; however, an estimated 30,000–60,000 enrolled law students nationwide ultimately battle anxiety and depression.
- The Socratic Method, the perceived competitive/adversarial nature of some law school discourse, and performance-oriented assignments like mandatory oral arguments can exacerbate anxiety for introverted, shy, and socially anxious students—even though these students are committed to their studies, prepare diligently, and think deeply about legal concepts.
- Legal educators and law practice mentors can remove at least one layer of anxiety for these law students and future lawyers (*without* reducing intellectual rigor) by:
  - Providing more *context* about oral communications in a transparent manner: First, overtly explaining and acknowledging that talking about the law in the classroom environment might be more stressful for some students than others, especially while they are learning a new legal language.

- ○ Indicating that it might take a bit longer for these students to find their authentic lawyer voices, and that this is normal and OK.
- ○ Emphasizing that this IN NO WAY means that these students are not cut out for law school or the practice of law.
- ○ Reinforcing the notion that quiet lawyers can be some of the most impactful advocates in our profession.
- With the right guidance and mindset, quiet law students can learn how to better prepare for and navigate classroom participation and other challenging law-related interpersonal scenarios, staying "in the moment" and working to manage—and ultimately minimizing—anxiety, so that they can shine.
- With open-mindedness and empathy, law professors can foster a learning environment in which quiet students can experiment with, and succeed in, finding their authentic impactful lawyer voices.
- With open-mindedness and an inclusionary mindset, law practice mentors can foster a training, development, and client-focused environment in which both introverts and extroverts thrive, are mentally and physically healthy, and contribute greatly to the profession.

BACKGROUND INFORMATION ABOUT INTROVERTS

- We are conscientious and perceptive readers and fact-gatherers.
- We are active listeners.
- We are careful decision-makers.
- We thrive in working independently, in quiet spaces with minimized or no external distraction or competing stimuli.
- We process a lot of external stimuli at once, so large classroom, office, and courtroom dynamics can pose a challenge if not managed mindfully and strategically.
- We often prefer writing to speaking, because it helps us vet and test nascent thoughts, ideas, and theories before taking them "prime time."
- While extroverts formulate answers and solve problems by thinking aloud, introverts naturally mull questions and generate answers *internally*.
  - ○ Thus, we are, or might appear, slower to join a dialogue than our extroverted counterparts. But really, we simply prefer to wait until our ideas are fully formed and can withstand scrutiny before sharing them aloud.

- Science links introversion with enhanced empathy and creativity.
- We resist inauthenticity and honor genuineness; thus, mantras like "fake it till you make it" are incongruent with our nature.
- We think deeply while we problem-solve.
- We can be impactful writers because we are choosy with words.
- We are comfortable with, and actually appreciate (and need), pauses and silence.
- Prodding introverts to act like extroverts and "just do it," "get over it," "just get involved," or "just speak up" does not work; it's like telling your dog, "be a cat." Many introverts have been told their entire lives to act like extroverts. This approach does not work and is antithetical to an introvert's peak performance.
- The Socratic Method can be challenging for introverts—no matter how substantively prepared we are for the dialogue—because of the expectation to speak spontaneously and extemporaneously without time for thought, deep analysis, and internal trial-and-error before sharing thoughts and responses aloud. This does not mean that we can't do it; instead, it means we need a thoughtful strategic plan.
- Introverts can be impactful transformative lawyers because of our natural tendencies toward active listening, deep thinking, creative problem-solving, contemplative writing, and empathic engaging—highly valued competencies in the legal profession.
- Even if we perform at peak levels in a law-related interpersonal interaction, eventually we need to retreat from everyone back into quietude to recharge.

BACKGROUND INFORMATION ABOUT SHYNESS AND SOCIAL ANXIETY

- Shyness and social anxiety reflect a fear of criticism or judgment from others, which can be grounded in (1) shame-based messages ingrained in childhood by past caregivers, coaches, mentors, and other authority figures, or (2) a single traumatic life event.
- This judgment-based fear can be debilitating for some individuals and can interfere in day-to-day functioning.
- The perceived judgment-based nature of the law classroom and legal practice arena can exacerbate social anxiety for some individuals.

- Perceived harsh criticism in the law classroom, office, or courtroom can trigger anxiety for shy and socially anxious folks because it ignites past messages deeply ingrained in our minds that play on an unhealthy soundtrack loop, blocking performance. Shy and socially anxious folks can eject the negative soundtrack but to do so takes self-awareness, a strong commitment, and a conscious strategic plan.

- Simply telling an anxious person to power through a nerve-wracking experience ("just do it and you'll get over it" or "fake it till you make it") does not work. Instead, we need a prudent, strategic plan to reframe unhealthy mental and physical habits and transform our thoughts and behaviors into empowering approaches to tackling each anxiety-producing event.

BACKGROUND INFORMATION ABOUT CULTURAL INTROVERSION

- Some law students and lawyers for whom English is a second language might experience *cultural introversion* in the law classroom or office.
  - These individuals might be confident extroverts in their native speaking environment, but fear of judgment based on accents or command of English grammar can foster self-censorship.
- Other law students and lawyers come from cultures in which disagreeing with or challenging a professor, a supervisor, or other authority figure is considered rude and disrespectful.
- Others have been raised in family environments with religious or cultural pressure toward quietude.

STRATEGIES FOR PROFESSORS TO FOSTER AN INCLUSIVE LAW CLASSROOM ENVIRONMENT

- Be explicit: State in class that you understand that the Socratic Method and other performance-oriented scenarios will invoke anxiety in some students and not others. Indicate that trepidation toward public speaking in the legal context does NOT mean these individuals are not cut out for the practice of law. With the right level of self-awareness and guidance, they can be impactful communicators.

- Model a Socratic dialogue on the first day of class and try to provide a sample "pattern" of questions, demonstrating to students that your goal is teaching and learning through conversation, not trick questions or a "hide-the-ball" test (which is how some students may perceive Socratic teaching without initial context).
- Give students practical advice regarding how to prepare for a Socratic dialogue—beyond just doing the assigned reading. Advise students to:
  - Use IRAC (Issue, Rule, Application/Analysis, Conclusion) or another easy-to-apply strategy or formula to organize concepts in the reading.
  - Create a glossary of unfamiliar words/terminology, with definitions.
  - Brainstorm alternative hypotheticals to apply the relevant legal rule from the assigned reading to different contexts.
  - Develop a "theme" for each case/rule/issue to use as "home base" if the student on-call does not understand the professor's question.
- Model for students how to "stay in the moment" in a Socratic Q&A if they do not understand or know the answer to the professor's question.
  - Give students practical advice on what to say in class if they do not understand or know how to answer a question.
- Advise students how to manage anxiety in the moment, such as:
  - Adopting a balanced seated stance to get oxygen, blood, and energy flowing in a constructive manner (i.e., rather than closing up into protective mode, with legs and arms crossed and shoulders hunched, opening up your frame).
  - Breathing.
  - Treating the classroom exchange like a conversation rather than a performance.
  - Making eye contact with the professor.
  - Projecting your voice loudly enough for the professor to hear.
  - Using the IRAC notes and themes.
- Foster a classroom dynamic of empathy when students are struggling:
  - Explain that you do not want to let students off the hook if the conversation becomes difficult, but instead you will guide them through the challenge.
  - Invite students to indicate if they do not understand a question, rather than fake their way through or shut down.

- If students do not understand a question, break the query down into shorter questions.

- Keep the student talking about what he or she DOES know, to help the student work through what he or she does NOT know.

- Encourage students to help each other out in an empathetic and collaborative way.

- Remind students that lawyers do not know the answer to every legal question posed; they read, think, research more if they need to, and collaborate to craft well-reasoned solutions to problems.

- Acknowledge students' efforts when they stay engaged during difficult moments.

- Invite students to visit you during office hours to forge a human connection, to help them engage and feel more comfortable in natural dialogue in the classroom.

- Please do NOT advise quiet and/or anxious law students to "just do it," "get over it," or "fake it till you make it." Instead, acknowledge and validate the reality of their anxiety, and provide or point them to additional, appropriate resources, so that they can work through their apprehension and become impactful, mentally healthy, empowered law students.

STRATEGIES FOR LAW OFFICE MENTORS TO FOSTER AN INCLUSIVE LAW OFFICE ENVIRONMENT

- Acknowledge the assets that quiet lawyers can bring to the table: active listening, deep thinking, thorough researching, creative problem-solving, contemplative writing, and empathic engaging.

- Afford quiet lawyers reasonable time and space to work in an environment in which they thrive: closed doors, minimized or no external distractions or competing stimuli, and reasonably appropriate time to read, think, and write deeply about legal concepts.

- Honor that quiet lawyers who take longer than more talkative colleagues to participate in group meetings likely are thinking about and processing legal strategy *internally*, and are vetting and testing theories before sharing them.

- Recognize that certain performance-driven scenarios might invoke more anxiety in quiet lawyers (especially, in quiet junior attorneys) than their extroverted counterparts:

  ○ Acknowledge that anxiety toward oral arguments, negotiations, presentations, depositions, and trial work does not IN ANY WAY mean that the quiet lawyer is not cut out for the legal profession or for the particular type of practice.

  ○ Provide reasonable context and training (or referrals to outside resources) for each of these performance-driven activities, not only substantively and procedurally, but with an eye toward mental, physical, and emotional strategies for minimizing anxiety and thriving in client representation. (Note: This type of training does not necessitate a significant amount of financial or time investment by the law firm, nor will it distract junior attorneys from their focus on billable client work. Conversely, even just one or two short training sessions or workshops focused on mental, physical, and emotional strategies for approaching interpersonal interactions in the legal context can go a long way toward reducing anxiety for new lawyers and fostering their mental health and well-being.)

  ○ Please do NOT advise quiet and/or anxious junior attorneys to "just do it," "get over it," or "fake it till you make it." Instead, acknowledge and address the reality of the anxiety, and provide them with or point them toward appropriate resources, so these lawyers can work through these challenges and become impactful, mentally healthy, empowered advocates.

In the clamor of the legal arena, let's start listening to the quiet ones.

Appendix B
Practical Suggestions for Law Professors and Law Practice Mentors

Although some law classrooms and law offices currently might not facilitate or encourage vulnerability or openness to discussing how to overcome challenging emotions, fears, and doubts about the practice of law,[415] it would take very little to adjust this mindset. To improve our profession, legal educators and attorneys shaping and coaching the next generation of lawyers can teach and train in a spirit of inclusion, recognizing and welcoming individuals who learn, analyze, and communicate legal concepts in a variety of ways. Some suggest this proposition could present an initial challenge; as law professor Alan D. Hornstein points out, "Law professors, after all, are not known for their intellectual humility or the grace with which they accept change."[416] Indeed, when we use training techniques like the Socratic Method in a manner that foments "an unhealthy need to appear knowledgeable and authoritative," unfortunately we can actively discourage intellectual curiosity.[417]

Max Maxwell, who studies and writes about the Socratic Method, contends that the most important characteristic of a Socratic teacher is to exhibit a Socratic temperament,[418] modeling attitudes of optimism and hope toward learning and self-scrutiny.[419] According to Maxwell, a teacher with a temperament conducive to the development of others exemplifies four traits; she (1) embraces discovery of her own lack of understanding; (2) vulnerably shares instances of her own intellectual boundaries; (3) radiates passion for knowledge-seeking; and (4) conveys excitement for self-evolution.[420] This type of educator and mentor shows "humility and grace," and inclusive respect and empathy for all types of learners.[421]

With subtle adjustments in classrooms, offices, and even courtrooms, we can create an environment conducive to healthy developmental growth without sacrificing intellectual rigor or standards. Indeed, intellectual humility does not connote weakness, or better said, "[b]eing humble does not mean being a doormat."[422] Even in high-stakes legal scenarios driven by the billable hour, a recognition by the profession that quiet lawyers can be some of our most impactful advocates can go a long way. In a profession that requires careful reading, critical thinking, thorough researching, contemplative writing, and thoughtful communicating to solve legal problems efficiently and intelligently, our quiet law students and lawyers can contribute great assets.

EMPATHICALLY IMPACTING QUIET LAW STUDENTS

Here are some suggestions for law professors and law school administrators to cultivate an inclusive educational environment and motivate and enable quiet students to shine:

- **Classroom Tone and Philosophy:**
  - Establish an educational message and classroom tone that overtly acknowledges and honors the variety of different ways in which individuals learn and process complex legal rules and concepts.
  - Resist the idea that traditional Socratic training (without sufficient and transparent context, empathy, and collaboration between teacher and student) is the only or best way to teach new legal learners to speak about the law.
  - Resist advising nervous or quiet students to "just do it," "get over it," or "fake it till you make it."
  - Explain that, just as students are learning unfamiliar legal rules and concepts and a new legal language, some students also might need to learn more about themselves, how they process complex concepts, and how they can best communicate about the law with the least amount of anxiety.
  - Emphasize that a new law student's hesitation or anxiety toward public speaking in the law context is absolutely *not* an indicator of the student's future success as a lawyer; with the right support and guidance, the student absolutely will find his or her *authentic* voice.
  - Model empathy for quiet students and avoid making assumptions about their reasons for holding back in the classroom (i.e., refrain from assuming that students who struggle with class participation are unprepared or not tough enough).[423]
  - Strive to broaden personal understanding of some introverts' natural hesitation toward interpersonal engagement, and acknowledge that

quiet personality traits (or potentially deeper-seated shame-based triggers that cause shy and socially anxious law students to self-censor) do not in any way indicate that such students cannot become transformational lawyers.

- ○ Model humility as teachers, and share personal journeys in overcoming personal challenges and becoming authentic advocates and educators.

- ○ Emphasize that students can continuously reinvent themselves as they develop and establish their professional identity and lawyer personas; however, introverted or naturally quiet students should not feel pressure to feign extroversion, but instead can learn how to capitalize on their quiet strengths and communicate most impactfully in their authentic voices.

- **Questionnaire:** To set an inclusive tone from the beginning of each new semester, professors can have students complete a confidential questionnaire, asking for students' names, hometowns, legal interests, and so on, but also posing questions like: "Do you have any concerns about class participation, the Socratic Method, group work, oral arguments . . . ?" "What are your concerns?" "Can I help alleviate those concerns?" Armed with these insights, professors expressly can address these concerns in the classroom, in small groups, or one-on-one with students.

- **Socratic Method:**
  - ○ Professors can overtly and transparently acknowledge—in syllabi and in class—the stress that on-the-spot intellectual exchange understandably can engender.

  - ○ Professors can start off 1L students' first exposure to the Socratic Method by stating, out loud, in class:
    - Yes, I understand that the Socratic Method can indeed be stressful and likely will be more intimidating for some students than others.
    - I acknowledge that it might feel stressful to some of you because it involves spontaneous dialogue in a public setting without a lot of time to think through answers.
    - The fact that you are nervous about the Socratic Method is not in any way an indicator that you do not deserve to be here or are not cut out to be a lawyer; if you are willing to work hard, you absolutely deserve to be in law school and can make an impactful lawyer.
    - I'm going to try to explain how the Socratic Method works in *general,* and how I *specifically* use it, and how you can best *prepare* for and *participate* in it (i.e., this is not a secret code you must earn).

- You might not get the Socratic dialogue exactly right the first time, or the first few times, and that is OK. This is new stuff.

- [*Explain the pattern of how the Socratic Method works in general, and in particular, how you use it*].

- Here is what the Socratic Method is designed to accomplish, and why we use it. [*Explain your goals in using the Socratic Method; however, instead of simply suggesting that the classroom mirrors the courtroom (a concept which can further intimidate quiet students, and which isn't exactly accurate), focus on (1) identifying tangible and practical purposes for Socratic questions (i.e., extracting key information from the reading, such as rules and policies and noticing how they apply to different factual scenarios), and (2) explaining what it means to "think like a lawyer."*].

- Here is some advice on how to prepare for, engage within, and support your classmates during a Socratic classroom exchange. [*Explain specifically how students should prepare for your class so that everyone can succeed in your style of Socratic dialogue; also provide advice to students regarding what to do if they invested a lot of effort in preparing for class but still do not know the answer to a Socratic question or do not understand a question.*].

- Here is my commitment to you as to how I will endeavor to use the Method to teach you and facilitate idea-sharing, and not accidentally shame or embarrass you. [*Describe your commitment to helping students succeed in the Socratic classroom.*] I might not always get it right; the law is hard; we are human; our conversations might get emotional; and teachers are not always perfect. But together, we will strive toward increasing rather than squelching our individual and collective knowledge in this room.

A renowned professor, scholar, and highly respected faculty member once asked me to come to his office to discuss scheduling issues that impacted our shared group of students. While we were talking, he mentioned that he was going to be "stricter this year" about class participation: Students who were unprepared would receive automatic grade deductions. Wincing internally, I described my own experience in law school, confiding that I was always prepared but I became so nervous in class that I routinely faltered during the Socratic Method. Exhibiting an enormous degree of open-mindedness, this professor—who has been teaching law for nearly four decades—invited me to come speak to his 1L classes, share my personal journey tackling public speaking anxiety in law school and during my litigation career, and offer the students strategies to: (1) prepare for a Socratic questioning; (2) show their professors that they *are* prepared even when nerves creep in; and (3) not only survive, but thrive in, the classroom Q&A experience. My colleague reported back that class participation picked up after the pep talk! And even better, one of his students reached out to me to construct a personal journey to overcome his particular challenge with law-related performance-oriented events. Since then, the student has volunteered in multiple classes. With this kind of collaborative approach, we truly can transform the learning experience for our students.

- **Empathy:** Professors should endeavor to model empathy toward students who are hesitant toward and within classroom exchange. As educators, we should strive for patience in navigating students through a bumpy Socratic dialogue so they learn better how to stay *within* the experience instead of opting out physically or emotionally, swallowing toxic anxiety, or resenting the teacher or classmates.

- **Seeking Help:** Professors can seek expert assistance (such as pedagogy workshops) in learning how to better handle heated classroom exchanges and student or professor missteps without dismissing the impact these classroom conflicts can have on students who already self-censor.

- **Class Participation Grade:** Although it certainly makes sense for professors to incorporate some aspect of class participation into students' grades, professors who teach first-year law students might consider alternate ways for quiet students to satisfy these criteria while they strengthen their "sea legs" in law school and learn *how* to speak about the law. For example, instead of cold-calling in class, professors could consider assigning self-identified anxious students certain days to be on-call, so they can prepare to handle their attendant apprehension on a scheduled date rather than worrying in *every* class session whether they will be the center of attention—which can detrimentally impact learning throughout an entire semester. For the first month or two of a new semester, professors also might assign on-call teams so students can help one another participate in class. For extreme cases of anxiety, professors could experiment with having students participate through writing rather than speaking (at least at first), and encourage such students to seek out school-provided resources for conquering trepidation. For example, professors could pose a series of Socratic questions on a PowerPoint slide, and require self-identified hesitant students to respond to the questions in writing by a same-day deadline.

- **Group-Based and Team-Based Classroom Work:** Although interactive and collaborative work inside and outside the classroom can be a wonderfully effective vehicle for student learning, professors should be mindful of potential extrovert-introvert dynamics within forced student groups. Dominant extroverts might naturally (unconsciously) take charge in these scenarios. Professors who like to assign group work can expressly address this situation: instead of just telling quiet students to speak up, and mandating participation as part of a grade, convey your recognition that group work can spark initial anxiety in some students. Encourage quieter students or those who prefer working independently to experiment with different roles within groups (for example, through writing: agenda-setting, note-taking, and post-meeting summarizing). Always motivate all students to be respectful to all voices within a group or team.

- **Oral Arguments and Class Presentations:** Many introverted, shy, and socially anxious first-year law students are hesitant toward public speaking, especially in the Socratic context, which requires extemporaneous reaction without a lot of reflection time, and can feel judgment-based. These same students strongly want to share their budding ideas about the law and do not want special treatment, but struggle with how to confront this anxiety without appearing weak. Professors who require oral arguments or class presentations should be mindful about student concerns, and rather than pushing students to simply perform before their peers without enough advance context, guidance, or training, first can expressly acknowledge in class that these experiences might be more stressful for some students than others. Professors can meet with these students individually or in small groups to discuss how best to prepare—not only substantively—but more importantly, *mentally* and *physically* for an oral argument or presentation. For professors who do not feel equipped to address the psychological aspects of preparing for oral arguments or class presentations, schools should provide small-group workshops and/ or one-on-one mentors to directly address public speaking anxiety. Oral argument workshops devoted to advocacy skills and techniques are great, but they are not enough to support students battling the emotional and physical reactions associated with public speaking anxiety. Professors also should be mindful that requiring nervous students to perform mock arguments or presentations to a peer audience before the actual event also might exacerbate rather than alleviate their anxiety; such students often perform better rehearsing privately or one-on-one with a peer, professor, or teaching assistant rather than in front of the entire class. Professors who require oral arguments or class presentations should: (1) provide advance explanation and guidance about the details and logistics of the event (these matters may seem obvious or inconsequential to a teacher who has required these types of assignments regularly, but taking the time to describe the setup or layout of the room, the sequence and timing of the argument or presentation, the composition of the audience, and so on, can go a long way toward helping a nervous speaker better visualize the *reality* of the event instead of *imagining* a much more stressful—and inaccurate—scenario); (2) demonstrate understanding that the experience might spark more anxiety in some students than in others; (3) emphasize that such apprehension is not in any way an indicator of a student's future success as a lawyer; and (4) refer students to tangible resources (small group workshops or one-on-one mentoring) to strategically tackle the mental and physical aspects of this challenge. When a professor is judging or grading an oral argument or presentation, if a student is visibly struggling, the professor should model empathy and inspire strength. Do not let the student abandon the assignment (unless it appears to be severely traumatizing), but prompt the student with questions and encouragement to keep going, to stay engaged throughout the experience, and to talk about what he or she *does* know. The nerves probably will block the student's clarity of thought, so it is important to guide the student back to what he or she *does* know. Let the student refer to notes. It is important for nervous students to try to complete the entire exercise, processing the rise and fall of mental and physical anxiety manifestations, so that they know they can survive the experience. Be supportive and encourage such students to understand that, with the right support, they will be impactful, authentic advocates *because* they care so much about doing it well.

- **Office Hours:** If a student visits a law professor or school administrator during office hours and admits trepidation toward public speaking in law school, we must acknowledge that this student wants to succeed in law school and is bravely and vulnerably asking for help. The best response is one that respects the student's courage in coming forward, recognizes and validates the student's fear or anxiety, and offers the student tangible and practical resources to work on exploring his or her strengths and weaknesses in a threat-reduced environment to amplify his or her authentic voice. We definitely should not advise the student to "just do it more and you'll get over it," or "fake it till you make it." Instead, professors can start by walking the student through the context, background, purpose, pattern, and logistics of the performance-oriented event (or point the student to someone who can do so effectively), and then provide additional resources (such as workshops and one-on-one mentoring) for building strength to strategically address this challenge. This is an opportunity for educators to further model empathy and show students that we do not need to be perfect; we just need to exhibit genuine effort and care.

- **Reaching Out to Students Who Do Not Come Forward:** As we consciously observe our classroom dynamics and notice quiet students or those who struggle in Socratic exchanges, we must not mistakenly or accidentally discount these individuals as disengaged, unprepared, or unassertive. Instead, we can reach out to students in person or in email and invite conversation: "How is law school going for you so far?" "I'd love to hear your thoughts in class about *X*." "Do you have concerns about class participation?" "Do you feel comfortable sharing your concerns?" "Can I help alleviate any concerns?"

- **Encouraging Legal Writing as a Vehicle for Amplifying the Quiet Law Student's Voice:** Law professors who observe quiet students struggling to find their place in law school should encourage legal writing as a medium for expressing thoughts and theories about the law. Quiet law students often are profoundly impactful advocates through the written word. Legal writing courses, short written assignments in lecture classes, seminar courses, and writing workshops offer tremendous opportunities for quiet students to test their legal theories, experiment with their lawyer voices, and demonstrate their depth of legal analysis.

- **Workshops:** Just like we offer law school workshops on outlining, test-taking, reading comprehension, legal research skills, oral arguments, time management, and career planning, we should offer workshops on tackling public speaking anxiety. These workshops should be distinct from oral advocacy workshops (customarily devoted to style and techniques) and rather should focus on understanding the *mental* and *physical* drivers of anxiety toward performance-oriented scenarios. These workshops can be scheduled throughout the year to address classroom participation (starting early in the fall semester) but also help students mentally and physically prepare for particularly stressful interactive events during the law school experience, such as oral argument assignments, moot court or trial team tryouts, negotiation and client counseling simulations, job interviews, etc. The arc of ongoing workshops could be structured around (1) mental and physical reflection; (2) mental and physical action; and (3) pre-game and game-day planning.

- **One-on-One Mentors:** Law schools can provide student and faculty mentors for students working through reticence toward interpersonal interaction in the law context. Faculty, administrators, and 2L/3L students who overcame similar struggles should vocalize and share their stories.

- **Career Planning and Job Interviews:** Many law schools' career development offices already are doing a wonderful job linking students with professional opportunities that fit their *substantive* legal interests. Pushing these efforts even further, career services departments can encourage students to study their skill sets and personality traits, through assessments such as the Myers-Briggs Type Indicator personality inventory,[424] to identify introversion and then study and understand personal strengths and particular challenges that might arise in job interviews and professional environments. Career counselors might consider providing interview workshops specifically devoted to introverted, shy, and socially anxious students, to develop pre-game and game-day strategies for preparing for and participating in job interviews. These workshops can focus on substantive, physical, and mental preparation, and techniques for staying calm, reducing anxiety, maintaining eye contact, breathing, answering difficult questions, and appropriately volunteering information about personal achievements and accomplishments.

EMPATHICALLY IMPACTING QUIET LAWYERS

- To empathically impact quiet lawyers and foster an environment where they can authentically amplify their lawyer voices, law offices, bar associations, supervising attorneys, and mentors can:
  - Establish a tone of inclusion, and while reinforcing intellectual rigor, professional standards, and expectations of excellence, expressly acknowledge that not all lawyers are, or should be, the same.
  - Demonstrate appreciation for careful reading, critical thinking, thorough researching, contemplative writing, and thoughtful communicating to solve legal problems efficiently and intelligently—recognizing that these are strengths of many quiet lawyers.
  - Resist the idea that, because all lawyers ultimately need to be able to speak about the law, pushing junior attorneys into depositions, negotiations, and trial work, etc.—without effective mentoring, training, and support—is a necessary rite of passage.
  - Emphasize that a junior lawyer's hesitation or anxiety toward depositions, negotiations, trial work, etc., is not an indicator of the attorney's future success—because, with the right context, training, self-awareness, and guidance, the junior lawyer will establish (and amplify) his or her *authentic* advocacy voice.

○ Acknowledge that depositions, negotiations, trial work, etc., can be stressful, but with the right context, training, self-awareness, and guidance, junior lawyers can conquer anxiety toward these lawyering activities.

○ Explain that, just as junior attorneys continue to learn new legal rules, concepts, and procedures as they develop and grow within an area of practice, some also might need to learn more about themselves and how they can best communicate about the law with the least amount of anxiety.

○ Resist making negative assumptions about quiet junior attorneys.

○ Enhance personal understanding of the different ways extroverts and introverts work, process legal concepts, produce their best written work product, and communicate about the law.

○ Cultivate an environment in which extroverted and introverted attorneys both can produce their best work product most efficiently; recognize that introverts might need to close their office doors to concentrate.

○ Strive to broaden personal understanding of introverts' natural hesitation toward certain contexts of spontaneous interpersonal engagement, and acknowledge that such quiet personality traits (or potentially deeper-seated shame-based triggers that fuel self-censorship in shy and socially anxious people) do not in any way indicate that such individuals cannot become transformational lawyers.

○ Acknowledge that quiet junior attorneys have a pivotal role to play in client representation (i.e., active listeners, thorough fact-gatherers and researchers, strategic thinkers, contemplative writers, creative problem-solvers, and so on).

○ Model humility as a leadership strength, and share professional journeys in overcoming personal challenges and becoming authentically powerful advocates.

○ Emphasize that introverted junior attorneys should not feel pressure to feign extroversion or aggressiveness, but instead should capitalize on their strengths and focus on communicating most impactfully about the law in their authentic voices.

• **Workload Management, Mentoring, and Training:** When we assign junior attorneys interactive and performance-driven tasks such as depositions, negotiations, trial work, etc., we can openly express that these tasks might indeed be stressful and intimidating. Quiet lawyers might experience more anxiety than their peers toward these activities, but with the right background context, training, and guidance, they certainly can master them. Law offices and bar associations can provide mentors to help junior attorneys prepare to handle these legal activities, to focus not only on the technical procedures, techniques, and intellectual strategy, but even more importantly, to learn how to step into each scenario with the greatest amount of mental and physical strength and least amount of anxiety. Training and mentoring programs can focus on helping junior attorneys understand *why* these tasks ignite anxiety, and (instead of glossing over that reality and prodding them to tough it out or push through it) provide resources to help junior attorneys adopt mental and physical strategies to reduce anxiety and develop their authentic advocacy personas.

- **Job Interviews:** Law students navigate countless job interviews, for internships, summer associate positions, clerkships, and full-time law office employment. Interviews can be a stressful experience for any law student or lawyer but often much more so for introverted, shy, and socially anxious job candidates. Interviewers in the legal market can alleviate some of this angst and pave the way for quiet applicants to showcase their strengths simply by being mindful of the differences between introverts and extroverts in interviewing, and by resisting making immediate assumptions about a quiet candidate's aptitude or ability to contribute to the law office environment. The more reserved applicants might be excellent legal writers, inquisitive thinkers, and deep analysts. Of course, legal interviewers are busy, they must plow through numerous applications, and they conduct an abundant number of interviews—so, speedy assessments indeed are often a reality. Nonetheless, with increased awareness of the possibility that quiet applicants just might be "diamonds in the rough," legal employers can increase the likelihood of finding outstanding candidates who will enhance the office environment, serve clients well, and contribute mightily to our profession.

- **Workshops:** Law offices and bar associations can offer workshops and accredited Continuing Legal Education (CLE) programs devoted to topics like: (1) understanding introversion, shyness, and social anxiety in the legal profession; (2) conquering public speaking anxiety in the legal profession; (3) enhancing the role of empathy in the legal profession; and (4) facilitating healthy, authentic expression in law-related interactions. Not only can we provide CLEs for interactive attorney tasks like depositions, negotiations, oral arguments, and trial work, we can incorporate a mental health aspect into this practical training, focusing on mental and physical manifestations of reticence or anxiety toward adversarial exchange. These workshops and programs should be designed to satisfy various states' mandatory requirements for CLE hours focused on mental health issues, professionalism, and advocacy skills.

EMPATHICALLY IMPACTING NERVOUS ADVOCATES IN THE COURTROOM

Judges can be some of the most influential figures in shaping a quiet junior lawyer's career path. Many introverted, shy, and socially anxious law school graduates find themselves in litigation careers either (1) intentionally, because they love legal research, writing, and problem-solving, and hope they can overcome anxiety toward performance-oriented activities like depositions, negotiations, and trial work, or (2) because of job market constraints or a lack of familiarity with other types of practice. Accordingly, many introverted, shy, and socially anxious lawyers will end up presenting oral arguments or conducting trials in courtrooms before judges. And they will be exceedingly nervous, although most likely overprepared.

I have never been a judge, and I have the utmost respect for the pressure judges are under to review myriad briefs, adjudicate countless cases in crowded dockets, and render reasoned decisions efficiently and fairly. I understand that judges need lawyers to not only follow procedural rules and submit quality briefs to facilitate efficient and just decision-making, but also to get to the point quickly in court proceedings and to know what they are doing. Judges can profoundly affect a quiet lawyer's career trajectory through even the most fleeting moments of understanding and empathy in courtroom scenarios. The quiet lawyer might have been the primary author of the party's pleadings and briefs. If so, she likely knows the facts, rules, and arguments inside and out. She cares deeply about the issues before the court. She probably has prepared and rehearsed her oral argument, opening statement, or witness examination numerous times. The authoritative, adversarial, and spontaneous nature of the courtroom experience likely will rattle her in the moment. She wants to communicate clearly and confidently. She might not do so. She has everything written down and is going to need to use her notes a lot. She's probably scared. She respects the judge and the process and wants to do a great job for her client. She wants to be better at this. She doesn't want to fake her way.

A federal district court judge exhibited great empathy to me when I was a very junior associate terrified of examining my first witness in my first trial. In the U.S. District Court for the Eastern District of Virginia, I needed to be sworn into the court before I could examine my first witness, and I was a sweaty, nervous, blushing wreck. The judge first took a few seconds to acknowledge the moment of my swearing in, smiled, openly acknowledged the significance of this moment in my new career, and patiently encouraged me to proceed with my short line of questioning of the witness. I wasn't eloquent, but I got through it, thanks to that empathetic judge. I wish I had willingly stepped into many more of those courtrooms, as my authentically empowered, quiet self, and learned from more judges like that one.

Quiet people have the loudest minds.

Stephen Hawking

Bibliography

A profound thank you to the many authors below who inspired me to embrace my introvert power and amplify my *authentic* lawyer voice, and gave me practical and understandable advice on how to do so.

Law Journal and Law Review Articles

Anderson, Vanessa; Downey, Geraldine; and London, Bonita. "Studying Institutional Engagement: Utilizing Social Psychology Research Methodologies to Study Law Student Engagement." *Harvard Journal of Law & Gender* 30 (2007): 389–407.

Brown, Heidi K. "Empowering Law Students to Overcome Extreme Public Speaking Anxiety: Why 'Just Be It' Works and 'Just Do It' Doesn't." *Duquesne Law Review* 53, no. 1 (Winter 2015): 181–214.

Brown, Heidi K. "The 'Silent but Gifted' Law Student: Transforming Anxious Public Speakers into Well-Rounded Advocates." *The Journal of the Legal Writing Institute* 18 (2012): 291–337.

Cain, Paul J. "A First Step Toward Introducing Emotional Intelligence into the Law School Curriculum: The 'Emotional Intelligence and the Clinic Student' Class." *Legal Education Review* 14, no. 1 (2004): 1–17.

Dysart, Sara E., and Foster, Ann D. "Practicing Law and Wellness: Modern Strategies for the Lawyer Dealing with Anxiety, Addiction, and Depression." *The Advocate* (State Bar of Texas) 4–17 (Spring 2011).

Gallacher, Ian. "Thinking Like Non-Lawyers: Why Empathy Is a Core Lawyering Skill and Why Legal Education Should Change to Reflect its Importance." *Legal Communication & Rhetoric: Journal of the Association of Legal Writing Directors* 8 (Fall 2011): 109–152.

George, Shailini J. "The Cure for the Distracted Mind: Why Law Schools Should Teach Mindfulness." *Duquesne Law Review* 53, no. 1 (Winter 2015): 215–244.

Gerdy, Kristin B. "Clients, Empathy, and Compassion: Introducing First-Year Students to the 'Heart' of Lawyering." *Nebraska Law Review* 87, no. 1 (2008): 1–61.

Glesner, B. A. "Fear and Loathing in the Law Schools." *Connecticut Law Review* 23 (1991): 627–668.

Gould, Emily J., Esq. "The Empathy Debate: The Role of Empathy in Law, Mediation, and the New Professionalism." *Vermont Bar Journal* 36, no. 3 (Fall 2010): 23–26.

Grover, Susan. "Personal Integration and Outsider Status as Factors in Law School Well Being." *Washburn Law Journal* 47 (2008): 101–134.

Hess, Gerald F. "Heads and Hearts: The Teaching and Learning Environment in Law School." *Journal of Legal Education* 52, no. 1 (2002): 75–111.

Jolly-Ryan, Jennifer. "Promoting Mental Health in Law School: What Law School Can Do for Law Students to Help Them Become Happy, Mentally Healthy Lawyers." *University of Louisville Law Review* 48 (2009): 95–137.

Korn, Jane. "Teaching Talking: Oral Communication Skills in a Law Course." *Journal of Legal Education* 54, no. 4 (2004): 588–596.

Larcombe, Wendy; Tumbaga, Letty; Malkin, Ian; Nicholson, Pip; and Tokatlidis, Orania. "Does an Improved Experience of Law School Protect Students against Depression, Anxiety and Stress? An Empirical Study of Wellbeing and the Law School Experience of LLB and JD Students." *Sydney Law Review* 35, no. 2 (June 2013): 407–432.

Lewinbuk, Katerina P. "Lawyer Heal Thy Self: Incorporating Mindfulness into Legal Education and Profession." *The Journal of the Legal Profession* 40, no. 1 (Fall 2015): 1–24.

Maloney, Bridget A. "Distress Among the Legal Profession: What Law Schools Can Do About It." *Notre Dame Journal of Law, Ethics & Public Policy* 15, no. 1 (2001): 307–331.

McKinney, Ruth Ann. "Depression and Anxiety in Law Students: Are We Part of the Problem and Can We Be Part of the Solution?" *The Journal of the Legal Writing Institute* 8 (2002): 229–255.

Montgomery, John E. "Incorporating Emotional Intelligence Concepts into Legal Education: Strengthening the Professionalism of Law Students." *University of Toledo Law Review* 39 (2008): 323–352.

Ricks, Sarah E. "Some Strategies to Teach Reluctant Talkers to Talk About Law." *Journal of Legal Education* 54 (2004): 570–587.

Rosenberg, Joshua D. "Teaching Empathy in Law School." *University of San Francisco Law Review* 36 (Spring 2002): 621–657.

Schulze, Jr., Louis N. "Alternative Justifications for Law School Academic Support Programs: Self-Determination Theory, Autonomy Support, and Humanizing the Law School." *Charleston Law Review* 5 (2011): 269–331.

Sexton, John. "'Out of the Box' Thinking About the Training of Lawyers in the Next Millennium." *University of Toledo Law Review* 33 (2002): 189–202.

Shanfield, Stephen B. and Benjamin, G. Andrew H. "Psychiatric Distress in Law Students." *Journal of Legal Education* 35 (1985).

Shapiro, Adam J. "Defining the Rights of Law Students with Mental Disabilities." *University of Miami Law Review* 58 (2004): 923–940.

Silver, Marjorie A. "Emotional Intelligence and Legal Education." *Psychology, Public Policy, & Law* 5, no. 4 (1999): 1173–1203.

Soonpaa, Nancy J. "Stress in Law Students: A Comparative Study of First-Year, Second-Year, and Third-Year Students." *Connecticut Law Review* 36 (2004): 353–383.

Sperling, Carrie and Shapcott, Susan. "Fixing Students' Fixed Mindsets: Paving the Way for Meaningful Assessments." *The Journal of the Legal Writing Institute* 18 (2012): 39–84.

Vance, Sheilah. "Should the Academic Support Professional Look to Counseling Theory and Practice to Help Students Achieve?" *University of Missouri-Kansas City Law Review* 69 (2001): 499–531.

Wellford Slocum, Robin. "An Inconvenient Truth: The Need to Educate Emotionally Competent Lawyers." *Creighton Law Review* 45 (2012): 827–852.

Zimmerman, Clifford S. "'Thinking Beyond My Own Interpretation': Reflections on Collaborative and Cooperative Learning Theory in the Law School Curriculum." *Arizona State Law Journal* 31 (1999): 957–1020.

Books about Introversion

Cain, Susan. *Quiet: The Power of Introverts in a World That Can't Stop Talking*. New York: Crown Publishing Group, 2012.

Dembling, Sophia. *Introverts in Love: The Quiet Way to Happily Ever After*. New York: Penguin Group, 2012.

Dembling, Sophia. *The Introvert's Way: Living a Quiet Life in a Noisy World*. New York: Penguin Group, 2012.

Helgoe, Laurie, Ph.D. *Introvert Power: Why Your Inner Life Is Your Hidden Strength*. Naperville, IL: Sourcebooks, Inc., 2008.

Kahnweiler, Jennifer, Ph.D. *Quiet Influence: The Introvert's Guide to Making a Difference*. San Francisco: Berrett-Koehler Publishers, 2013.

Kahnweiler, Jennifer, Ph.D. *The Introverted Leader: Building on Your Quiet Strength*. San Francisco: Berrett-Koehler Publishers, 2013.

Kozak, Arnie, Ph.D. *The Everything Guide to the Introvert Edge*. Avon, MA: Adams Media, 2013.

Laney, Marti Olsen, Psy.D. *The Introvert Advantage: How to Thrive in an Extrovert World*. New York: Workman Publishing, 2002.

McHugh, Adam. *Introverts in the Church: Finding Our Place in an Extroverted Culture*. Downers Grove, IL: InterVarsity Press, 2009.

Tanner, Mark. *The Introvert Charismatic: The Gift of Introversion in a Noisy Church*. Grand Rapids, MI: Monarch Books, 2015.

Newspaper Articles about Introversion

Brown, Heidi K. "Harness the Skills of the Introverted Lawyer." *New York Law Journal*, August 15, 2016.

Cain, Susan. "The Rise of the New Groupthink." *New York Times*, January 13, 2012.

Schultz, Katherine. "Why Introverts Shouldn't Be Forced to Talk in Class." *Washington Post*, February 12, 2013.

Legal Education Wellness Websites

Association of American Law Schools' (AALS) Section on Balance in Legal Education: http://www.law.du.edu/index.php/aals-balance-in-legal-education-bib (with bibliography)

Law School Wellness Project Blog: https://law.stanford.edu/blog/?taxand terms=4971

Law Student Division's Mental Health Initiative, the Young Lawyers Division's Health and Wellness Initiative, and the Commission on Lawyer Assistance Programs: www.americanbar.org

Introversion Websites

www.theintrovertedlawyer.com

introvertspring.com/category/blogs/

introvertdear.com/

www.psychologytoday.com/blog/the-introverts-corner

introvertzone.com/

www.quietrev.com/

www.quietlyfabulous.com/

introvertretreat.com/

www.sheepdressedlikewolves.com/

Books about Shyness, Social Anxiety, and Public Speaking Anxiety

Breggin, Peter R., MD. *Guilt, Shame, and Anxiety: Understanding and Overcoming Negative Emotions*. Amherst, NY: Prometheus Books, 2014.

Cho, Jeena, and Gifford, Karen. *The Anxious Lawyer: An 8-Week Guide to a Joyful and Satisfying Law Practice Through Mindfulness and Meditation*. Chicago: Ankerwycke Books, 2016.

Esposito, Janet E., MSW. *In the Spotlight: Overcome Your Fear of Public Speaking and Performing.* Bridgewater, CT: Strong Books, 2000.

Fensholt, M. F. *The Francis Effect: The Real Reason You Hate Public Speaking and How to Get Over It.* Ontario, CA: Oakmont Press, 2006.

Flowers, Steve, MFT. *The Mindful Path Through Shyness.* Oakland, CA: New Harbinger Publications, Inc., 2009.

Hilliard, Erika B., MSW, RSW. *Living Fully with Shyness and Social Anxiety.* Philadelphia: Da Capo Press, 2005.

Markway, Barbara G., Ph.D.; Carmin, Cheryl N., Ph.D.; Pollard, C. Alec, Ph.D.; and Flynn, Teresa, Ph.D. *Dying of Embarrassment: Help for Social Anxiety & Phobia.* Oakland, CA: New Harbinger Publications, Inc., 1992.

Markway, Barbara G., Ph.D., and Markway, Gregory P., Ph.D. *Painfully Shy: How to Overcome Social Anxiety and Reclaim Your Life.* New York: Thomas Dunne Books, 2001.

Naistadt, Ivy. *Speak Without Fear.* New York: HarperCollins, 2004.

Rogers, Natalie H. *The New Talk Power.* Sterling, VA: Capital Books, Inc., 2000.

Books about Public Speaking and Oral Advocacy Skills for Lawyers

Diaz-Bonilla, Rebecca. *Foolproof: An Attorney's Guide to Oral Communications.* LexisNexis, 2014.

Johnson, Brian K., and Hunter, Marsha. *The Articulate Attorney: Public Speaking for Lawyers.* Phoenix: Crown King Books, 2013.

Sayler, Robert, and Shadel, Molly. *Tongue-Tied America: Reviving the Art of Verbal Persuasion.* New York: Aspen Publishers, 2014.

Books about Socrates

Gross, Ronald. *Socrates' Way: Seven Master Keys to Using Your Mind to the Utmost.* New York: Jeremy P. Tarcher/Putnam, 2002.

Johnson, Paul. *Socrates: A Man for Our Times.* New York: Penguin Books, 2011.

Phillips, Christopher. *Socrates Café: A Fresh Taste of Philosophy.* New York: W.W. Norton & Co., 2001.

Notes

1. Jennifer B. Kahnweiler, Ph.D., *Quiet Influence: The Introvert's Guide to Making a Difference* (Oakland, CA: Berrett-Koehler Publishers, 2013), 7.

2. Stephanie B. Goldberg, "Beyond the Socratic Method," *Student Law* 36 (October 2007): 18–19. ("While the Socratic Method forces students to think on their feet, it also replicates the tension of standing before a judge in court, knowing he or she can humble you at any moment.")

3. Susan Cain, *Quiet: The Power of Introverts in a World That Can't Stop Talking* (New York: Crown Publishing Group, 2012), 6.

4. Burton Raffel, reply by P. N. Furbank, *Lost in Translation*, November 16, 2006, http://www.nybooks.com/articles/2006/11/16/lost-in-translation/.

5. Lawyers & Depression, http://www.daveneefoundation.org/scholarship/lawyers-and-depression/. *See also* Jennifer Jolly-Ryan, "Promoting Mental Health in Law School: What Law School Can Do for Law Students to Help Them Become Happy, Mentally Healthy Lawyers," *University of Louisville Law Review* 48 (2009): 95, 103 (quoting Susan Grover, "Personal Integration and Outsider Status as Factors in Law School Well Being," *Washburn Law Journal* 47 (2008): 419, 421 n.16). ("Empirical research shows that entering law students possess 'normal psychological markers.' However, they 'shift quickly to major psychological distress during the first year of law school.'").

6. Dan Lukasik, "Law School Depression," http://www.lawyerswithdepression.com/law-school-depression/.

7. Grover, 419, 426. *See also* Hollee Schwartz Temple, "Speaking Up: Helping Law Students Break Through the Silence of Depression," *ABA Journal* (February 2012): 23.

8. Susan Daicoff, "Lawyer, Be Thyself: An Empirical Investigation of the Relationship Between the Ethic of Care, the Feeling Decisionmaking Preference, and Lawyer Wellbeing," *Virginia Journal of Social Policy & the Law* 16 (Fall 2008): 87.

9. Leonard Riskin, "The Contemplative Lawyer: On the Potential Contributions of Mindfulness Meditation to Law Students, Lawyers, and Their Clients," *Harvard Negotiation Law Review* 7 (Spring 2002): 1, 10.

10. Temple, 23, citing Professor Krieger's statistics.

11. Michael L. Perlin, "'Baby, Look Inside Your Mirror': The Legal Profession's Willful and Sanist Blindness to Lawyers with Mental Disabilities," *University of Pittsburgh*

Law Review 69 (Spring 2008): 589, 592 n. 14, citing David M. Wooldridge, "Addressing the Unthinkable: How You Can Constructively Deal with the Problem of Suicide," *Alabama Law Review* 68 (2007): 154, 155. Online: http://www .alabar.org/publications/pastissues/0107/addressing_ suicide.pdf.

12. Cain, 104.

13. Marti Olsen Laney, Psy.D., *The Introvert Advantage: How to Thrive in an Extrovert World* (New York: Workman Publishing, 2002), 252.

14. Ibid.

15. Many of the ideas, language, and sources in the next few chapters were previously published in Heidi K. Brown, "Empowering Law Students to Overcome Extreme Public Speaking Anxiety: Why 'Just Be It' Works and 'Just Do It' Doesn't," *Duquesne Law Review* 53 (Winter 2015): 181–214; Heidi K. Brown, "The 'Silent but Gifted' Law Student: Transforming Anxious Public Speakers into Well-Rounded Advocates," *The Journal of the Legal Writing Institute* 18 (2012): 291–337; and Heidi K. Brown, "Harness the Skills of the Introverted Lawyer," *New York Law Journal*, August 15, 2016, http://www.newyorklawjournal.com/id=1202764878620.

16. Quiet law students and lawyers might consider taking the Myers-Briggs Type Indicator (MBTI) personality inventory. As explained on The Myers & Briggs Foundation website (http://www.myersbriggs.org/my-mbti-personality-type/ mbti-basics/), "[t]he theory of psychological type was introduced in the 1920s by Carl G. Jung. The MBTI tool was developed in the 1940s by Isabel Briggs Myers and the original research was done in the 1940s and '50s. This research is ongoing, providing users with updated and new information about psychological type and its applications. Millions of people worldwide have taken the Indicator each year since its first publication in 1962." Certified administrators conduct the "instrument," comprised of 93 questions, and then provide written results— which can unveil deep insights into personality preferences, including the introversion and extroversion dichotomy. The Myers & Briggs Foundation website provides resources for finding a local certified administrator, or for accessing the instrument online. See http://www.myersbriggs.org/my-mbti-personality-type/ take-the-mbti-instrument/.

17. There are two different spellings of *extravert/extrovert*. Jung used the former.

18. MBTI Basics: Extravert and Introvert. http://www.myersbriggs.org/my-mbti-personality-type/mbti-basics/extravert-and-introvert.htm (adapted from Gordon Lawrence & Charles Martin, *Building People, Building Programs: A Practitioner's Guide to Introducing the MBTI to Individuals and Organizations* (2001)).

19. Erika B. Hilliard, MSW, RSW, *Living Fully with Shyness and Social Anxiety* (Philadelphia: Da Capo Press, 2005), 10.

20. Laney, 21.

21. Sophia Dembling, *The Introvert's Way: Living a Quiet Life in a Noisy World* (New York: Penguin Group, 2012), 52.

22. Laney, 37.

23. Mark Tanner, *The Introvert Charismatic: The Gift of Introversion in a Noisy Church* (Grand Rapids, MI: Monarch Books, 2015), 207. ("[P]ublic intimacy . . . can be quite oppressive for introverts. Many do not really want to be in 'group hug' sessions or invited to bear their souls with no notice or preparation time.")

24. Cain, 11.

25. Sophia Dembling, *Introverts in Love: The Quiet Way to Happily Ever After* (New York: Penguin Group, 2012), 20.

26. Dembling, *The Introvert's Way*, 29, referring to Carl Jung's characterization of introverts.

27. Ibid., 101.

28. Laurie Helgoe, Ph.D., *Introvert Power: Why Your Inner Life Is Your Hidden Strength* (Naperville, IL: Sourcebooks, Inc., 2008), 13. ("Introverts appear to do their best thinking in anticipation rather than on the spot; it now seems clear that this is because their minds are so naturally abuzz with activity that they need to shut out external distractions in order to prepare their ideas.")

29. Ibid., 234.

30. Kahnweiler, *Quiet Influence*, 13.

31. Dembling, *Introverts in Love*, 20.

32. Dembling, *The Introvert's Way*, 29.

33. Ibid., 30.

34. Ibid., 31.

35. Dembling, *Introverts in Love*, 32.

36. Laney, 69.

37. Ibid.

38. Ibid.

39. Ibid., 69–70.

40. Ibid., 72.

41. Ibid., 72–73.

42. Ibid., 71.

43. Neurotransmitters: Serotonin, GABA, Dopamine, and Acetylcholine. http://knowmental.com/neurotransmitters-serotonin-gaba-dopamine-acetylcholine/.

44. Laney, 51.

45. Arnie Kozak, Ph.D., *The Everything Guide to the Introvert Edge* (Avon, MA: Adams Media, 2013), 25.

46. Laney, 243.

47. Ibid., 48.

48. Cain, 46.

49. Tanner, 38, citing Adam McHugh, author of *Introverts in the Church* (Downers Grove, IL: InterVarsity Press, 2009).

50. Laney, 86.

51. Cain, 122.

52. Laney, 197.

53. Flanagan, Bill, *U2: At the End of the World* (New York: Delacorte Press, 1995), 44–45.

54. Laney, 197.

55. Ibid., 83.

56. Tanner, 16.

57. Laney, 191–192.

58. Ibid., 192.

59. Dembling, *The Introvert's Way*, 157.

60. Kahnweiler, *Quiet Influence*, 8–9.

61. Researchers note that public speaking is "an inherently stimulating activity," and that overstimulation can interfere with focus and memory. Cain, 126.

62. Cain, 122.

63. Laney, 19.

64. Ibid., 23.

65. Dembling, *The Introvert's Way*, 34.

66. Tanner, 32.

67. Kahnweiler, *Quiet Influence*, 19.

68. Laney, 141.

69. Ibid., 152.

70. Ibid., 52.

71. Ibid., 193.

72. Ibid., 133.

73. Kahnweiler, *Quiet Influence*, 11.

74. Laney, 123.

75. Kozak, 135.

76. Laney, 184.

77. Ibid.

78. Ibid., 171.

79. Cain, 129.

80. Kozak, 21.

81. Dembling, *The Introvert's Way*, 22.

82. Ibid., 87.

83. Kahnweiler, *Quiet Influence*, ix.

84. Laney, 166.

85. Dembling, *The Introvert's Way*, 144.

86. Laney, 53.

87. Ibid., 28.

88. Ibid., 156.

89. Ibid., 55.

90. Peter R. Breggin, MD, *Guilt, Shame, and Anxiety: Understanding and Overcoming Negative Emotions* (Amherst, NY: Prometheus Books, 2014), 114.

91. Ibid., 125.

92. Ibid., 116.

93. Laney, 43.

94. Ibid., 156.

95. Ibid., 43.

96. Hilliard, 10.

97. Steve Flowers, *The Mindful Path Through Shyness* (Oakland, CA: New Harbinger Publications, 2009), 19.

98. Ibid., 18.

99. Barbara G. Markway, Ph.D. and Gregory P. Markway, Ph.D., *Painfully Shy: How to Overcome Social Anxiety and Reclaim Your Life* (New York: Thomas Dunne Books, 2001), 13; Flowers, 2.

100. Flowers, 2.

101. Ibid., 19.

102. Laney, 157.

103. Ibid., 156.

104. Ibid., 43.

105. Breggin, 77.

106. Ibid., 78.

107. Ibid., 79.

108. Ibid., 164.

109. Flowers, 95.

110. http://www.valhl.org/wp-content/uploads/2015/07/6Challenges-of-Practicing-Law-While-Struggling-with-Depression-and-Anxiety.pdf; http://www.daveneefoundation.org/scholarship/lawyers-and-depression/.

111. http://www.valhl.org/wp-content/uploads/2015/07/6Challenges-of-Practicing-Law-While-Struggling-with-Depression-and-Anxiety.pdf; http://www.daveneefoundation.org/scholarship/lawyers-and-depression/.

112. http://www.valhl.org/wp-content/uploads/2015/07/6Challenges-of-Practicing-Law-While-Struggling-with-Depression-and-Anxiety.pdf; http://www.daveneefoundation.org/scholarship/lawyers-and-depression/.

113. Paul Foxman, in Hilliard, *xi.*

114. Kozak, 47.

115. Foxman, in Hilliard, *xi.*

116. Flowers, 20 (citing the American Psychiatric Association, 2004).

117. Ibid., 69. ("Social anxiety is essentially created and perpetuated by the words in our heads about ourselves and other people. Anxiety feeds on the things we say to ourselves and therefore requires frequent verbal maintenance to keep regenerating itself.").

118. Kozak, 47.

119. Hilliard, 9.

120. Flowers, 21 (citing D. H. Barlow, *Anxiety and Its Disorders: The Nature and Treatment of Anxiety and Panic,* 2d. ed. (New York: Guilford Press, 2002)); *see also* Hilliard, 12, 19, 28.

121. Kozak, 47; Hilliard, *xvi.*

122. Hilliard, 25.

123. Christopher Phillips, *Socrates Café: A Fresh Taste of Philosophy* (New York: W.W. Norton & Co., 2001).

124. William A. Bablitch, "Reflection on The Art and Craft of Judging," *The Judges' Journal* 42, no. 4 (2003): 7, 8.

125. Paul Johnson, *Socrates: A Man for Our Times* (New York: Penguin Books, 2011), 29–31.

126. Ibid., 28.

127. Ibid., 95.

128. Phillips, 8.

129. Ronald Gross, *Socrates' Way: Seven Master Keys to Using Your Mind to the Utmost* (New York: Jeremy P. Tarcher/Putnam 2002), 82.

130. Johnson, 7.

131. Plato, *Phaedrus,* 230a.

132. Johnson, 78.

133. Gross, 8.

134. Phillips, 200.

135. Ibid., 11.

136. Ibid., 18.

137. Ibid., 20.

138. Gross, 53.

139. Phillips, 235. *See also* Johnson, 112 (emphasizing "Socrates' importance in revealing the need for definition of terms").

140. Phillips, 234.

141. Gross, 59.

142. Johnson, 79.

143. Ibid., 88.

144. Ibid., 106.

145. Phillips, 49 (emphasis added).

146. Ibid., 210.

147. Ibid., 49.

148. Ibid., 159.

149. Gross, 65.

150. Ibid., 37.

151. Ibid., 85.

152. Ibid., 37.

153. Tanner, 182.

154. Cain, 255 ("Extroverts tend to like movement, stimulation, collaborative work. Introverts prefer lectures, downtime, and independent projects.").

155. Ibid., 253.

156. Ibid.

157. Kozak, 152.

158. Katherine Schultz, "Why Introverts Shouldn't Be Forced to Talk in Class," *Washington Post* (February 12, 2013).

159. "Socrates Café are gatherings around the world where people from different backgrounds get together and exchange thoughtful ideas and experiences while embracing the central theme of Socratizing; the idea that we learn more when we question, and question with others." http://www.philosopher.org/Socrates_Cafe .html.

160. Phillips, 29.

161. Cain, 51.

162. Ibid., 167.

163. Ibid., 168–169.

164. For more information about the Myers-Briggs Type Indicator (MBTI) personality inventory, please see Note 16.

165. Cain, 108.

166. Ibid., 265.

167. Gross, 92.

168. Kahnweiler, 10.

169. Michael Sullivan, "The Lawyer as Counselor," *Defense Counsel Journal* 76 (April 2009): 253, 254.

170. Ibid.

171. William Prewitt Kralovec, "Contemporary Legal Education: A Critique and Proposal for Reform," *Willamette Law Review* 32 (1996): 577, 578.

172. Kevin Houchin, Esq. https://lawyerist.com/29242/attorney-counselor-law-ambiguity/.

173. Ibid.

174. Jack W. Burtch, Jr., "The Lawyer as Counselor," *Virginia Lawyer* 58 (April 2010): 27.

175. Ibid.

176. Thomas J. Ryan, "Attorney and Counselor at Law," *Michigan Bar Journal* 79 (December 2000): 1624.

177. Ibid.

178. Ibid., 1625–1626.

179. Marjorie M. Shultz and Sheldon Zedeck, "Predicting Lawyer Effectiveness: A New Assessment for Use in Law School Admission Decisions" (July 31, 2009). CELS 2009 4th Annual Conference on Empirical Legal Studies Paper; http://www.albanylaw.edu/media/user/faculty_scholarship/wkshops/Presentation_Materials/Lawyering_Effectiveness.pdf.

180. http://www.merriam-webster.com/dictionary/sympathy.

181. http://www.merriam-webster.com/dictionary/empathy.

182. The Difference Between Sympathy and Empathy. http://themindunleashed.org/2015/01/difference-sympathy-empathy.html.

183. http://www.boundlessawareness.com/.

184. Kahnweiler, *Quiet Influence*, 76.

185. Joshua D. Rosenberg, "Teaching Empathy in Law School," *University of San Francisco Law Review* 36 (Spring 2002): 621, 632.

186. Emily J. Gould, Esq., "The Empathy Debate: The Role of Empathy in Law, Mediation, and the New Professionalism," *Vermont Bar Journal* 36, no. 3 (Fall 2010): 23.

187. Ian Gallacher, "Thinking Like Non-Lawyers: Why Empathy is a Core Lawyering Skill and Why Legal Education Should Change to Reflect Its Importance," *Legal Communication & Rhetoric: JALWD* 8 (Fall 2011): 109–110.

188. Rosenberg, 632.

189. Gallacher, 110.

190. Rosenberg, 637–638.

191. Gould, 23.

192. Gallacher, 113.

193. Gould, 23.

194. Janeen Kerper, "Creative Problem Solving vs. The Case Method: A Marvelous Adventure in which Winnie-the-Pooh Meets Mrs. Palsgraf," *California Western Law Review* 34, no. 2 (1998): 351, 366.

195. Bablitch, 8.

196. Aharon Barak, "Let There Be Law: Judging as a Way of Life," *Legal Affairs* 28 (2002). ("A judge should show intellectual humility. The strength of his judgments is displayed in his ability to admit errors."); Aharon Barak, "The Role of a Judge in a Democracy," *Judicature* 88 (March-April 2005): 199, 200. ("The strength of our judgment lies in our ability to be self-critical and to admit our errors in the appropriate instances. Law has not started with us. It will not end with us."); Wayne D. Brazil, Jordan Eth, Thelton E. Anderson, "In Memory of Chief Judge Robert F. Peckham," *Hastings Law Journal* 44 (1993): 973, 977. (In a memoriam to a Chief Judge of the U.S. District Court for the Northern District of California: "Perhaps because of this fundamental intellectual humility, he could hear others without a trace of that defensiveness that can impede real access to other people's suggestions or insights.") Notably, Justice and Professor Aharon Barak was appointed Justice of the Supreme Court of Israel in 1978, and served as Supreme Court President from 1995 until 2006.

197. *American Federation of Labor v. American Sash and Door Co.*, 335 U.S. 538, 557 (1949) (Frankfurter J., concurring).

198. John Sexton, "Structuring Global Law Schools," *Dickinson Journal of International Law* (Spring 2000): 451, 452. ("[A]n essential feature of the defining perspective embraced by the global law school is intellectual humility. It is understanding that there is wisdom outside of our narrow world—and delighting in being asked the question that you would (have) never asked inside your own thought system.") John Sexton, "'Out of the Box' Thinking About the Training of Lawyers in the Next Millennium," *University of Toledo Law Review* 33 (2002): 198–199. ("[P]erhaps the most profound impact of globalization on the enterprise of legal education can be captured in the word 'humility.' Discovering a premise that unconsciously shaped one's thinking is a dramatic moment intellectually, and the repetition of such discoveries should instill intellectual humility and a reluctance to assume that there is a single right answer.")

199. Brett Scharffs, "The Role of Humility in Exercising Practical Wisdom," *University of California, Davis Law Review* 32, no. 127 (1998): 162.

200. Phillip H. Miller, "Critical Thinking in Litigation," *2013 Annual American Association for Justice Papers* (2013): 35.

201. Kahnweiler, *Quiet Influence*, 9.

202. Scharffs, 162.

203. Laney, 35.

204. Ibid., 198.

205. Kozak, 17.

206. Ibid., 97.

207. Ibid.

208. M. F. Fensholt, *The Francis Effect: The Real Reason You Hate Public Speaking and How to Get Over It*, 67 (Ontario, CA: Oakmont Press 2006).

209. Flowers, 137.

210. Anna LeMind, "Science Associates Social Anxiety with High IQ Levels and Empathic Abilities," http://themindunleashed.org/2015/05/science-associates-social-anxiety-with-high-iq-levels-and-empathic-abilities.html (May 15, 2015) (emphasis in original).

211. Hilliard, *xvi.*

212. Ibid., 38.

213. Kahnweiler, *Quiet Influence*, 1–2.

214. Ibid., 78.

215. Tanner, 36.

216. Ibid., 158.

217. Adam Clayton, Dave Evans, Larry Mullen, Paul David Hewson. Lyrics © Universal Music Publishing Group.

218. Kahnweiler, *Quiet Influence*, 73.

219. Cain, 57.

220. Kahnweiler, *Quiet Influence*, 54.

221. Jennifer Kahnweiler, *The Introverted Leader: Building on Your Quiet Strength* (Oakland, CA: Berrett-Koehler Publishers 2013), 39.

222. Barbara Roberts attributes her first therapist for those words.

223. Dembling, *The Introvert's Way*, 39.

224. Laney, 19.

225. Tanner, 162.

226. Ibid., 41.

227. https://en.wikipedia.org/wiki/Groupthink.

228. Kozak, 95.

229. Ibid., 132.

230. Tanner, 163.

231. Kozak, 118.

232. Ibid., 156.

233. Cain, 74 (italics in original).

234. Susan Cain, "The Rise of the New Groupthink," *New York Times*, January 13, 2012, SR1.

235. Helgoe, 88.

236. Kozak, 80.

237. Cain, *Quiet*, 74.

238. Kerper, 366. ("Creative problem-solving begins with an assumption of not knowing, a confession of ignorance, a kind of bafflement, and a surrender to curiosity.")

239. Ibid.

240. Cain, 11.

241. Kozak, 17.

242. Kahnweiler, *Quiet Influence*, 111.

243. Thoughts from Places: The Tour, Nerdfighteria Wiki, January 17, 2012; https://www.youtube.com/watch?v=qy6FdaJ6Ayc&feature=BFa&list=UUGaVdbSav8x-WuFWTadK6loA.

244. Gallacher, 110.

245. Ibid., 147.

246. Ibid., 112.

247. Kahnweiler, *Quiet Influence*, x.

248. Laney, 204.

249. Gould, 24, citing Dorothy J. Della Noce, "Seeing Theory in Practice: An Analysis of Empathy in Mediation," 15 *Negotiation Journal* 15, no. 3 (1999): 271.

250. Rosenberg, 633. *See also* Gould, 23. ("[E]mpathy is a valuable skill for creating good outcomes.")

251. http://www.huffingtonpost.com/2013/02/21/women-talk-more-than-men-study_n_2734215.html.

252. Other introverts concur. See http://introvertspring.com/introverts-stay-quiet/ (Michaela Chung).

253. Tanner, 182.

254. Dembling, *The Introvert's Way*, 32.

255. Tanner, 176.

256. Theoi Greek Mythology: Exploring Mythology in Classical Literature and Art. http://www.theoi.com/Daimon/Nike.html.

257. *The Simpsons*: "Bart's Inner Child" (#5.7) (Fox 1993).

258. Many of the ideas, language, and sources in the second half of this book were previously published and cited in Heidi K. Brown, "Empowering Law Students to Overcome Extreme Public Speaking Anxiety: Why 'Just Be It' Works and 'Just Do It' Doesn't," *Duquesne Law Review* 53 (Winter 2015): 181–214.

259. Barbara G. Markway, Ph.D.; Cheryl N. Carmin, Ph.D.; C. Alec Pollard, Ph.D.; and Teresa Flynn, Ph.D., *Dying of Embarrassment: Help for Social Anxiety & Phobia* (Oakland, CA: New Harbinger Publications, Inc., 1992), 24–25.

260. Flowers, 2 (citing J. J. Gross and R. W. Levenson, "Hiding Feelings: The Acute Effects of Inhibiting Negative and Positive Emotion," *Journal of Abnormal Psychology* 106, no. 1 (1997): 95–103; C. Purdon, "Thought Suppression and Psychopathology," *Behavior Research and Therapy* 37, no. 11 (1999): 1029–1054).

261. Markway, Carmin, et al., 14.

262. Flowers, 41.

263. Ibid.

264. Markway & Markway, 63.

265. Flowers, 108.

266. Plato, *Apology*, 38a.

267. Flowers, 90.

268. Markway & Markway, 50.

269. Cara Santa Maria, *Insanity: The Real Definition*, Huffington Post (Feb. 19, 2012), http://www.huffingtonpost.com/2011/12/20/insanity-definition_n_1159927.html; Daniel D'Addario, *"The definition of insanity" is the most overused cliché of all time*, Salon (Aug. 6, 2013, 10:33 AM), http://www.salon.com/2013/08/06/the_definition_of_insanity_is_the_most_overused_cliche_of_all_time/; Michael Becker, *Einstein on misattribution: 'I probably didn't say that.'*, Becker's Online J. (Nov. 13, 2012), http://www.news.hypercrit.net/2012/11/13/einstein-on-misattribution-i-probably-didnt-say-that/.

270. Flowers, 43 (citing M. G. Williams, J. Teasdale, Z. Segal, & J. Kabat-Zinn, *The Mindful Way Through Depression: Freeing Yourself from Chronic Unhappiness* (2007)).

271. Ibid., 43.

272. Ibid.

273. Ibid., 44.

274. Markway & Markway, 165.

275. Flowers, 84. ("These are the habits of mind and behavior that can get you lost in your shyness patterns and keep you there. So, the more you can illuminate them, the more you may be able to uncouple from some of these automatic reactions.")

276. Gross, 193.

277. Ibid., 195.

278. Flowers, 148–149.

279. Ibid., 90.

280. Ibid., 42.

281. Breggin, 123.

282. Ivy Naistadt, *Speak Without Fear* (New York: HarperCollins, 2004), 75.

283. Ibid., 18. As Naistadt emphasizes: "Authenticity is what we respond to most strongly as listeners." Individuals want to "achieve a style of communicating that is a reflection of who they truly are, not a false notion or imitation of something or someone else they think they should be." Ibid., 74. Similarly, legal communication experts Brian K. Johnson and Marsha Hunter reiterate that "[g]ood public speaking is not based on pretending, acting, or faking it; you must look, sound, and feel authentic to appear confident, comfortable, and credible." Brian K. Johnson & Marsha Hunter, *The Articulate Attorney: Public Speaking for Lawyers* (Phoenix: Crown King Books, 2013), 6.

284. Markway & Markway, 152.

285. Laney, 132.

286. Tanner, 17.

287. Naistadt, 3–4.

288. Ibid., 16.

289. Ibid., 18.

290. Flowers, 31.

291. Ibid., 27.

292. Ibid., 38.

293. Phillips, 114.

294. Ibid., 94.

295. Ibid., 95.

296. Ibid., 94.

297. Ibid.

298. Ibid., 97.

299. Naistadt, 30.

300. Ibid., 31 (emphasis in original)

301. Breggin, 35.

302. Flowers, 26 (2009) (citing J. Kagan, *Galen's Prophecy: Temperament in Human Nature* (1994)).

303. Ibid., 105.

304. Hilliard, 20–21.

305. Markway & Markway, 38.

306. Naistadt, 57.

307. Ibid., 62.

308. Markway & Markway, 37.

309. Flowers, 175 (adults can "learn how to give [them]selves the safe and secure base of self-compassion that [they] never had before").

310. Naistadt, 62.

311. Ibid., 66.

312. Breggin, 123.

313. Ibid., 200 ("promise yourself not to act on painful feelings as they arise inside you.").

314. Markway & Markway, 115 (encouraging labeling the messages "misleading and maladaptive").

315. Ibid., 112.

316. Flowers, 102.

317. Hilliard, 141.

318. Flowers, 104.

319. Ibid., 119 ("When you shift your awareness into a physical place grounded in the body and attend to what's happening right now, your attention can stop contracting around some idea of a future calamity and expand to take in the whole spectrum of sensations, emotions, and thoughts occurring right now. Notice the changing and impermanent nature of each of these mental and physical events and allow your attention to settle in the physical sensations. You might acknowledge that this is just another anxiety event, and that it too will pass."); *see also* Markway & Markway, 57 ("[I]f you're feeling anxious, you're feeling anxious. That's all. It doesn't mean it's horrible or catastrophic. It doesn't mean the anxiety will last forever. It doesn't mean you won't be able to handle it. It doesn't mean anything except that you're feeling anxious at a particular moment.").

320. Flowers, 99.

321. Ibid., 103.

322. Ibid., 118 (". . . [A]cknowledge or note 'anxiety,' give it some space, and feel into it with gentle curiosity. You stay. You breathe. You let the feeling of anxiety just be there.").

323. Ibid., 91.

324. Ibid., 118, 145–146.

325. Ibid., 119.

326. Ibid., 106.

327. Naistadt, 62.

328. Hilliard, 43.

329. Flowers, 119.

330. Hilliard, 44.

331. Ibid., 166.

332. Flowers, 109.

333. Hilliard, 58.

334. Breggin, 142.

335. Ibid., 143–144.

336. Hilliard, 63 (encouraging individuals to "take ownership" of blushing by stating, "I am blushing myself.").

337. Ibid., 60.

338. Ibid., 64.

339. Ibid., 62.

340. Johnson & Hunter, 10.

341. Ibid.

342. Ibid., 59.

343. Naistadt, 146.

344. Ibid., 33.

345. Ibid., 145–146.

346. Ibid., 147.

347. Johnson & Hunter, 10.

348. Ibid., 12.

349. Breggin, 237.

350. Markway, Carmin, et al., 69.

351. Ibid.

352. Ibid.

353. Ibid., 70.

354. Ibid.

355. Hilliard, 151.

356. Laney, 179.

357. https://www.youtube.com/watch?v=lfsf2gbR4K8.

358. Breggin, 237.

359. The suggestions in this chapter were inspired by and adapted from Ivy Naistadt's list: balance, breath control, eye contact, hand placement and gestures, and vocal power. Naistadt, 147.

360. Naistadt, 148.

361. Johnson & Hunter, 50.

362. Naistadt, 146.

363. http://www.ted.com/talks/amy_cuddy_your_body_language_shapes_who_you_ are?language=en.

364. Johnson & Hunter, 21.

365. We just need to be sure that the tangible object is not an obvious or distracting one, like a pen. No matter how hard we try not to, we will inevitably click a pen, or flick it against the podium.

366. Johnson & Hunter, 60.

367. Naistadt, 165.

368. Ibid.

369. Ibid.

370. Kahnweiler, *The Introverted Leader*, 90.

371. http://www.nhs.uk/Conditions/blushing/Pages/causes.aspx. The irrational fear of blushing is called erythrophobia.

372. Hilliard, 63 (encouraging individuals to "take ownership" of blushing by stating, "I am blushing myself.").

373. Ibid., 60.

374. Flowers, 145.

375. Markway, Carmin, et al., 81.

376. Flowers, 149.

377. Ibid.

378. Ibid., 163.

379. Markway & Markway, 152. ("The trick is to break your fears into a series of steps, with the first few steps being only mildly challenging, with later steps increasing in difficulty. To do this, you create what's called a 'hierarchy'—a list of the situations that elicit anxiety, rank ordered by the amount of distress each would lead to if you entered the situation.").

380. Markway, Carmin, et al., 107 (citing a 1981 study by Drs. Andrew Matthews, Matthew Gelder, and Derek Johnson).

381. Hilliard, 175.

382. Flowers, 120.

383. Markway & Markway, 153.

384. Ibid.

385. Hilliard, 180.

386. Markway & Markway, 146.

387. Hilliard, 175.

388. http://www.merriam-webster.com/dictionary/habituation.

389. https://www.google.com/webhp?sourceid=chrome-instant&rlz=1C1CHWA_enUS64
4US644&ion=1&espv=2&ie=UTF-8#q=habituation%20definition.

390. http://www.merriam-webster.com/dictionary/desensitize.

391. Markway, Carmin, et al., 82.

392. Fensholt, 67.

393. Markway & Markway, 152.

394. Hilliard, 124.

395. Johnson & Hunter, 13.

396. Naistadt, 176.

397. The Honorable Kenneth F. Ripple, "Legal Writing in the New Millennium: Lessons from a Special Teacher and a Special 'Classroom,'" *Notre Dame Law Review* 74 (March 1999): 925, 926.

398. http://www.nytimes.com/2014/06/03/science/whats-lost-as-handwriting-fades
.html?_r=0 (Maria Konnikova, June 2, 2014).

399. http://www.medicaldaily.com/why-using-pen-and-paper-not-laptops-boosts-
memory-writing-notes-helps-recall-concepts-ability-268770 (Lizette Borreli, February 6, 2014); http://pss.sagepub.com/content/early/2014/04/22/09567976
14524581.abstract.

400. Ibid.

401. Some of the suggestions in this chapter also appear in Heidi K. Brown, *The Mindful Legal Writer: Mastering Predictive Writing*, Appendix F (New York: Wolters Kluwer Law & Business (Aspen Publishers) 2015) and Heidi K. Brown, *The Mindful Legal Writer: Mastering Persuasive Writing*, Chapter 11 (New York: Wolters Kluwer Law & Business (Aspen Publishers) 2016).

402. Flowers, 104.

403. http://www.musicnotes.com/blog/2014/08/19/popular-pre-show-rituals/
(Aug. 19, 2014).

404. http://www.nytimes.com/1999/08/22/sports/baseball-between-pitches-twist-
tap-a-game-within-the-game.html (Buster Olney, August 22, 1999).

405. Gross, 97.

406. http://ignitedleadership.com/6-ways-to-destroy-your-fear-of-public-speaking/
(May 21, 2013); www.jasonconnell.co.

407. Naistadt, 190.

408. Ibid.

409. Some of the suggestions in this section (and in the section on courtroom appearance) also appear in Heidi K. Brown, *The Mindful Legal Writer: Mastering Predictive*

Writing, Appendix F (New York: Wolters Kluwer Law & Business (Aspen Publishers) 2015) and Heidi K. Brown, *The Mindful Legal Writer: Mastering Persuasive Writing*, Chapter 11 (New York: Wolters Kluwer Law & Business (Aspen Publishers) 2016).

410. See, for example, Roger C. Park, *Trial Objections Handbook 2d*, Appendix B (New York: McGraw-Hill, 1991).

411. Kozak, 163.

412. This phrase is attributed to Gotham Writing Workshop teacher and author Stephanie Elizondo Griest, who is now a writing professor at the University of North Carolina at Chapel Hill. During critiques of our memoir-writing, she asked participants to identify one aspect of each writer's piece that "we love" and one "that could use more love."

413. Tanner, 182.

414. Friedrich Nietzsche, *Twilight of the Idols, or, How to Philosophize with a Hammer* (1889).

415. Rosenberg, 646. ("Obviously, the typical law school environment is often not conducive to students feeling that kind of safety.")

416. Alan D. Hornstein, *Tributes to Professor Edward Tomilson*, 64 Md. L. Rev. 947, 952 (2005); Kralovec, 32 Willamette L. Rev. at 586 ("Progress in [the quest for a shared professional identity] can be made, however, only if the legal professorate is willing to lay down its extraordinary mantle of power and assume greater intellectual humility vis-à-vis students.").

417. Kerper, 367 n.62.

418. Max Maxwell, "The Socratic Temperament, PDF Files," http://www.socratic method.net/essays/ST_pdf_versions.html.

419. Ibid., 2.

420. Ibid., 2–3.

421. Ibid., 3–4.

422. Scharffs, 162.

423. https://www.insidehighered.com/blogs/just-visiting/failure-empathy#.V5_1z-vRTxPA.facebook (John Warner, Aug. 2, 2016) (discussing empathy in teaching).

424. *See* http://www.myersbriggs.org/my-mbti-personality-type/take-the-mbti-instrument/.

Index

Note: The letter *A* following a page number indicates appendix.